The Santa Monica Farmers' Market Cookbook

The Santa Monica Farmers' Market Cookbook

Seasonal Foods, Simple Recipes, and Stories from the Market and Farm

Amelia Saltsman

Foreword by Deborah Madison

Designed by Ph.D

blenheim
PRESS

Library of Congress Control Number: 2007901323

ISBN 978-0-9790429-0-4   0-9790429-0-9

Design by Ph.D, www.phdla.com
Copyediting by Sharon Silva
Photographs copyright © 2007 by Anne Fishbein on back cover, spine, and pages ii, vi, viii, 9, 11, 14, 16
Photographs copyright © 2007 by Hill Street Studios on front cover and pages 10, 12, 13, and 15
Photographs copyright © 2007 by Amelia Saltsman on page 15

Published by Blenheim Press
1223 Wilshire Blvd., Suite 800
Santa Monica, CA 90403
For sales visit: www.blenheimpress.com

Printed in China

First Edition
10 9 8 7 6 5

For the California farmers of the Santa Monica Farmers' Market

Contents

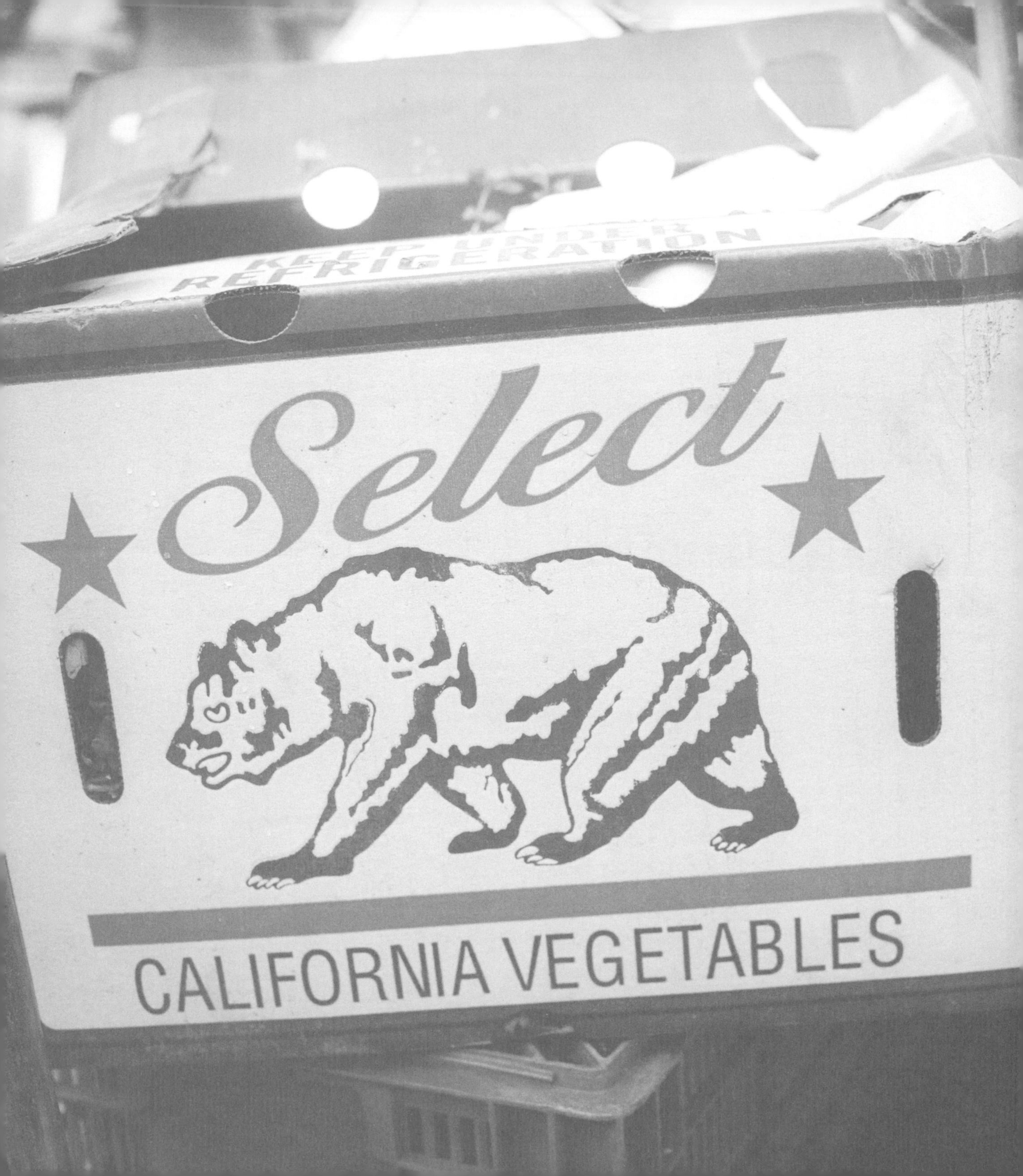
KEEP UNDER
REFRIGERATION
Select
CALIFORNIA VEGETABLES

Foreword

I'm thrilled to see Amelia Saltsman's beautiful work, *The Santa Monica Farmers' Market Cookbook*, in print. I know this is a true labor of love, one whose labor I've had the pleasure of observing for some time both close up and from a distance. Amelia cares about many things in life, one of which is this farmers' market, *her* market, where she has shopped for many years. Another is her family, and a third is cooking beautiful food. All three meet on the pages of this book, a seamless work that expresses a keen sensibility based on passion, intelligence, and real sense of caring.

When I set out to write a book on farmers' markets (*Local Flavors: Cooking and Eating from America's Farmers' Markets*), I was quite involved with the running of my own local market—and much in love with it. But I didn't want to write about it alone. Instead, I wanted to bring into view the look and feel of farmers' markets across the nation. So I used my market, which I knew well, as a springboard from which I made a hundred-odd visits to other markets across the country. The result was a painting of America's passion for small-scale farming and local eating as expressed in our country's farmers' markets, from east to west and from north to south.

Amelia, however, has taken the opposite tack in this book. Using one market as a lens, she has looked long, carefully, and lovingly at those who grow, raise, and otherwise produce some extraordinary foods that thousands of Angelenos enjoy throughout the year, either at home or in restaurants. In *The Santa Monica Farmers' Market Cookbook*, we too get to know these foods and their growers in a way that we might like to but can't when we are mere visitors to the market, shoppers in a hurry, or maybe just shy. We can finally make deep sense out of this market because Amelia has been talking with its producers for years. What she shares with her readers are the Santa Monica market's extraordinary foods and their producers, both of which are richly endowed with stories and histories. In the end, this sustained look at a single market lacks nothing. If anything, it conveys what is at the heart of all true farmers' markets, which is the richness that comes out of a culture of growing and selling food at a particular intersection of time and place.

There were a few scary decades, the 1950s and 1960s in particular, when our produce choices had atrophied severely, despite the enormous diversity in the plant world. That amazing wealth of difference had been thinned to the supermarket's paltry offerings of, say, two kinds of lettuces, three varieties of apples, boiler and baker potatoes. Fortunately, humans like and need variety, and eventually we reacted to this unnecessary poverty with sufficient fire to create farmers' markets, the ultimate showcase for diversity. Even though supermarkets now offer far more choices than they used to, farmers' markets are always many steps ahead of them. You might find fifteen potato varieties at a single stand, or Lebanese and Zephyr zucchini, or three or four different kinds of limes.

2

But as much as we crave difference and variety, we are also capable of stalling when it comes to adventures with food, unless someone can show us the way. However wonderful they may be, fruits and vegetables, meats and nuts, honeys and cheeses don't mean much unless we understand their natures and know their possibilities. We need a guide for such explorations, and Amelia Saltsman is a very good one, indeed. What is the nature of a Meiwa kumquat that sets it apart from another variety? (It's sweet throughout.) What is a Japanese dried persimmon, and what do you do with it? (You'll find out.) Have you been intrigued by those gorgeous fresh grape leaves but unsure of how to proceed? (You'll learn.) I didn't know that there were low-acid pomegranates and that their paler color is just as it should be, not a sign of some deficiency. Next time I have the opportunity, I'll be sure to pick some up.

Amelia's work is really three volumes in one: gleanings from the culture of farming; a guide to produce, meats, and cheeses found at this extraordinary market; and a great cookbook. Her recipes make it possible to translate the market's exceptional raw materials into something good for dinner. Amelia knows many Los Angeles chefs and their food well, yet she is very much a home cook. This is great for her readers because what she does is suggest utterly doable dishes that have uncommon flair. These are recipes that let us cook not just well, but even brilliantly. I read them and I think to myself, "Why didn't I think of that? How smart! How good!" Fresh and utterly original, they possess an internal logic that tells you they will work. And they do. Imagine Black Cod with Green Tomatoes, Meyer Lemon Sundae with Cara Caras and Tangelos, Nettle and Potato Frittata—these are enough to make me want to move from New Mexico to within walking distance of the Santa Monica market. Although I can't do that, really, I can keep my eyes open for parallel experiences that my own high-desert market might offer. Not the fish and crabs perhaps, but definitely the green garlic, a fresh goat milk ricotta, a great Hubbard squash. And when I travel, particularly to the Santa Monica Farmers' Market, but really to any of the farmers' markets that draw from the beneficent climate of Southern California, I know that I am well prepared to understand the food I see there, know something about how it was grown and who grew it, and, of course, know what to do. That final point is very important, because I'll be sure to get on that plane home with a few sturdy bags filled with treasures from the Santa Monica market.

In the end, my wish for our country is that every farmers' market will have such a keen and passionate biographer as Amelia Saltsman. When that happens, we will truly have a food culture with deep, delicious roots!

Deborah Madison

Introduction

Every Wednesday, Saturday, and Sunday, the bustling, boisterous Santa Monica Certified Farmers' Market emerges from the early-morning mist like a beachside Brigadoon, only to disappear again by midafternoon, loose lettuce leaves and carrot tops swept up, farm trucks easing toward home. This urban oasis is my village square. It is where I catch up on all the news with neighbors, chefs, and farmers who have become friends, and where we shoppers find endless inspiration from the freshest, tastiest seasonal ingredients that are all the richer for how they are grown.

Anchored at one end by a landmark row of palm trees standing sentinel over the Pacific Ocean, the original downtown Wednesday Santa Monica Farmers' Market (there are now four in three locations) at Second and Arizona was founded in 1981, making it one of the oldest certified farmers' markets in California. It is also one of the largest, and because of its focus on an astonishing year-round abundance of varied produce (as opposed to crafts or prepared foods) proudly grown by California family farmers, it is one of the most important in the country. The market has changed the way its farmers farm and the way Southern California chefs and home cooks think about food, shop, cook, and eat. For locals, this microcosm of cultural diversity—farmers, customers, and ingredients—is a way of life. For visitors, the Santa Monica Farmers' Market offers the truest California souvenirs: impossibly sweet local citrus, meltingly tender desert dates, and for those with stars in their eyes, innumerable celebrity-chef sightings. This book is a celebration of the market's more than twenty-five years of excellence and of the farmers who have made it that way.

The Santa Monica Farmers' Market is part of an increasing national desire for local ingredients (there are now more than three thousand certified farmers' markets across the country) that has substantially changed restaurant and home cooking from seasonless, recipe-driven dishes to a cuisine where hours-old seasonal ingredients are the stars. In spring, when even the humble carrot has innate flavors of surpassing complexity, the best recipe is often the simplest: a slick of olive oil, a sprinkling of good salt, and a hot oven. This isn't a new idea, but a return to a sense of place, time, taste, and variety as we relearn what years of shopping out of context has wiped from our memory.

But the fact is many home *and* professional cooks are overwhelmed by the choices and new rules. How are white zucchini different from green, or ripe green tomatoes from red? What are amaranth, sapote, and ramps? Does shopping at the farmers' market really make a difference?

Culling from my twenty years of shopping, talking with farmers and visiting their farms, researching, and experimenting, and many more years of cooking for my family, I have written *The Santa Monica Farmers' Market Cookbook* to offer novice and market-savvy shoppers a seasonal guide to both familiar and exotic crops, with tips on how to select, store, and prepare these interesting finds. From everyday to company fare, the straightforward recipes show ways to combine the contrasting flavors, textures, and colors created by nature and hardworking farmers into delicious, fresh, and, for the most part, quick-to-assemble dishes.

These days, busy cooks need farmers' markets more than ever, because the tastier the raw ingredients, the easier it is to prepare delicious food. The biggest surprise, even to regulars, is that a good farmers' market offers much more than fruits and vegetables. It is also one-stop shopping for carefully produced meat, eggs, line-caught fish, handcrafted cheeses, olive oil—just about everything you need to prepare a meal. Using the farmers' market as my primary food source, I have discovered many exciting flavor combinations and at the same time have simplified my larder and often reduced my time in the kitchen.

To say that cooking from the farmers' market is more "nutritious" or "healthier" makes it sound medicinal instead of the delectable pleasure it is. Yes, I believe local crops nourished by the sun, picked at their peak, and brought to market fresh are more nutrient rich. Knowing where my food comes from gives me peace of mind about its safety. That simpler cooking is often lighter I consider added value. But I've been shopping the market so long, to me these are givens. Simply put, if you feed your family from the full spectrum at the market, you will indeed feed them well.

As a writer, I've always been drawn to stories about family, and the Santa Monica Farmers' Market is most assuredly about families: those who farm together and those who gather at the table to enjoy the market's bounty. The dishes offered here are recipes I've been inspired to cook for my own family: my husband, who used to think he didn't like beets and now asks for seconds; our three children, who grew up thinking kale and cauliflower were fine things; and now our granddaughter, who smacks her lips for collards and chard and whose appreciation for lush red strawberries reassures me that a taste memory for excellence will carry to the next generation.

Whenever I give a cooking demonstration at the farmers' market, I find myself smiling in anticipation as I make my early-morning rounds to collect supplies and say a quiet good morning to the farmers setting up. Soon, I'll be helping shoppers become "market cooks" who look first at what's available, then at a recipe. I'll get to tell them there are only two things required for good cooking: great ingredients and just enough technique to tweak them into a tasty meal. And I'll get to see their smiles and hear my favorite words, "I could do that," as they head off to make their purchases.

The People Who Grow Our Food

Farming isn't for the faint of heart. In winter, you wait for the early-morning frost to dissipate so you can cut kale and chard without damaging the leaves' veins and cell walls. Mud sucks at your boots as you work the row, your hands are numb from the near-freezing damp, and by afternoon, pounds of wet clay cling to your boots and your clothes are soaked with the odd mix of sweat and chill. In summer, the stench of rotting melons and tomatoes hangs in the air as you race the heat to claim ripe fruits before they turn. It's a miracle so much perfect produce makes it to the market.

And that's just the harvest. Farmers spend the year gambling against the elements, often in the face of encroaching urban development. Century-old farms lose land to eminent domain. Los Angeles County farms, once part of a vast agricultural landscape, become pin dots in a sea of suburban housing. Landlords sell to developers and uproot farmer lessees who have to relocate without missing a selling season. Long rains and cold can delay harvest by several weeks, or a heat wave can wipe out crops days before harvest, crops that will take another year's cycle to reappear. And old-timers worry about who will carry on the tradition.

Yet for all this, farmers have an abiding passion for the land, for the smell of the damp, rich soil when they pull winter root crops from the flatlands of the San Joaquin Valley, and for quiet, after-dinner sowing and weeding on a summer evening when the surrounding Sierras glow pink from the lowering sun. Farmers wouldn't have it any other way.

They came to it by many routes. Phil McGrath and Truman Kennedy come from generations of farmers. Molly Iwamoto Gean and her family emigrated from rural southern Japan in the 1950s. Vang Thao and Phong Vang are Hmong refugees from Laos. Barbara Spencer was a cellist, Rusty Hall an architect, James Birch an irrigation specialist. Chemistry teacher Sid Weiser realized a lifelong dream when the family started farming in Tehachapi in 1977. Dr. Bob and Rose Polito's retirement land in northern San Diego County became a thriving citrus ranch through son Bob's efforts. Longtime shoppers note which of the farmers' kids inherited their parents' passion: Romeo Coleman, Armando Garcia, Edgar Jaime, and Alex Weiser are the next generation growing the family business.

Ask farmers why they rise well before dawn to drive their crops to market, and the answers are the same: "We wouldn't have survived otherwise." Selling directly is often the only way small farmers financially sustain their farms. It is the difference between earning a dollar for a head of lettuce and a dollar a box, and it is the point of the state's certified farmers' markets. Tsugio Imamoto and Elmer Lehman have been at the Santa Monica Farmers' Market since it opened and others nearly as long. Sure it's business, but it's personal. Farmers make the drive because they appreciate the opportunity and because "putting what we grow into a customer's hand gives us the energy to go on."

Direct selling also has given the market its crop diversity. Years ago, shoppers simply saw fresher versions of the same familiar varieties, such as Red and White Rose and Yukon Gold potatoes. But as farmers have seen customers' response firsthand, learned what works and what doesn't, their inner horticulturalists have blossomed. Chefs request specific crops, and farmers can oblige. Today we find at least fifteen kinds of potatoes, a dozen kinds of carrots and broccoli, all grown first for flavor. We see *puntarella*, *agretti*, and Costoluto tomatoes, kaffir limes, lemongrass, and kari leaf. This biodiversity isn't just a chic indulgence. Besides preserving an array of species and varieties for future generations, growing multiple crops protects the land and prevents plant disease and disaster (the Great Potato Famine was an extreme consequence of monocropism).

When Santa Monica market farmers choose to sell locally and directly instead of supply large commercial concerns, it requires a shift in philosophy and method. "We can either play it safe and sell commercially for low gain," Ventura farmer Phil McGrath explains, "or gamble, work harder, and sell it ourselves." California's mild climate challenges farmers to resist overmanipulating the seasons. "It's tempting to grow a lot year-round to accommodate unknowing customers, including chefs," Phil says, "but things really grow and taste best in their true season. I've always been told a farmer needs to achieve consistency. Now consistency within the season is my goal."

Growing local, fully ripe produce requires greater oversight and seasonal variety. Phil plans four years ahead for each block of rows planted, planting two acres every two to three weeks so that he's constantly harvesting and rotating crops. The Geans, whose motto is "Growing ordinary foods with extraordinary flavor," farm strawberries, snap beans, and tomatoes intensely in small plots so nothing slips by their quest for perfection.

And nothing goes to waste. The Geans, who do not resell unsold produce at another market, turn leftovers into preserves, salsa, and irresistible spicy dill beans, growing their own herbs, onions, and peppers to do it. The Spencers dry and smoke tomatoes and chiles to preserve them, and Alex Weiser replants unsold baby spring onions and reharvests them when they're full size. Think arugula flowers and onion tops are foodie affectations? Instead, consider them ingenious, delicious ways to wring every last bit of use from a crop. Anything left after that is plowed under as compost. Even irrigation hoses and farm machinery parts get recycled, the former to build hoop houses, the latter, if you are creative like Rick Gean, to become whimsical giant sculptures.

Many small farmers, who grow food with and for their own families, have a deep sense of personal responsibility about being good stewards of the land. Some have chosen to become certified organic. Others farm organically without certification or are in the certification process. And some exceptionally conscientious farmers are cantankerous iconoclasts who won't be told what to do. Certified or not, many Santa Monica market farmers employ practices that far exceed minimum organic requirements. A better question when you approach a farm stand is "How do you farm?" (For these reasons, I don't actively distinguish farms as organic in the book. For a listing of certified organic farms at the Santa Monica Farmers' Market, see pages 200 to 204.)

Locally grown means farming close enough to drive, not fly, crops to market. Most Santa Monica market growers who come year-round farm within 250 miles, many within 20, 50, or 100 miles—not bad considering the urban sprawl that separates us from where our food is grown. Some seasonal farmers, such as the excellent Stockton and Lodi cherry growers, drive longer distances for a short time of the year. California farmers often find they use fewer petrochemical dollars driving farther but to fewer, more populated urban markets than doing a dozen markets in their neighborhoods.

These are the farmers of the Santa Monica Farmers' Market. Their wisdom (and cooking advice) fills the pages of this book. If Santa Monica isn't your local market, I hope their stories and their portraits, beautifully captured by Lawrence Manning and Betty Mallorca of Hill Street Studios and Anne Fishbein, inspire you to meet the farmers in your own hometown and support your farmers' market.

They could stay in their offices and check off items on a produce list, but instead many chefs spend their Wednesdays (and sometimes Saturday and Sunday mornings) maneuvering carts piled high with fresh produce destined for some of the most interesting dishes at many of the city's best restaurants. "Once you start cooking with seasonal farm produce, it drives what you're going to make," says Suzanne Goin, chef-owner of Lucques and A.O.C. and author of *Sunday Suppers at Lucques: Seasonal Recipes from Farm to Table*. "It's a structure bigger than you are, and it's impossible to go back."

There's a special symbiosis between chefs and farmers. The market is a wellspring for culinary creativity, and farmers, who depend on chefs' large steady orders, are a constant resource for new, exotic foodstuffs. Farm names listed on menus are no gimmicky frill. Instead, they confirm the quality of ingredients and pay tribute to the chefs' sources of inspiration. Committed chefs and restaurateurs like Christopher Blobaum of Wilshire Restaurant and Josh Loeb of Rustic Canyon in Santa Monica now get up to 80 to 90 percent of their produce from local farmers

One of the godfathers of contemporary California cuisine, Michael McCarty, whose eponymous restaurant founded in 1979 is located just one block from the Santa Monica Farmers' Market, has been a supporter since the market's early years. The longtime restaurateur sums up the connection this way: "When we began, focusing on seasonal fresh produce was revolutionary. The revolution has succeeded. Today, we're eating better than we ever have at home and in restaurants."

In *The Santa Monica Farmers' Cookbook*, you'll meet many of these chefs the way I do, at the market, shoulder to shoulder at farm stands discussing the merits of this or that ingredient. Look for their Chef's Tips throughout the book, the ideas, advice, and professional "trucs" (cooking tricks) they've generously given me that I now pass on to you.

So grab your shopping bags and let's visit the Santa Monica Farmers' Market where you'll quickly discover that shopping the market does make a big difference.

A History of the Market

by Laura Avery, Market Supervisor of the Santa Monica Farmers' Markets

The Santa Monica Farmers' Market opened at noon on July 15, 1981, in what was then an ailing downtown business district. It was one of the first markets implemented through the California Department of Food and Agriculture's Direct Marketing Act of 1977, which enabled farmers to sell nonstandard pack produce—specifically "fresh, unprocessed fruits and vegetables"—to consumers at locations designated as certified farmers' markets. Commercial concerns weren't interested in this nonstandard produce: fully ripe peaches or tomatoes are not shippable or storable. But customers of the new market loved them. And even though state regulations did not include such processed agricultural products and nonproduce items as dried fruits, fruit juices, jam, eggs, shelled nuts, honey, plants, bread, and seafood, they made their way to the market, too.

The framers of the direct-marketing regulations understood that these new markets would divert some fruits and vegetables from the packinghouse to the consumer. But they did not foresee that small family farms in California would seize on this new opportunity to save and reenergize their farms. For the first time, California farmers were allowed to sell directly to their customers at a realistic price that reflected the cost of growing their crops. On the market's opening day, raisin farmer Jay Scott of Dinuba arrived with several of twelve hundred boxes of golden yellow Thompson seedless grapes that were deemed too ripe for commercial sale. They were a big hit, and over the next few weeks, he sold all twelve hundred boxes to customers who sang their praises. Today, approximately three thousand of California's thirty-three thousand small family farms rely on the state's farmers' markets to make all or part of their living.

During its first fifteen years, the Santa Monica market grew from one location to four. In 1991, lack of shopping opportunities for weekday workers led to the opening of a Saturday market at the same location. The next year, Santa Monica's east-side community mounted a campaign to bring a farmers' market to its neighborhood, and the Saturday Pico Market, in the heart of the now beautiful Virginia Park, was born. The Sunday Main Street Market, with its block-party atmosphere, opened in 1995, following the efforts of residents and businesses who wanted to see their storied street return to a lively walking, shopping, and meeting area. Today, some 180 seasonal and year-round farmers participate in Santa Monica's four markets. Together, they represent a combined total of more than eight thousand acres of farmland under cultivation and four thousand years of farming experience.

By the late 1990s, local chefs such as Nancy Silverton, cofounder of Campanile and Mozza restaurants and founder of La Brea Bakery; Bruce Marder, chef-owner of Capo and Brass Cap; and Suzanne Tracht, chef-owner of Jar restaurant, were spending hours at the Wednesday farmers' market finding one-of-a-kind produce to inspire their cooking. Other chefs followed, many bringing farmers

FARMER TO YOU
BEEF
FARMER TO YOU
PORK

Harry's Berries

special seeds and requesting that certain items be harvested at a particular moment. Soon, tiny fennel bulbs, marble-sized Brussels sprouts, and bite-sized turnips were turning up on restaurant menus.

Immigrants from Iran, Mexico, Africa, and the Philippines found that they could buy such favorite items as fenugreek, *hoja santa*, and bitter-melon leaves from farmers who also valued the ingredients. And farmers were discovering that it made good business sense to invest some of their land in such venerable but neglected crops as Blenheim apricots, Persian mulberries, heirloom apples and pears, Nantes carrots, and pastel cauliflower.

Being so close to the source of their food has been an education for shoppers. They have learned about California's seasons, when to buy which crop, and how to factor in weather conditions that would cause heirloom tomatoes to show up a month late or cherries to come in two weeks early. Santa Monica's school students have benefited, too. In 1997, the local school district launched a summer farmers' market salad bar program at McKinley Elementary School that expanded into a district-wide lunch option at all sixteen campuses within two years. The farmers' markets are also the embodiment of Santa Monica's "sustainable city" initiative. They provide its citizens with locally grown food, its student population with nutrition education through garden programs and market tours, and have implemented a "zero waste" market on Sunday, at which all trash, including plates and forks, is either composted or recycled.

The Santa Monica Farmers' Market is still home to about a dozen of its original farmers and their families. Jim Tamai's granddaughter Julia brings vegetables, sweet corn, and strawberries to market with her mother. Every Wednesday, Tsugio Imamoto sells herbs, celery root, and watercress in the same place he parked on opening day in 1981. Some of the farmers have passed their farming operations along to longtime employees; others have seen offspring grow up at the market who are now ready to take over the farm. At eighty-two, Elmer Lehman, who farms in Fresno, still comes to market each week when his peaches and grapes are in season, but now he lets his helper drive. He says that without the Wednesday market, he would have quit farming years ago.

Over the years, many people, all of them with stories to tell and recipes to share, have talked about writing a Santa Monica Farmers' Market cookbook. But Amelia Saltsman made it happen. The talented home cook and food writer has filled these pages with the foods and the farmers that make the market so special. And in doing so, she has celebrated its rich history.

18   A Day in the Life of the Market Manager

It is mid-May and a shimmering one hundred degrees in the Central Valley when we leave the paved road just outside downtown Fresno. Laura Avery, market supervisor of the Santa Monica Farmers' Market; Howell Tumlin, executive director of Southland Farmers' Market Association; and I are headed to visit three Hmong (a Southeast Asian ethnic minority group) farmers to learn more about what they grow. As we bump along a dirt road in a Santa Monica city-owned Prius, billows of dust wafting over us from the white pickup truck leading the way, I wonder, "Is this part of the market manager's job description?"

It is if you're Laura Avery, whose dedication and high standards of excellence for over twenty years have nurtured the Santa Monica Farmers' Market to become what it is today. Our visit is officially a farm audit, a program that protects both farmers and customers by ensuring compliance with the state regulation that farmers who participate in certified farmers' markets must grow everything they sell. (Resale is considered unfair practice by hardworking small farmers who already must compete with large domestic and foreign operations; selling strictly sorted-out produce that is too small or blemished for commercial markets compromises quality.)

Unofficially, and equally important to Laura, the visit is an opportunity to foster communication and understanding. Many managers leave inspections to county officials, but Laura believes the oversight program builds bridges and wants to see as many farms as she can. "You don't really know your farmer until you visit the farm. I feel so edified after a visit, so plugged into the farmers' lives."

There is a lot to learn on this visit, and Richard Molinar and Michael Yang, of the University of California Cooperative Extension, Fresno County, are with us to interpret (Michael is fluent in the Hmong and Lao languages) and teach us about Hmong farming techniques. (Fresno has the greatest concentration of Hmong farms in the United States.) It is early afternoon when we pull up amid the crop rows, and Vang Thao and his wife, Khoua Her, who sell at the downtown Saturday market; Yee Her of Fresno Evergreen, who can be found at the Saturday Pico market; and Phong Vang and Houa Moua, whose stand is at the Sunday Main Street market, are eager to show us what they grow and how they farm.

We walk each of their farms (the families lease the land together, but subdivide it), peeking inside steamy hoop houses at okra-leaf plants (an okra relative grown for its greens), stopping at the lean-to packing shed to admire pristine bundles of late-spring garlic ready for market. The farmers grow familiar and, to us, unfamiliar Asian crops such as bitter melons, luffas, and yam leaves, as well as fragrant Laotian highland rice for their own use that we encourage them to bring to the market.

The farmers talk to Laura and Howell about their desire to participate in more markets, which would make the trip to Los Angeles more productive, and the two administrators offer suggestions. [Update: Several months after our visit, a spot opened up at the Wednesday market for the appropriate crop mix, and Laura offered it to Yee Her and another Hmong farmer who alternate weeks.]

Certified farmers' markets are meant to create just these types of selling opportunities. Within each market, it's up to the manager to bring in a good balance of crops and experienced growers who set the bar high. An astute manager has to make sure farmers are well placed to help improve their sales. There's only one way to do that. "When I started at the market," Laura says, "I spent all day hanging out with the farmers getting to know them and the market as much as I could. I realized that the manager's booth was not where I belonged. I never sit down until the end of the day when it's time to help farmers check out and get on their way quickly."

When asked what makes the Santa Monica Farmers' Market successful, Laura lists its central location to business and residential areas, ample parking, and the city's tremendous support. True, but her respect for the farmers, her passion for small-farm produce, and her patient building of the market and ceaseless promoting of it and its growers are what make Santa Monica a destination market. The general sense of mutual respect that permeates the market makes it a good place to be.

Laura is pleased with the trip, certain it opened better lines of communication and opportunity. It is nearly nine o'clock when we get back to Santa Monica. We've been on the road thirteen hours and hundreds of miles, talking about farming and markets the whole way. It's been quite a day.

How to Use this Book

To make it easy to find what you are looking for, I've organized this book by the traditional divisions of starters, soups, salads, and so on, partly because that's how most of us think about recipes. More important, crop seasons vary depending on where you live, and they don't have absolute dividing lines, especially in California, arriving instead in overlapping waves throughout the year. While this yields wonderful intersections where cooks can pair late-winter citrus with early-spring green garlic, or late-summer tomatoes with autumn pumpkins, it makes it a challenge to categorize recipes by season.

So, to let you know at a glance when you are most likely to find its ingredients at the market, each recipe is clearly labeled by season or seasons at the upper left-hand side (along with the yield). If you see the word *evergreen*, it means the dish can be made year-round. And both recipes and ingredients are listed by season at the back of the book.

But before you begin shopping and cooking, read through the next several pages for tips on how to shop at the farmers' market and for suggestions for pantry items and tools to have on hand that will be especially useful for the recipes in this book. In Basic Kitchen Techniques, you'll find instructions for the fundamentals used throughout the book, such as how to zest, peel, and segment citrus; toast nuts; roast winter squash; and cook both fresh and dried shell beans.

Many of the recipes include information on how to choose and store market produce, as well as recommendations on which varieties to use and where and when to find them. In contrasting color so they are easy to spot, you'll also discover produce glossaries; farmer's, cook's, and chef's tips; and stories about crops, farms, and farmers, all of which I hope will enrich your understanding of the food you buy and the effort it takes to grow it.

See the back of the book for the locations and hours of the four Santa Monica Farmers' Markets and for a list of all the farmers who sell there, including what crops they grow, the farm location and acreage, organic certification, and contact details for mail order.

How to Shop

Once upon a time, when grocery stores only stocked locally grown fruits and vegetables, even city dwellers could read the changing seasons in the produce bins. With today's global air freight, we have forgotten when and where things want to grow. It's time to undo our years of seasonless, solitary shopping experience and replace it with a willingness to use all our senses—sight, sound, smell, taste, touch—to relearn the seasons and the joy of anticipation. The key to knowing your farmers' market is to remember that all crops have seasons. And the best way to learn about the seasons is at the market.

1. **MAKE YOUR LIST.** But keep it loose. It can be as simple as "green vegetable, salad fixings," until you are more attuned to planning by season. Leave room on your list for surprise finds, as the chefs do. "The market is constant discovery that you can't predict from the [home or] office," says chef-owner Mark Peel of Campanile restaurant. "I see what's there and start making the connections."

2. **NOTICE THE MARKET LAYOUT.** To protect the small farmer, the two most important rules of California certified farmers' markets are that only farmers are allowed to sell within the formal boundaries of the market, and they must grow the produce they sell. The market operator (manager) and the farmers (producers) must be certified by the local county agricultural commissioner, and farmers must prominently display their "certs" listing field location and quantities and varieties grown. Market managers who want to include sellers of nonagricultural products must place them outside the formal boundaries of the certified farmers' market. Figure out these demarcations and you will know which markets feature real farmers.

3. **RESPECT MARKET ETIQUETTE.** If a sampling tray is not out, ask for a taste. Be patient; think about how hard the farmer worked to grow the crop and to get it to market before dawn within a day of harvest. California farmers' markets are not the place to work on your bargaining skills. Discounts are at the farmers' discretion and are usually tokens of appreciation for being a loyal customer. Come prepared with small bills to avoid cleaning out farmers' cash drawers.

4. **LOOK AT WHAT'S AVAILABLE.** If it's not there, it's not in season or locally grown. Notice the waves of crops as they appear throughout a season. An early-spring market is filled with bright young greens; a late-spring market overflows with color. Exactly when items first appear depends on weather idiosyncrasies from planting through harvest time. Learn to distinguish a fully ripe tomato or a peach saturated with color from its paler cousin that needs a couple of days on the counter to finish ripening (buying some of both is a good way to extend your purchases through the week in prime condition). Note the differences in color depth between citrus picked early season and late

season: the longer it sits on the tree, the more it "colors up." Look for the fresh leafy tops and juicy appearance of just-dug root vegetables.

5. **LISTEN TO THE SNAP AND CRUNCH OF FRESH PRODUCE.** Moreover, listen to the farmer. Growers are proud of a particularly great harvest and willingly teach how to choose and store their crops, when they will be ready to use, and how to prepare them. Farmers want your repeat business and will answer forthrightly about which variety is in better shape that day or about whether something is "early, peak, or late." They cook their own produce, learn from their chef and home-cook customers, and are happy to share recipe tips and expertise. If a farmer doesn't engage or has sent an indifferent employee to sell there, shop at another stand. Nothing is more educational or rewarding than a visit with an enthusiastic grower.

6. **BREATHE IN THE AROMA.** The scents of fully ripe strawberries, cantaloupes, citrus, and apples and of rich earth clinging to vegetables are important clues to quality. Cradle a fruit in your hand to feel the give that comes with ripeness. Ask the farmer to confirm your findings as you learn how to choose.

7. **TASTE THE PRODUCE.** Sampling is a farmer's greatest selling tool. Taste to educate your palate, to learn which varieties are your favorites, and to distinguish between ripe and unripe, early and high season, who and what areas are having a good year. Quality differences can be due to climate, soil, weather, time of year, or the variety grown. At home, note how the ingredient handles and tastes when cooked and share your findings with the farmer, who will be glad for the feedback.

8. **CARPE DIEM.** If you find something amazing, buy it on the spot and change your cooking plans. Some varieties or even whole crops are in the market a fleeting week or two. Ask the farmer how long he or she will have it.

9. **JUDGE HOW MUCH YOU NEED.** Bunches are standardized by weight, such as ½ pound or 1 pound including tops. Visualize herbs in handfuls, keeping in mind most small handfuls yield 2 tablespoons leaves. A small onion will yield about 1 cup chopped, while a large onion will yield 1½ to 2 cups. A generous handful of nuts weighs about 1 ounce and measures ¼ to ⅓ cup.

10. **STORE YOUR PURCHASES.** Tips on storing specific items appear throughout the book. In general, never wash produce until you are ready to use it, and never refrigerate it until it is fully ripe.

VARIETIES AND CULTIVARS. These terms are often used interchangeably (cultivar is short for cultivated variety), but they don't necessarily distinguish among open-pollinated, hybrid, or heirloom members of a plant species. Celebrity, Early Girl, and Brandywine are all tomato varieties or cultivars. Some cultivars aren't officially named by breeders, and farmers occasionally give a crop a whimsical moniker you won't find in any horticultural book, such as Mr. McNulty, Fitz Kelly's title for a white nectarine–plum cross. Varieties and cultivars may be bred or seed-selected to resist disease; bear early, middle, or late season; or do better in cooler or warmer areas, which gives farmers the ability to grow crops suited to their climate and to harvest a continuous stream of different varieties, extending the selling season. That's why you find June Lady peaches at the beginning of summer and Autumn Ladies towards the end.

HEIRLOOMS AND HYBRIDS. Heirlooms are open-pollinated varieties—pollinated by wind or insect and capable of reproducing genetically consistently from generation to generation—that typically have been around for at least four decades. Hybrids are crosses between two varieties to create a new variety. They cannot reproduce "true," however, and must be cross-pollinated anew each season. Using examples given above, Celebrity and Early Girl are hybrids, while the century-old Brandywine is an heirloom.

FAMILY, GENUS, AND SPECIES. Fruits and vegetables related to one another are grouped in widening circles of connection from species to genus to group to family. Melons, squash, and cucumbers are all cucurbits; cabbage, broccoli, cauliflower, beets, and kale are brassicas; celery, parsley, parsnips, and carrots are in the Apiaceae family; and tomatoes, peppers, eggplants, and potatoes are all solanums. It's fun to begin to understand the relationships through taste, texture, and growth characteristics.

MATURE AND RIPE. Many fruits can be picked mature—fully developed—but not necessarily fully ripened to peak flavor and softness. Picking mature stone fruits a day or two before peak ripeness protects the fruits from bruising during transport and gives shoppers a little more time to enjoy them at home. However, if fruit is harvested immature, it won't ripen satisfactorily if at all. But fruit picked fully ripe—sloppy, fragile, and fleeting as it is—is an extraordinary taste experience. Some crops, such as strawberries or watermelons, don't get any better after picking, while others, such as winter squash, improve with age once off the vine, getting sweeter and meatier with storage. Ask the farmer.

FIELD RUN AND CULLS. Field run produce is "as is": boxed without first being sorted for size. Culls are the sort outs, or seconds, removed during sorting.

Basic Kitchen Techniques

HOW TO ZEST CITRUS. Zest, the colored part of citrus skin, contains highly flavored oils, but the white layer, or pith, that lies beneath it is bitter. A sharp paring knife will do, but handy tools exist to simplify removing just the zest. For long, thin strands, scrape a five-hole zester against the fruit, pressing deeply enough to remove only the skin. For tiny zest bits, use a Microplane grater, and for wide strips, try a stripper or channel knife, the tool bartenders use. Whenever possible, work over the other ingredients in the dish to catch the spray of oils that is released as you work.

HOW TO PEEL AND SEGMENT CITRUS. Using a sharp, small- to medium-sized knife, cut a thin slice off the top and bottom of the fruit, exposing the flesh. Stand the fruit upright and cut downward to remove the peel and its pith in wide strips, tracing the curve of the fruit with your knife to expose the pulp. Hold the fruit in one hand over a bowl and slice along both sides of each segment to free it from the membrane, dropping the segments into the bowl as you go. Reserve the juice-laden membranes for use in dressing or seasoning the dish, squeezing them with your hand to extract the juice.

HOW TO PEEL AND SEED TOMATOES. Drop whole tomatoes into a pot of boiling water for 30 seconds. Immerse only two at a time to prevent lowering the water temperature. Use a skimmer, slotted spoon, or tongs to remove the tomatoes from the pan. The skins will slip off easily. Use the tip of a paring knife to cut out the core. Cut the tomatoes in half crosswise, and gently squeeze each half to remove the seeds, easing the seed sacs out with a fingertip if necessary. To reserve tomato juices, work over a sieve set over a bowl. Very firm or green (unripe) tomatoes can be peeled with a swivel-blade vegetable peeler.

HOW TO PEEL PEACHES. Drop whole peaches into a pot of boiling water for 30 seconds. Immerse only two at a time to prevent lowering the water temperature. Use a skimmer, slotted spoon, or tongs to remove the peaches from the pan. The skins will slip off easily. Very firm fruits can be peeled with a swivel-blade vegetable peeler.

HOW TO STRIP HERBS AND GREENS. Leaves of woody-stemmed herbs such as thyme, bay, and rosemary can be "plucked" by grasping the top of the sprig and pulling sharply downward. For greens such as kale, grasp the stem end with one hand and, with your other hand, fold the leaf in half lengthwise and pull both sides of the leaf sharply downward.

HOW TO MAKE BREAD CRUMBS. For soft crumbs, tear country bread (with or without crusts) into small pieces and dry on the countertop or in a 250-degree oven until no longer moist but still pliable. Pulse in a food processor to desired consistency. For dry crumbs, tear stale bread into large pieces and dry until hard. Grate on a box grater or pulverize in a food processor.

HOW TO ROAST AND PEEL PEPPERS. Place sweet peppers and chiles over a hot fire on a grill, over the direct flame of a gas burner, or under a broiler close to the heat source and roast, turning as needed, until blackened on all sides. The heat source must be very hot so the peppers roast quickly, which preserves their flavor, color, and texture. Remove the peppers to a plate, cover with a dish towel, and allow to steam for at least 10 minutes to loosen the skins. Peel when cool enough to handle. Much of a chile's heat is in the seeds and interior membranes, or "ribs," and the meat closest to the stem is hotter. Remove or retain the seeds to taste.

HOW TO TOAST NUTS. Preheat oven to 350 degrees. Spread the nuts on a baking sheet and toast in the center of the oven until fragrant and the nuts are lightly golden in the center, 10 to 15 minutes for almonds, hazelnuts, and pistachios, 7 to 10 minutes for oil-rich pecans and walnuts. Set aside to cool; the nuts will continue to take on color and crisp as they cool. With hazelnuts and walnuts, place hot nuts in a dish towel and rub to remove the skins. Use a chef's knife to chop nuts to desired size. To grind nuts, use a Mouli hand grater or pulse in a processor to the desired texture (add 1 tablespoon of the sugar in a dessert recipe to the processor to prevent the nuts from turning to butter). Toast the nuts the day you intend to use them to retain crispness and freshness.

HOW TO COOK FRESH SHELL BEANS. Shell the beans and place in a pot with water to cover. Bring to a gentle boil, reduce the heat, cover partially, and simmer until the beans are tender but still hold their shape, 30 to 40 minutes. Add salt to taste, turn off the heat, cover the pot, and let the beans cool. Refrigerate the beans in their liquid, then drain before using and reserve the liquid for enriching soups and stews. Fresh beans do not expand much in cooking. Plan on about 1 cup cooked beans from ½ pound beans in the pod.

HOW TO COOK DRIED BEANS. If you have the current season's dried beans, there is no need to presoak them. Otherwise, soak beans in a bowl of cool water to cover for at least 6 hours or up to overnight. Drain, place in a pot with water, using 4 cups water for each cup of beans. Bring to a gentle boil, reduce the heat to low, cover, and simmer gently until the beans are tender but still hold their shape, 45 to 60 minutes. Add salt to taste, turn off the heat, cover the pot, and let the beans cool in the liquid. Refrigerate the beans in their liquid, then drain before using and reserve the liquid for enriching soups and stews. Dried beans will triple in volume when cooked.

HOW TO ROAST LARGE WINTER SQUASH OR PUMPKINS. Preheat oven to 375 degrees. Pierce the squash in a few places with a knife or meat fork and place on a baking sheet. Roast until the squash is browned, shiny, beginning to lose its shape, and easily pierced with a knife, about 1 hour for a 5-pound squash. When cool enough to handle, cut in half crosswise and scoop out and discard the seeds and strings (or save seeds for another purpose). Scoop the pulp from the "shell." A 5-pound squash yields about 6 cups cooked pulp. Use as is, or puree or mash with a food processor or a fork and freeze in 2-cup containers for convenient use throughout the season.

HOW TO ROAST SMALL WINTER SQUASH. Preheat oven to 375 degrees. Cut a long squash, such as a butternut, in half lengthwise and scoop out the seeds and strings. Brush the cut sides with olive oil and season with kosher or sea salt. Place cut side down on a baking sheet with at least 1 inch between the halves, and roast until the skins are browned and shiny and the squash is easily pierced with the tip of a knife, about 40 minutes. For a small round squash, such as a Sweet Dumpling, leave whole. Or, cut off the top, scoop out the seeds and strings, brush the cavity with olive oil, season with salt, and roast cut side down, as above. Serve as is, or scoop pulp from the shell as for large squash.

HOW TO SAUTÉ AND BROWN. To sauté ingredients without browning, place them with the olive oil in a cold pan and heat (or melt butter briefly before adding other ingredients). When you want a sizzle and quick browning, heat the pan and the fat before adding the ingredients, and if using butter, add a little oil to prevent burning (butter has a lower smoking point).

HOW TO SEASON WITH SALT. Add a little salt at each stage of your recipe—when starting to sauté, after adding liquid, and again just before serving—to deepen the flavor of the finished dish. The final layering adds textural sparkle without making the dish salty. When boiling foods, salt the cooking water generously: a good handful added to a pasta pot is only ¼ teaspoon salt per cup of water—not enough to make food salty, but the bare minimum to add flavor to the food being cooked.

HOW TO MEASURE FLOUR. Spoon into a dry measure (½ cup, 1 cup, or the like) to heaping full. Do not shake or tap the cup to settle the ingredients. Using the edge of a metal spatula or the back of a knife, sweep across the top of the cup, leveling the flour flush with the rim.

Handy Pantry Items

These items can be found in most supermarkets, but specialty shops or ethnic markets often carry more authentic, better-quality brands. Starred items are available at the Santa Monica Farmers' Market.

SALT. Perhaps the single most important and versatile flavoring tool, salt comes in many types, each of which delivers its own distinctive qualities to a dish. Only a handful of the many varieties available are described here. **Kosher salt**, which is inexpensive and has a pure salt flavor, is your main cooking salt for savory foods, and the best brands (Diamond Crystal is recommended) contain no additives or anticaking agents. Its coarse texture gives it more volume, which means the cook has more control when salting foods. Keep an open bowlful handy for easy pinches. **Sea salt**, available coarse grain and fine grain, is a bit more expensive than kosher salt and has a "marine" taste and a milder saltiness. Coarse or fine grain is used for general cooking, while fine grain is a good choice for baking. The moist sea salt crystal "blossoms" of pricey ***fleur de sel*** are harvested by hand from the surface of salt beds. Its sweet marine taste and crunchy texture make it a wonderful finishing salt. Moderately priced, lovely large-flaked **Maldon sea salt** from England is used for both cooking and finishing.

CAPERS. Salt-packed capers are preferred over brined capers, which have a more assertive "pickled" taste. Rinse salt-packed capers, then soak in water for 10 to 20 minutes to remove excess saltiness. Rinse brined capers before using.

ANCHOVY FILLETS. Dissolved in warm olive oil, oil-packed anchovy fillets add savoriness but not fishiness to many dishes, making them a great secret seasoning. Look for fillets packed in olive oil. Salt-packed anchovies taste even better, but require rinsing and boning.

FISH SAUCE, THAI OR VIETNAMESE.

SOY SAUCE.

PANCETTA. This salt-cured (rather than smoked), rolled Italian bacon is seasoned with black pepper and sometimes other spices. Store ¼-inch-thick slices in the freezer for up to 6 months. Cut into dice with scissors while still partially frozen.

MUSHROOMS, DRIED PORCINI AND SHIITAKE.*

PEPPERCORNS. Black peppercorns are not-quite-ripe berries. White peppercorns are fully ripe, skinned berries. They have a milder taste and are invisible in light-colored dishes.

RED PEPPERS, GROUND DRIED. Among the mild choices are *togarashi*, the popular Japanese table condiment available in most supermarkets that also comes as part of a sesame-ginger-seaweed spice blend (*nanami togarashi*); Argentine *ají molido*, and Spanish smoked paprika (*pimentón de la Vera*). Hot examples include red pepper flakes and Hungarian paprika.

CHILES, WHOLE DRIED. Chipotles* (dried and smoked jalapeños) are widely available canned in *adobo* sauce, but you'll find whole dried ones at the farmers' market. Árbol chiles, which are small and mild and most often found dried, are used whole to add depth and broken to add zing.

RED-PEPPER SAUCES. Tabasco and *harissa* (Moroccan hot sauce).

TOMATOES, SUN-DRIED AND SMOKED.*

VINEGARS. Red wine, white wine, sherry, cider, rice, and good-quality balsamic, such as Fini brand.

DIJON MUSTARD. Maille brand preferred over sharper-flavored Grey Poupon.

OLIVE OIL. Look for cold-pressed extra-virgin oils,* filtered or unfiltered, and preferably with a harvest date on the label. Different olives, sources, and processes yield different colors and flavors, from a light gold to deep green, from mild and buttery to fruity and peppery. Store away from light, ideally in a dark glass container, and use within 6 months.

OTHER COOKING OILS. Canola, grape seed, and soybean are mild-tasting oils with a high smoking point.

NUT AND SEED FINISHING OILS. Walnut,* hazelnut, almond, pistachio,* and sesame oils are used for flavoring and for dressing salads. They have a low smoking point and are highly perishable; store in the refrigerator and use within 6 months.

PARMIGIANO-REGGIANO CHEESE. This is the king of Italian cheeses, often imitated (Parmesan), but never equaled. It is long aged and has a sweet, nutty flavor, slightly granular texture, and excellent melting properties. Purchase in a chunk, wrap tightly in plastic wrap, and grate or shave as needed.

Helpful Kitchen Tools

OFFSET SPATULA. Large (3 by 10-inch blade) with short handle for turning fish or lifting pastry.

TONGS. Have on hand both short and long, easy-to-squeeze tongs.

LONG-BLADED OFFSET SERRATED KNIFE. Handy for slicing bread, tomatoes, and meat.

SCISSORS. Heavy-duty for everything from snipping chives to splitting a chicken.

OYSTER KNIFE. Stubby blade with wide guard, for coring quince, chunking cheese, and shucking oysters.

CUTTING MATS. Flexible plastic sheets for easy transport of chopped ingredients.

GRAPEFRUIT SPOON. Serrated spoon great for removing the fuzzy core of an artichoke.

BENRINER SLICER. Inexpensive Japanese mandoline, for cutting paper-thin slices. For safety, leave an inch of vegetable stem attached to hold onto as you slice.

PEPPER MILLS. Have one for black and one for white peppercorns. The difference between freshly ground pepper and long-stored preground pepper is night and day. Peugeot brand recommended.

MORTAR AND PESTLE. For pulverizing garlic, spices, and herbs.

REAMER. Small, handheld conical tool for juicing citrus.

STRIPPER KNIFE, FIVE-HOLE ZESTER, AND MICROPLANE GRATER. Tools for zesting citrus (see page 24).

MOULI GRATER. Small, rotary French hand grater for nuts and cheese.

CHINOIS AND TAMIS. For fine straining. A chinois is a cone-shaped fine-mesh sieve. A tamis is a drum-shaped sieve, often fitted with worsted fabric. When fitted with wire mesh, it is used as a sifter.

FOOD MILL. Hand tool used for pureeing foods that simultaneously removes the skin, seeds, and fibers. Some models have a fixed blade and others have changeable blades, from coarse to fine.

IMMERSION OR STICK BLENDER. Handheld electric blender, for pureeing soups right in the pot.

BAKING SHEETS. Heavy-duty pans with 1-inch rims, indispensable for roasting, baking, carrying, and organizing. Popular sizes are the half sheet (12 by 18 inches) and quarter sheet (9 by 12 inches).

PARCHMENT PAPER. Handy for lining baking sheets (instead of greasing them), for twisting into cones for piping, and for speeding cleanup. Unlike waxed paper, it is not coated.

Starters

Teasers, as celebrated food writer M. F. K. Fisher called hors d'oeuvres, should do just that, tease and awaken the appetite for the meal to come. The farmers' market offers a vast seasonal array of contrasting flavors and textures to amuse the mouth well beyond the usual bowl of salted nuts—though there's nothing wrong with still-warm roasted almonds liberally seasoned with crunchy sea salt! For example, I like to serve crisply roasted tiny chanterelle mushrooms or balsamic-glazed baby Brussels sprouts as predinner morsels with a crisp, minerally white wine.

The recipes in this chapter range from Fisher's cocktail teasers to more substantial appetizers and plated first courses. Some can be served buffet style, echoing an assortment of mezes, or they can be expanded into sides and main courses. And don't limit your starter options to the offerings here. You will find recipes in the Soups, Sides, and Mains chapters that work beautifully in miniature portions, including those Glazed Brussels Sprouts (page 126), Green Zebra Gazpacho (page 60), the deviled eggs in Bacon and Egg Salad (page 92), Albacore, Bay Laurel, and Bacon Skewers (page 146), and fresh Hachiyas and prosciutto (Cook's Tip, page 152).

Local Olives and Almonds Roasted with Garlic, Lemon, and Herbs

This zesty starter showcases several of California's most famous crops. In fall, you'll find freshly harvested olives for home curing, and sweet, fresh-cured green Manzanillo olives from Adams Olive Ranch in Tulare County. These have been cured in water and sea salt for only a week, which results in a buttery taste, and will last for a week or two in your refrigerator. If you cannot find them, soak brined green or black olives to remove some of their saltiness. Fresh bay laurel leaves are at their peak in summer and fall, but are available much of the year from Maggie's, Coleman, and Flora Bella farms.

MAKES ABOUT 3 CUPS

Autumn, Evergreen

¾ pound (about 2 cups) green or black olives or a mixture

1 cup whole raw almonds

2 large cloves garlic, slivered

2 tablespoons fresh rosemary leaves

6 sprigs thyme

8 fresh bay leaves

1 lemon

3 tablespoons olive oil

Kosher or coarse sea salt

1 teaspoon or more *ají molido* (page 28) or hot Hungarian paprika

Preheat oven to 400 degrees. If using olives in brine, soak in water to cover for 20 minutes, then drain. Place the olives, almonds, garlic, rosemary, thyme, and bay leaves on a baking sheet. Cut the zest from the lemon in long strips (page 24), working over the pan so the olives receive the lemon oils that spray as you work. Give a generous squeeze of lemon juice over all. Add the oil, toss, season with salt and *ají molido*, toss again, and spread the mixture evenly over the pan.

Roast in the upper third of the oven until the nuts are fragrant and toasted and bay leaves crisp, about 15 minutes, stirring once halfway through cooking. While still hot, add salt to taste. Cool for at least 20 minutes before placing in a serving bowl. Serve warm or at room temperature.

A California Tradition

With its Mediterranean climate, California has been an olive oil culture from the time the missionaries first planted olive trees here in the eighteenth century. By the nineteenth century, when the rest of the country's favorite cooking medium was lard, Californians regularly dressed their salads and cooked their foods with local olive oil. The Adams family began growing and curing olives in Oak Park (now Sunland) in northern San Fernando Valley in the late 1800s, when Los Angeles County was known for abundant quality produce. In 1953, Alfred Adams moved to Tulare County, the historic epicenter of U.S. olive production, and Fred Jr. began selling olives at farmers' markets in the 1980s.

Chanterelle Popcorn

Roasted to earthy crispness and liberally salted, "mini-chanties" make a decadent munchy. One-inch chanterelles are available roughly July to November from David West of Clearwater Farms, and larger ones through winter from Louie Mello. A pound of raw chanterelles fills two baking sheets, but yields just two cups roasted. This also makes a rustic-elegant topping for roast chicken or sautéed spinach.

MAKES ABOUT 2 CUPS

Summer, Autumn

1 pound button-sized chanterelle mushrooms, brushed clean

2 to 3 tablespoons extra-virgin olive oil

Kosher or sea salt and freshly ground black pepper

Fleur de sel or other finishing salt

Lemon

Preheat oven to 425 degrees. Divide the mushrooms between 2 baking sheets. Drizzle each pan with the oil, season with kosher salt and pepper, and toss to coat. Spread evenly no more than 2 deep.

Roast in the upper third of the oven until the mushrooms have shrunk substantially and released some of their moisture, about 10 minutes. Toss or loosen with a spatula, and return to the oven until no moisture is visible in the pans and the mushrooms are crisp and dry looking, about 10 minutes more. Toss the mushrooms with *fleur de sel*, then let cool slightly before placing in a serving bowl. Add a squeeze of lemon just before serving.

HOW TO CHOOSE CHANTERELLES: Look for golden orange, firm, heavy-for-their-size, dry (but not dried out) mushrooms. Trim away any dark reddish, dried-out areas (a sign of toughness) on otherwise good specimens. Store the mushrooms in a brown paper bag, never plastic. If they are damp from rain, add a paper towel to the bag to absorb the moisture. If too dry, add a damp paper towel, but watch that they don't get too wet. Clean mushrooms with a damp brush; avoid rinsing with water.

Eureka!

Louie Mello discovered a different sort of gold on the land he has owned in San Luis Obispo's fertile See Canyon for twenty-five years. It turns out that his cool, damp coastal property is chanterelle rich, "but," explains the former postal worker, "I didn't have time to forage them until I retired." Since 2004, Louie and wife Jan have been harvesting golden "chanties." He says their floral, nutty aroma is a "ladylike perfume" compared to the primal scent of porcini or truffles. Because See Canyon is much farther south than most coastal chanterelle areas, Louie doesn't start picking until December or January and typically goes through March or later.

Dried Persimmons, Sheep's Milk Cheese, and Walnuts

Sweet, spicy persimmons, salty, aged cheese, and toasty walnuts are delicious together on a winter's evening, especially with a glass of champagne or lightly fruity Sauvignon Blanc. Try farmer Jeff Rieger's remarkable *hoshigaki*, hand-dried Hachiya persimmons (opposite), or chewy dried Fuyu persimmons from Burkart Farms. Chandler Farms grows sweet, crisp Franquette walnuts, an old French cultivar, and Rancho La Viña brings La Nogalera walnut oil to the market. At the Windrose Farm stand, you'll find Rinconada Dairy's handcrafted pozo tomme, an aged, pressed, natural-rind cheese reminiscent of Spanish Manchego.

MAKES 6 SERVINGS

Autumn, Winter

3 *hoshigaki* (whole dried persimmons),
  or 3 ounces dried persimmon slices
  (thickest slices possible)
¼ pound aged sheep's milk cheese such
  as pozo tomme or Manchego, broken
  into 1-inch chunks

⅔ cup walnut halves, toasted (page 25)
1 to 2 teaspoons walnut oil
1 teaspoon black peppercorns, toasted
  and crushed (see Cook's Tip)
Fleur de sel or other finishing salt

Use scissors to cut the *hoshigaki* lengthwise into long, narrow strips. If using persimmon slices, cut off tough persimmon skins and leave slices whole. Scatter persimmon pieces, cheese, and walnuts onto a serving plate. Drizzle with the oil to taste and season with the crushed pepper and *fleur de sel*.

HOW TO CHOOSE WALNUTS: Stock up on fresh walnuts soon after the fall harvest. Light-skinned varieties generally have less astringency. Inside, the nutmeat should be opaque and creamy looking; darkening or translucence can signal the beginnings of rancidity. Store the nuts away from the light in airtight containers in the refrigerator or freeze for longer keeping.

COOK'S TIP: Toasting black peppercorns brings out their fruity flavor, a trick I learned from Karen Bates and Sally Schmitt of The Apple Farm in Philo, near Mendocino. Toast 1 to 2 tablespoons peppercorns in a small, heavy skillet over medium heat until they are fragrant and begin to pop, 6 to 7 minutes. Let cool briefly, then crush with the back of a large spoon or a broad knife handle, or put them in a pepper mill and grind as needed.

Farmers are always looking for ways to extend the life of their crops. Since only so many ripe persimmons can be sold on any given day, Jeff Rieger of Penryn Orchard in Placer County has taken up extreme preserving.

Hoshigaki means "dried persimmon," but that hardly describes the painstaking traditional Japanese technique that produces this winter delicacy. Oblong Hachiya persimmons are picked in October, carefully peeled, hung by string from poles to dry, and kneaded every few days to help the fruit dry evenly, bring sugars to the surface, and create a soft, chewy texture without added sulfur or preservatives. If all goes well, after four to six weeks the persimmons are ready: not-too-sweet, plump, dusky ovals "powdered" with their own sugar. Because they are prime soon after processing, *hoshigaki* are an auspicious New Year's food, but if stored in a cool, dry place or even frozen, they can last a year.

Japanese immigrants brought the Oriental persimmon (*kaki*) and the tradition of drying them to the area northeast of Sacramento in the late nineteenth century. (While Placer County doesn't lead state production, California does produce almost all U.S.-grown persimmons). Renewed interest by growers like Jeff, who learned the craft from their older Japanese American neighbors, has helped make Placer the American center for this endangered art. Slow Food, the international organization dedicated to conserving agricultural biodiversity and food traditions, has included *hoshigaki* in its Ark of Taste.

Grilled Goat Cheese Wrapped in Fresh Grape Leaves

Tangy, young fresh grape leaves are available during late spring and early summer when farmers trim back new shoots from the developing grapes. Grape growers Alex Weiser, Scott Peacock, and John Hurley, among others, will bring cuttings to market on request. Ask for large leaves that aren't deeply lobed (indented). The leaves will keep wrapped in paper towels in resealable plastic bags in the refrigerator for a week. Sandy Garber and Ralph Meyer, owners of Topanga Vineyards, first introduced me to this classic vineyard starter that is lovely with a Viognier or rosé.

MAKES 8 SERVINGS

Spring, Summer

16 large, young grape leaves
¾ pound mild goat cheese such as Redwood Hill plain chèvre

½ cup extra-virgin olive oil
2 tablespoons fresh thyme leaves
Freshly ground black pepper

Soak the grape leaves in ice water to cover for 30 minutes. Meanwhile, use a fork to mix together the cheese, 1 tablespoon of the oil, thyme leaves, and a few generous grinds of pepper. Drain the leaves, pat dry, and snip off each stem close to the leaf. Pour the remaining oil onto a shallow plate. To form each package, dip the dull underside of 1 leaf into the oil and place, oiled side up, on a work surface. Place 1 tablespoon of the cheese mixture in the center. Fold the sides of the leaf over the cheese and then the top and bottom over to make a square package. Place seam side down on a clean plate, and repeat with the remaining leaves and cheese mixture. (The packages may be covered and refrigerated overnight before continuing.)

Heat a grill to medium-high. Grill the packages, beginning seam side down, until the leaves are no longer bright green and are nicely scored, about 2 minutes on each side, using a spatula to turn them. Serve warm or at room temperature.

RADICCHIO VARIATION: Use radicchio leaves, which lose their bitterness when cooked, when grape leaves aren't available. Dip them in hot water to soften and omit brushing the undersides with oil. Fold the core end of the leaf over the filling, fold in the sides, roll up, and brush with oil to grill as above. Radicchio leaves are also delicious stuffed with smoked Cheddar from Redwood Hill Farm and topped with a little balsamic vinegar.

COOK'S TIP: Wrap fish in grape leaves to add tart flavor and to keep fish moist on the grill. Season salmon or bass fillets with salt and pepper, wrap in oiled grape leaves (overlapping the leaves as necessary to cover fish fully), and grill over a medium fire.

Bruschetta

Bruschetta (broos-KEH-ta) is a smoky slice of grilled bread perfumed with garlic and slicked with olive oil. Delicious on its own, it adds dimension to a variety of toppings (see the next several recipes). To make bruschette (plural), lightly grill or broil country bread slices on both sides, then rub one side with the cut side of a garlic clove and brush it with olive oil. When a simpler or less rustic base is desired, make crostini, oven-toasted bread slices. Several artisanal bakers sell bread at the Santa Monica Farmers' Market, including Röckenwagner Bakery, The Bread Man, Bezian's, and La Brea Bakery, which donates all of its proceeds to the 24th Street School Gardens Project and the Santa Monica Farmers' Market School Garden Project.

Tomato-Mint Topping

Placing a mixture of perfectly ripe tomatoes—a classic red such as Early Girl or Celebrity, yellow-and-red supersweet Pineapple, bright red Brandywine, or dusky Purple Cherokee heirloom—and aromatic mint (basil's cousin) on top of bruschetta at the height of tomato season is so satisfying that you won't need to add much more than a slice of cheese or ham to the plate to call it supper. Or, try arugula or thyme in place of the mint—live a little.

MAKES ABOUT 2 CUPS

Summer

1 pound very ripe tomatoes, cored and cut into ½-inch dice

1 tablespoon extra-virgin olive oil

About 1½ tablespoons chopped fresh mint

Kosher or sea salt

Bruschette for serving

In a bowl, mix together the tomatoes, oil, mint, and salt to taste. Allow to rest for 10 to 20 minutes so the flavors blend. Serve with bruschette.

Sfranta

Evan Kleiman, chef-owner of Angeli Caffe and host of KCRW's *Good Food* show, shared Edda Servi's traditional Italian Jewish recipe for cooking summer squash until it falls apart. It's a great bruschetta topper, but Evan also serves it as a side dish, stirs it into risotto and pasta, and sometimes thins leftovers with stock to make a soup. Use medium-sized white or Lebanese zucchini for their creamy flavor and texture and for uniform color throughout the dish. Lemon thyme adds sparkle, but you can use regular thyme, Italian parsley, or basil.

MAKES ABOUT 3 CUPS

Summer, Autumn

2 pounds zucchini (about 6), preferably white or Lebanese, cut into ½-inch pieces

2 cloves garlic, chopped

¼ cup extra-virgin olive oil, or as needed

1 cup water

Leaves from several sprigs lemon thyme

Kosher or sea salt and freshly ground white pepper

Bruschette (page 37) for serving

Put the zucchini, garlic, ¼ cup oil, water, thyme, and a little salt in a deep pot, cover, and cook over medium heat for 10 minutes. Uncover, reduce the heat to low, and continue cooking, stirring occasionally, until the zucchini break down, the liquid is absorbed, and the mixture looks glossy, 30 to 40 minutes. Adjust the seasoning with salt, pepper, and oil. Serve warm or at room temperature with bruschette. Or, refrigerate for up to 3 days; bring to room temperature before serving.

CHEF'S TIP: Amy Sweeney, owner of Ammo Café in Hollywood, takes the opposite approach with summer squash, using a mandoline to shave raw yellow and green zucchini into long ribbons and dressing them with olive oil, mint, lemon, sea salt, and a scattering of green Lucques olives.

Flame-Roasted Eggplant Spread with Lemon and Garlic

From midsummer through early fall, eggplants of all shapes and sizes abound at the market, from psychedelic Neons to finger-sized Millionaires and Ichibans perfect for pickling. My favorite is the purple-and-white Rosa Bianca globe eggplant with creamy white flesh and few seeds that Scott Peacock and Alex Weiser bring to market. This spread, which can also be served as a salad, is an old family recipe handed down from my grandmother. Although a bit messy, roasting eggplant over an open flame adds sweet smokiness and keeps the flesh white.

MAKES ABOUT 2 CUPS

Summer, Autumn

2 large eggplants (about 1 pound each)
4 to 6 tablespoons canola or other mild cooking oil
1 scant teaspoon minced garlic
Juice of ½ lemon

Kosher or sea salt
Cucumber and tomato for garnish
Bruschette (page 37), pita wedges, or crackers for serving

Place the whole eggplants directly on the burners of a gas stove turned to medium-high or close to a medium-high fire on a grill. Roast, turning often, until the skins blacken and flake and the eggplants collapse and are meltingly tender, 10 to 15 minutes. As the eggplants start to char, the skins will tear and release steam and juices. If the skin burns before the flesh is tender, lower the flame slightly.

Remove each eggplant to a plate (use 2 large spoons or spatulas to manage this). While still hot, split them open flat like a book. Scoop the pulp into a sieve set over a bowl, scraping as much as possible from the skin and leaving any juices behind. If there are a lot of seeds, remove some, and pick out any black bits of skin. Drain for 10 minutes, discard the juices, and place the pulp in a bowl.

Using a whisking motion, mash the pulp with a fork, adding the oil gradually until the mixture is light and fluffy. Stir in the garlic, lemon juice, and salt to taste. The mixture will be a pale gold. It can be refrigerated for up to 1 day before serving. Serve at room temperature garnished with cucumber and tomato. Accompany with bruschette.

HOW TO CHOOSE EGGPLANTS: Look for firm, shiny eggplants that are heavy for their size and free of soft spots. Store unwrapped in the refrigerator crisper.

Marinated Grill-Roasted Lipstick Peppers

Rutiz, Tutti Frutti, and Beylik farms grow these succulent, sweet, deep red, pointed pimiento peppers that are meatier than red bell peppers. Summer through fall, have a batch of marinated peppers on hand to serve at a moment's notice with bruschetta or as a condiment for sandwiches and roasted or grilled meats. They will keep well, covered, in your refrigerator for a couple of weeks.

MAKES ABOUT 3 CUPS

Summer, Autumn

8 Lipstick peppers, or 4 red or yellow bell peppers

3 tablespoons extra-virgin olive oil

2 or 3 cloves garlic, chopped

Roast and peel the peppers as directed on page 25, then slice open lengthwise and discard the stems and seeds. Cut vertically into 1-inch-wide strips and place in a shallow serving dish. Drizzle with the oil and sprinkle with the garlic, tucking some in between the layers. Refrigerate for up to 3 days before serving to develop flavors. Serve at room temperature.

Winter Squash Puree with Shaved Parmesan

There's no need to add sugar to already sweet winter squash. Instead, play up its natural attributes through contrast—savory herbs, cheese, chiles—to welcome the season with this autumnal starter. Roast and freeze winter squash such as La Estrella, kabocha, butternut, or Queensland Blue, so you can easily make this spread all winter. Also try stirring it into a risotto (page 136), or make a double batch to serve alongside roast chicken or turkey. For more about winter squash, see page 69. Winchester Cheese Company milks Holsteins to produce its Dutch-style farmstead Gouda, which is aged from two months (creamy and mild) up to one year (extra sharp).

MAKES ABOUT 2 CUPS

Autumn, Winter

½ cup finely chopped onion

1 large clove garlic

1 tablespoon chopped fresh sage

1 dried árbol chile, or pinch of red pepper flakes

Kosher or sea salt

2 tablespoons extra-virgin olive oil

2 cups roasted winter squash (page 25)

About ½ cup vegetable or beef stock

2 to 4 tablespoons grated Parmigiano-Reggiano or Winchester sharp Gouda cheese, plus cheese for shaving

1 tablespoon pumpkin seed or extra-virgin olive oil

Bruschette (page 37) for serving

In a skillet, sauté the onion, whole garlic clove, sage, chile, and a little salt in the olive oil over medium-low heat until the onion is translucent and soft, 5 to 7 minutes. Stir in the squash, a little more salt, and ¼ cup of the stock. Reduce the heat to low, cover, and cook to a thick puree, about 15 minutes, stirring frequently and adding stock as needed to keep the mixture smooth and prevent sticking. If the mixture seems too wet, uncover during the last few minutes of cooking.

Remove the pan from the heat, discard the chile, and mash the garlic clove into the squash. Stir in the grated cheese and salt to taste along with the pumpkin-seed oil. The puree can be made a day ahead and refrigerated. Top with cheese shavings and serve at room temperature with bruschette.

Cannellini Bean Puree

This popular classic tastes best when made with fresh or new-season dried beans available from such farmers as Bill Coleman, Phil McGrath, and Richard Sager. Cannellini are a kind of white kidney bean with a lovely creamy texture. This puree is also delicious made with ruddy-colored cranberry beans. You can turn this recipe into a soup by thinning the puree with stock or water. See page 118 for more about beans at the farmers' market.

MAKES ABOUT 1¾ CUPS

Evergreen, Autumn

½ cup finely chopped onion

Kosher or sea salt and freshly ground black pepper

3 tablespoons extra-virgin olive oil

2 cloves garlic, minced

1 generous teaspoon minced fresh rosemary or sage

2 cups drained, cooked cannellini beans (from fresh or dried), page 25

About 1 cup bean cooking liquid, Chicken Stock (page 53), Vegetable Stock (page 52), or ½ cup canned stock diluted with ½ cup water

Bruschette (page 37) for serving

In a skillet, sauté the onion and a little salt in 2 tablespoons of the oil over medium-low heat until the onion is translucent and soft, 5 to 7 minutes. Stir in the garlic and rosemary and cook until fragrant, about 1 minute longer. Add the beans, a generous sprinkling of salt, several grinds of pepper, and about ¼ cup of the bean liquid. Bring to a simmer, stirring and mashing the beans with the back of a spoon. Reduce the heat to low, cover, and cook for 10 minutes, stirring and mashing frequently and adding cooking liquid ¼ cup at a time as needed to keep the mixture loose and prevent sticking. The mixture should be creamy with some texture.

Remove from the heat, stir in the remaining tablespoon oil, and season with salt and pepper. Serve warm or at room temperature with bruschette. The puree can be made a day ahead and refrigerated.

COOK'S TIP: Here's a legume starter idea that calls for chickpeas in the pod. In early summer, James and Dawn Birch of Flora Bella Farm in Three Rivers bring armloads of chickpea (garbanzo) cuttings that have fuzzy, light green, puffy pods containing one or two nutty, tender green peas hidden amid the foliage. Arrange the "branches" in a vase and let guests pick and eat the chickpeas raw. Or, toss the unopened pods and a handful of kosher salt into a heavy skillet and place on a grill until the pods are blackened in places and some pop open. Serve as you would roasted peanuts in the shell.

Sautéed Escarole

Common and inexpensive escarole looks like sturdy lettuce but is an often-overlooked mild endive related to radicchio and other chicories. Quick cooking, versatile, and nutritious, escarole has a slight bitterness that makes it an appealing rustic topping for bruschetta. Although it is available most of the year, you'll find especially tender and tasty giant heads of escarole at the stands of Flora Bella Farm and Coleman Family Farm. Try this recipe with Swiss chard, dandelion greens, or beet tops. Double the recipe for a side dish, stir into a pot of risotto, toss with pasta, or mix with cooked white beans.

MAKES ABOUT 2 CUPS

Evergreen

1 head escarole (about ½ pound)

3 tablespoons extra-virgin olive oil, or more to taste

1 cup chopped onion

2 large cloves garlic, minced

1 dried árbol chile, or pinch of red pepper flakes

Kosher or sea salt and freshly ground black pepper

Bruschette (page 37) for serving

Cut away and discard the core from the escarole, then chop the leaves. In a large skillet, heat 2 tablespoons of the oil over medium heat. Add the onion and sauté until soft and turning golden, 7 to 10 minutes. Add the garlic and chile and sauté until fragrant, about 1 minute. Add the escarole, reduce the heat to medium-low, and cook, stirring occasionally, until the escarole wilts and turns tender and dark green, about 10 minutes, adding a little water if it begins to stick.

Remove from the heat, discard the chile (if used), and season to taste with salt and pepper. Finely chop the escarole, place in a serving bowl, and stir in the remaining tablespoon oil. The dish can be made 6 hours ahead. Serve at room temperature with bruschette.

CHEF'S TIP: Amaranth is another underappreciated green worth trying. Magenta-splashed or solid-green varieties have a "grainlike flavor," says Mary Sue Milliken, chef-owner of Border Grill and Ciudad restaurants, who was introduced to the nutritious green on a long-ago trip to Greece. She boils the leaves in generously salted water for 5 minutes, drains and spreads them on towels to cool quickly, squeezes gently to remove moisture, and serves them at room temperature tossed with olive oil, lemon, salt, and pepper as an appetizer, salad, or side dish. Delicious with a wedge of feta cheese.

Persian-Style Herb and Cheese Platter

Herbs and alliums (onions and garlic) are at their most tender in spring, which is when Persian cooks especially like to assemble sprightly platters of *sabzi*—aromatic herbs, spring onions, and crisp radishes—with slabs of salty, creamy feta cheese, flat bread, and sweet halvah for guests to combine into bite-sized sandwiches of contrasting flavors. This also makes a savory and healthful afternoon snack, or a light lunch with a bowl of Green Garlic and New Potato Soup (page 56). Coleman Family Farm in Carpinteria and Rutiz Farms in Arroyo Grande specialize in Persian herbs, including cool mint (*na'nah*), sweet tarragon (*tarkhoun*), spicy pepper cress (*shahee*), and pungent leek-chive (*tareh*).

MAKES 6 TO 8 SERVINGS

Spring

1 bunch each Persian or regular mint, tarragon, Persian leek-chive, pepper cress, and/or cilantro

1 pound feta cheese

½ pound halvah (optional)

1 bunch radishes, sliced

1 bunch small spring or green onions, white part only, halved or quartered lengthwise

Flat bread, focaccia, lahvosh, or pita

Select any variety of herbs. Rinse and dry herbs up to 6 hours ahead, wrap in paper towels, and refrigerate. At serving, snip the herbs into large sprigs or individual leaves, discarding tough stems. Cut the cheese and halvah into ¼-inch-thick slices and the bread into small serving-sized pieces. (If using focaccia, halve horizontally first, then cut into pieces.) Arrange the herbs, radishes, onions, cheese, halvah, and bread on a platter. To eat, place a slice of cheese, several herb sprigs, a radish slice or two, some onion, and halvah onto a piece of bread.

FARMER'S TIP: Dennis Peitso of Maggie's Farm says the secret to storing herbs and salad greens is a not-too-cold fridge—no colder than 40 degrees. Keep delicate leafy herbs and greens such as chervil, winter hothouse basil, chives, and salad mixes unwashed in plastic bags with air trapped inside and refrigerate until needed. Shrubby herbs such as rosemary, thyme, or sage can be stored in a glass without water on the counter away from light. As the herbs dry, they are easier to pluck and crush right into your dish. Keep summer basil at room temperature with the stems in water.

Eggs at the Farmers' Market

Fresh eggs laid by hens who roam the farm pecking at field grains, bugs, and dirt have deep yellow, perky, upright yolks; thick, cloudy whites; and a rich, eggy flavor with little sulfur taste. And fresh eggs make the prettiest poached and hard-boiled eggs and the most stable meringues. You can't do much better than the eggs that Lily's Eggs, Schaner Farms, Peacock Family Farm, and Rocky Canyon Produce bring to market within twenty-four to forty-eight hours of gathering them.

At Lily's Eggs in Fillmore, Dianne Tuomey and Robert Tropper, who started egg farming about thirty years ago because they couldn't find good-tasting eggs for their bakery, average twenty-thousand dozen eggs a year from fifteen hundred to twenty-three hundred Rhode Island Reds (frequent layers), greenish black Australorps (larger eggs), Aurcanas (blue and green eggs), and some beautiful black-and-white Japanese Silkies (petite, sometimes green eggs), who are particularly maternal and willing to sit on other hens' eggs. Customers can place orders at Lily's market stand for quail and duck eggs, some goose eggs, and even the occasional giant, leathery emu egg.

On a smaller scale, the Schaners collect eggs from four hundred Rhode Island Reds and Aurcanas, and forty Khaki Campbell and Blue Swedish ducks at the Valley Center family farm in northern San Diego County. Besides a desire for top-quality eggs, fruit and vegetable farmers like Peter Schaner and Greg Nauta raise chickens to contribute to sustainability on their farms: the birds nourish the soil.

If you pay close attention, you'll see that eggs are seasonal, with spring, appropriately enough, being the most prolific time. Hens don't lay as much during hot weather, and small operations, like Peter Schaner's, offer fewer eggs in the summer. At Lily's, Dianne and Robert give a lot of thought to keeping the birds cool. They have built *palapas* (dried-palm-leaf umbrellas), installed sprinklers on the roofs of the open-door chicken houses, and provide lots of shady trees and bamboo. Eggs are collected twice a day at Lily's, more often when it's hot. If you notice smaller eggs among your dozen, they are most likely from younger hens, rather than a sign of an inferior product.

To test eggs for freshness at home, place them in a bowl of water. The freshest eggs lie flat. As they age and the air pocket at the large end increases, the eggs stands upright (the larger air pocket explains why you sometimes get hard-boiled eggs with a concave bottom). Superfresh eggs are harder to peel, so refrigerate them for several days before boiling. Fresh eggs will keep refrigerated up to six weeks.

Jessica's Aioli

My daughter Jessica has perfected the art of making fluffy aioli, the garlicky Provençal mayonnaise. She even knows how to fix it when it "breaks" (separates). You can make aioli or mayonnaise in a food processor, but it's more magical and the results more delicate when made with a bowl and whisk. Aioli served with a few well-chosen dippers makes a hearty appetizer. Instead of the usual raw, steamed, or boiled vegetables, try an assortment of roasted seasonal vegetables (pages 102 to 105).

MAKES ABOUT 2 CUPS

Evergreen

1½ cups canola or other mild cooking oil
½ cup extra-virgin olive oil
3 large cloves garlic
Kosher or sea salt

2 egg yolks
1 lemon, halved
2 to 3 tablespoons water

Stir together the oils in a 2-cup liquid measure and set aside. Remove any green shoots from center of the garlic cloves to make them easier to crush. To make aioli by hand, in a mortar, mash together the garlic and 1 teaspoon salt with a pestle until the garlic is completely pulverized, using a rubber spatula to scrape down the sides of the mortar as you work. Scrape the garlic paste into a large, deep ceramic bowl, add the egg yolks and a pinch of salt, and whisk to combine. While whisking constantly, begin adding the blended oils 1 drop at a time. After adding 1 to 2 tablespoons oil, the mixture will become very stiff. Whisking constantly, blend in 1 tablespoon of the water. When the mixture looks smooth, resume adding the oil drop by drop until the mixture again becomes stiff (you will have added about ½ cup oil at this point). Whisk in the juice of ½ lemon. When the mixture smoothes out, resume adding oil, this time in a thin stream. When the mixture is again stiff (you will have used about 1 cup oil), whisk in 1 more tablespoon water and add the remaining oil in a thin stream while whisking constantly. Taste the aioli and add salt as needed. It should taste more garlicky than lemony and the consistency should be looser than mayonnaise. If it's too thick, stir in a little water (or lemon juice if it won't upset the flavor balance). Refrigerate until ready to serve. It will keep for up to 3 days. Discard any aioli that sits out at room temperature more than an hour or two.

To make aioli in a food processor, with the motor running, add the garlic and 1 teaspoon salt through the feed tube and process until pureed. Add the egg yolks and process until blended, then begin adding the oil drop by drop through the feed tube as described for the hand method. Proceed as directed for the hand method.

COOK'S TIPS FOR SUCCESS

- It's easier to produce an emulsion in a narrow-bottomed ceramic bowl than a broad-bottomed one.
- Have ingredients and equipment at room temperature.
- Don't cut the recipe in half. It's easier to make 2 cups than 1 cup.
- If you don't have a mortar and pestle, place the garlic and salt on a cutting mat (page 29) and use the edge of a heavy pot to pulverize the garlic.
- If in the early stages of whisking the sauce turns thin, almost like a grainy salad dressing, it means the emulsion has "broken." Set it aside and place another egg yolk in a clean, deep bowl. Start whisking and add the broken aioli drop by drop until you have restored the emulsion. The ratio of yolks to oil is always 1 yolk to 1 cup oil; you have now used 3 yolks, so you must use a total of 3 cups oil. Adjust the amount of oil in your measuring cup and resume whisking in oil as directed. You will have 3 cups aioli.

Crab Cakes with Meyer Lemon Relish

Good crab cakes should be light, tender, and taste like crab, so handle them gently, season sparingly, and sauté rather than deep-fry. Fisherman Dennis Tsunoda of Anjin II traps rock (Dungeness-like texture) and spider or sheep (sweet) crabs off the Channel Islands, and sister Kathy steams them, picks the meat, and brings a blend of the two to the market within twenty-four hours. The local crab supply is most abundant in the spring. Happily, delicate Meyer lemons (a Eureka lemon–sweet orange cross) are plentiful at the same time, and are a perfect accent to crab. I got the idea for this simple raw lemon relish from chef and market regular Chris Kidder of Literati II Restaurant. It's like a fresh version of Moroccan preserved lemons—salty and tangy—and is great with other fish dishes. This recipe won't work with Eureka lemons, which have too much pith and are too tart.

MAKES TEN 2-INCH CRAB CAKES

Spring

30 Ritz crackers
½ pound lump crabmeat such as Channel Island rock-spider blend or Dungeness
1 egg, beaten
2 tablespoons mayonnaise
1 tablespoon lemon juice
Few drops hot-pepper sauce such as Tabasco

Kosher or sea salt
1 tablespoon unsalted butter
1 tablespoon canola or other mild cooking oil
Meyer Lemon Relish (recipe follows)
1 bunch frisée, tough stems removed and tossed with extra-virgin olive oil and salt (optional)

Place the crackers in a plastic bag and crush with a rolling pin to a texture coarser than commercial bread crumbs, with some small chunks remaining. Measure out ⅓ cup crumbs. Pour the remaining crumbs onto a dinner plate and set aside. Have another clean dinner plate ready nearby for holding the shaped crab cakes.

In a bowl, break the crabmeat apart with a fork, leaving some larger (about ½-inch) pieces intact. Using a fork and a gentle whisking motion, blend in the egg, mayonnaise, lemon juice, hot-pepper sauce, ½ teaspoon salt, and the ⅓ cup crumbs. The mixture will be wet and rather loose. Spoon a small handful (a scant ½ cup) of the crab mixture into the palm of your hand and lightly shape into a patty about 2 inches in diameter. Don't worry if the edges are ragged. Place the patty on the plate of crumbs and coat it well, gently turning and shaping the patty until it is straight sided and about ¾ inch thick. The patty will become more stable as it is coated. Place the crab cake on the clean dinner plate and repeat with the remaining crab mixture. You should have 10 crab cakes. Cover and chill the cakes for at least 30 minutes and up to 4 hours before cooking.

In a large skillet, heat the butter and oil over medium heat until the butter starts to color and sizzles when a drop of water is added. Add the crab cakes without crowding and sauté until the undersides are golden brown, 3 to 5 minutes. Flip the cakes and sauté until cooked through and lightly springy to the touch, 3 to 5 minutes. Resist the temptation to press on the cakes with the spatula! Season with a little salt and serve hot with the lemon relish as an hors d'oeuvre, or plated with the relish and a tangle of frisée as a first course.

Meyer Lemon Relish

MAKES ¾ TO 1 CUP

1 large shallot, minced (about ⅓ cup)

1½ to 2 teaspoons kosher or sea salt

2 or 3 Meyer lemons

4 sprigs Italian parsley, chopped

In a small bowl, mix together the shallot and 1½ teaspoons salt. With a sharp knife, pare the yellow zest from 2 of the lemons and reserve. Trim and discard the white pith from the 2 lemons, then quarter them and remove the seeds and center pith. On a cutting board, chop together the lemons, zest, and salted shallots until finely minced. Scrape the mixture and its juices into a small serving bowl. Add more salt or the third lemon to taste. Stir in the parsley and let the relish stand for 30 minutes before serving. It will keep refrigerated for up to 4 days.

HOW TO CHOOSE MEYER LEMONS: Look for deep golden yellow, smooth-skinned fruits that are heavy for their size and feel full of juice.

FARMER'S TIP: According to Kathy Tsunoda, "Taste cooked crabmeat for saltiness before using it at home. You never know how much seawater taste it will have retained. Keep it refrigerated and use within two days."

CHEF'S TIP: Josiah Citrin, chef owner of Melisse, makes quick Moroccan-style preserved Meyer lemons for year-round use in everything from simple pan sauces for fish to fancy apricot-date confiture. Josiah considers them "a great 'seasoning' that adds complex lemon flavors to many foods." Slice lemons crosswise into ½-inch-thick slices and pick out the seeds. Layer the slices in a perforated pan or on a rack placed in a pan, season heavily with equal amounts kosher salt and sugar, cover, and refrigerate for 48 hours. Pack the lemon slices into jars and pour in equal parts grape seed and olive oil to cover the lemons completely, allowing the oil to sink to the bottom (weight lemons if necessary). Refrigerate at least 5 days before using (3 weeks is even better). They'll keep refrigerated up to 6 months.

Soups

Farmers' market produce offers endless soup possibilities, from homey tomato to elegant mosaics of bright vegetables floating in clear broth. Even humble root vegetables such as parsnips and rutabagas reveal their splendor when transformed Cinderella-like into shimmering purees.

Whether designed to warm or refresh us, comfort or impress, soups are straightforward to make. Once ingredients are prepared for the pot, it's usually a matter of briefly sautéing and then simmering them for either a few minutes or a couple of hours, depending on the recipe. And some soups require no cooking at all. Here are six simple steps for flavorful results.

Soup Basics

1. Sauté or roast—but don't burn—the flavor base (vegetables, spices, meats) to intensify flavors before adding liquid to the pot. Use a wide pot so the ingredients caramelize rather than steam.
2. Add stock in batches to deepen flavors. After the sauté stage, add part of the liquid and simmer until reduced by about one-third. Then add more, but not so much your soup looks anemic. For pureed soups, add the last of the liquid after pureeing to reach the desired consistency.
3. If a pureed soup ends up too thin, cook it uncovered a little longer to allow some liquid to evaporate, or thicken it by adding a diced boiled potato and then pureeing it again. If it is too thick, add water or more stock to maintain the flavor balance.
4. A good homemade stock produces the tastiest soup (keep some frozen for convenience), but when pressed for time, you can use good-quality canned stock diluted with water to half strength. Also, you can substitute vegetable stock in most recipes calling for a meat stock and get a satisfactory result.
5. Salt stock lightly. It is a building block and will concentrate as the soup cooks. Dilute homemade stock to half strength (or 1 cup canned to 2 cups water) for a **light stock** when you want depth and richness but not meatiness. Taste and adjust the seasoning again before serving.
6. If using a stand blender to puree hot soup, cool the soup briefly and puree in batches, never filling the jar more than half full, and covering the lid with a folded towel for extra protection.

Vegetable Stock

This is a rough guide for what to include in your vegetable stock, depending on what is in season or in your refrigerator. For example, you can add a tomato, a piece of winter squash, some spring parsley roots, and/or a few dried mushrooms, or you can skip the red pepper. Be sure to avoid strong-flavored vegetables, however, such as cabbage, cauliflower, or broccoli, and go light on garlic to keep the stock versatile. You can easily double this recipe and freeze the extra. For a deeper, heartier stock, roast the vegetables instead of sautéing them: toss them with the oil, spread them on baking sheets, and roast in a 375-degree oven until nicely browned but not blackened, about 1 hour.

MAKES 7 TO 8 CUPS

Evergreen

1 large leek, split lengthwise with greens and roots intact

3 carrots

1 large or 2 medium onions (about ½ pound total)

2 ribs celery with leaves

2 zucchini

Few large Swiss chard leaves with stems

1 red bell pepper (if doubling recipe, don't double pepper)

½ bunch parsley with stems (about 20 large sprigs)

6 sprigs thyme

2 bay leaves, preferably fresh

Kosher or sea salt

A few black peppercorns (optional)

1 to 2 tablespoons olive, canola, or other mild cooking oil

Cut all the vegetables into 1- to 2-inch pieces and put into an 8-quart stockpot. Add the herbs, 1 tablespoon salt, the peppercorns, and the oil and set over medium heat. Sauté the vegetables until wilted, 10 to 15 minutes. Raise the heat to medium-high and add water barely to cover the vegetables (8 to 10 cups). Cover and bring to a boil, reduce the heat to low, adjust the lid to cover partially, and simmer gently for 1 hour.

Strain the soup through a fine-mesh sieve, pressing on the vegetables to extract all their goodness. Discard the vegetables. If the flavor is weak, boil the stock uncovered to reduce and concentrate the flavor. Lightly salt the stock to taste. Use immediately, or let cool completely, cover, and refrigerate for up to 4 days or freeze for up to 3 months.

Chicken Stock

This is my mother's recipe, and it results in a stock so full of protein that it jells completely when chilled. Bones, skin, and long cooking make a tasty stock, so don't use boneless, skinless chicken breasts and expect a rich broth after only an hour on the stove. Remember, too, any fat is easily removed after cooking. My mother often adds a parsnip, parsley root, or a piece of summer or winter squash and sometimes a leek or two. Use the stock as is, or thin it with water to half strength for a light stock when you want depth but a less intense chicken flavor in your finished soup. For a rich poultry stock, add turkey wings to the mix as cookbook author Lynne Rosetto Kasper suggests (see below). Use a 12- or 16-quart pot to make a double recipe and freeze the extra stock in 2- or 4-cup containers for convenient use later.

MAKES 6 TO 8 CUPS

Evergreen

4 pounds chicken wings and backs

2 onions, halved

2 or 3 ribs celery with leaves, preferably from heart, broken in half

2 large carrots, cut in half

½ bunch parsley with stems (about 20 large sprigs)

Kosher or sea salt

Rinse the chicken and discard any large pockets of fat from the backs. Put the chicken into an 8-quart stockpot and pour in cold water barely to cover (8 to 10 cups). Cover, set over medium-high heat, and bring almost to a boil (avoid a rolling boil or the stock will be cloudy). Reduce the heat to low and skim off any foam as it rises to the top. Add the onions, celery, and carrots and push them down into the liquid. Cover the pot partially and simmer over low heat (you want to see bubbles coming up from the bottom of the pot) for 3 to 4 hours, adding the parsley during the last 30 minutes.

Strain the stock through a fine-mesh sieve and discard the meat and vegetables. If you want a clearer stock, strain the stock again through a sieve lined with a paper towel or a paper coffee filter. Season to taste with up to 1 tablespoon salt. If using the stock immediately, skim the fat off the surface with a large spoon. If not using immediately, let cool completely, cover, and refrigerate until well chilled, then lift off and discard the congealed fat. The stock can be refrigerated for up to 4 days or frozen or up to 3 months.

RICH POULTRY STOCK: Reduce the chicken backs and wings to 3 pounds and add 1½ pounds turkey wings. Proceed as directed.

Simple Beef Stock

Use a mix of beef and veal bones and collagen-rich beef shank meat, which gives heft to the stock. The addition of dried mushrooms and tomato amps up the savory meatiness, what the Japanese call *umami*, of this stock. For a richer, deeper-flavored stock, roast the bones first in a 375-degree oven until they are nicely browned, about 45 minutes.

MAKES 4 TO 5 CUPS

Evergreen

4 pounds mixed beef shanks and beef or veal bones
1 large carrot
1 rib celery with leaves
1 tomato
1 large onion, cut in half

4 dried shiitake mushrooms
6 large sprigs parsley with stems
1 bay leaf
2 large sprigs thyme
Kosher or sea salt

Put the shanks and bones in an 8-quart stockpot and pour in cold water barely to cover (6 to 8 cups). Cover, set over medium-high heat, and bring almost to a boil (avoid a rolling boil or the stock will be cloudy). Reduce the heat to low and skim off any foam as it rises to the top. Add all the vegetables and herbs and push them down into the liquid. Cover the pot partially and simmer over low heat (you want to see bubbles coming up from the bottom of the pot) for 3 to 4 hours.

Strain the stock through a fine-mesh sieve and discard the meat, bones, and vegetables. If you want clearer stock, strain the stock again through a sieve lined with a paper towel or a paper coffee filter. Season to taste with up to 1 tablespoon salt. If using the stock immediately, skim the fat off the surface with a large spoon. If not using immediately, let cool completely, cover, and refrigerate until well chilled, then lift off and discard the congealed fat. The stock may be refrigerated for up to 4 days or frozen or up to 3 months.

Indian-Style Cauliflower Soup with English Peas

Cauliflower was once considered a gardener's delicacy, because it was a challenge to grow the pristinely white compact heads we take for granted today. Cauliflower is sweetest grown in cool weather and does well in coastal climates. Suncoast Farms and Green Farms in Lompoc, Two Peas in a Pod in Arroyo Grande, and Coastal Farms in Santa Paula bring beautiful specimens to the market. Make this soup in spring when sweet English, or garden, peas are available from McGrath Family Farms, Two Peas in a Pod, Tutti Frutti, and Fairview Gardens. The peas float in this golden soup like emeralds.

MAKES 6 TO 8 SERVINGS

Spring

2 tablespoons canola or other mild cooking oil

1 teaspoon cumin seeds

1 teaspoon ground turmeric

½ teaspoon ground coriander

½ teaspoon ground cumin

⅛ to ¼ teaspoon red pepper flakes

1 teaspoon kosher or sea salt

1 onion, chopped

1 large clove garlic, finely chopped

1 tablespoon minced fresh ginger

1 large head cauliflower (about 2 pounds), cut into small florets

½ cup water

4 to 6 cups Chicken Stock (page 53), Vegetable Stock (page 52), or 2 to 3 cups canned diluted with 2 to 3 cups water

1 cup shelled English peas (about 1 pound in the pod)

½ lime

Small handful each of fresh mint leaves, chives, and cilantro leaves, chopped

In a wide pot, heat 1 tablespoon of the oil over medium heat. Add the cumin seeds and stir until brown, 1 to 2 minutes. Add the ground spices, pepper flakes, and salt and cook until fragrant, 30 to 60 seconds. Reduce the heat to medium-low, add the remaining tablespoon oil and the onion, and sauté until translucent and soft, 5 to 7 minutes. Add the garlic and ginger and cook 1 minute. Stir in the cauliflower and water, cover, raise the heat to medium, and cook for 5 minutes. Add 4 cups stock, re-cover, and bring to a boil. Reduce the heat to low and simmer gently until very tender, 15 to 20 minutes.

Use an immersion or stand blender to puree the soup, leaving a little texture. Add the remaining 2 cups stock as needed to achieve the consistency of heavy cream. Return the soup to medium-low heat, add the peas, cover, and simmer until the peas are tender but still bright green, about 5 minutes. Give the soup a squeeze of lime and serve with a sprinkling of the herbs.

HOW TO CHOOSE ENGLISH PEAS: Look for plump, bright green, slightly tender pods. Harder, overly full pods signal starchy overly mature peas. Because their sugars turn to starch quickly, peas are sweetest when eaten as soon as possible after harvest, but will keep refrigerated for up to 1 week.

Green Garlic and New Potato Soup

This pink-and-green soup is a favorite of mine, because it shows how delicious a soup made with only a few ingredients can be. Spring or green garlic, admired in Asian and European cooking, looks like a skinny leek and is the mild-tasting immature garlic plant pulled before the bulb forms cloves. Traditionally, it showed up in markets when farmers thinned the field to make space for maturing "heading" bulbs. Today, growers such as Peter Schaner of Schaner Farms and his cousin William Stehley of Sycamore Hill treat it almost like a separate first crop.

MAKES 6 TO 8 SERVINGS

Spring

3 bunches green garlic (about 1 pound)
4 to 5 tablespoons extra-virgin olive oil, plus more for finishing soup (optional)
1 onion, chopped
Kosher or sea salt and freshly ground black pepper

1 pound red-skinned or completely red potatoes such as French Fingerling, Red Thumb, or All Red, preferably new, cut into ½-inch pieces
5 to 6 cups water

Trim the root end and tops off the garlic, so that you have the white part and about 4 inches of the green. Discard any yellowed or old-looking leaves. Cut the garlic plants in half lengthwise and then cut crosswise into thin slices (you should have 5 to 6 cups). In a wide pot, heat 3 tablespoons of the oil, garlic, and onion over medium-low heat. Add ½ to 1 teaspoon salt, stir, and cook, stirring occasionally, until the garlic is wilted but still bright green, 5 to 10 minutes. Reduce the heat to low, cover, and cook until the garlic and onion are tender, about 10 minutes more.

Add the potatoes, 2 cups of the water, a little salt, and several grinds of pepper and re-cover the pot. Raise the heat and bring to a gentle boil. Reduce the heat to a simmer, cover the pot partially, and cook for 5 minutes. Add 3 cups of the water and continue cooking until the potatoes are tender, and soup flavors develop, about 15 minutes.

Add the remaining 1 cup water if the soup seems thick. Season to taste with salt, pepper, and 1 to 2 tablespoons oil. Drizzle each serving with additional oil.

HOW TO CHOOSE GREEN GARLIC: The youngest, most delicately flavored green garlic has a straight bulb end ½ to 1 inch thick and bright green leaves. As the season progresses, plants develop fat-bottomed bulbs, tougher, yellowed leaves, and a sharper taste. If you can find only these mature plants, reduce the number of plants called for and use less of the green. The soup will have a heartier flavor, and the garlic may take longer to soften.

One Potato, Two Potato

It wasn't long ago that market shoppers found just a few kinds of potatoes—Red and White Rose, Yukon Gold, the occasional russet—until it dawned on farmers (Alex Weiser gets credit for starting the movement at the Santa Monica Farmers' Market) and chefs that such a homely staple could be a thing of infinite variety, beauty, and seasonality. Weiser Family Farms, Windrose Farm, Tutti Frutti Farms, Fairview Gardens, Rutiz Farms, and others grow an exceptional array, from starchy Purple Peruvians, descended from the ten thousand-year-old South American spud, to silky French Fingerlings.

Texture is the biggest difference among potatoes. Dry, starchy, or floury potatoes mash well; moist, waxy potatoes hold their shape better for salads. Many potatoes fall somewhere between the two extremes and are considered "all-purpose." All varieties range from bite-sized peewees to large "bakers."

"New" refers to freshly dug potatoes of any variety and size, not just round red ones. These have delicate skins easily rubbed off with your thumb and flesh that is juicy, sweet, and crisp. Alex Weiser hand-digs new potatoes at the beginning of each harvest (there are several each year) in Tehachapi and Edison, two historic California potato-growing regions, and leaves the remaining potatoes in the field for a couple of weeks to cure and toughen up their skins, which is how we are used to seeing them.

Choose unblemished potatoes with no sprouting eyes or green tinge, signs of age and improper storage (exposure to light). New potatoes of any size have flaky skin. Store potatoes out of the plastic bag in a cool (not cold), dark place, and use new potatoes within a few days. If potatoes develop patches of green (a toxic reminder they are part of the nightshade family), peel deeply—about 1/16 inch—to remove them. Here are some recent market favorites.

ALL BLUE AND PURPLE PERUVIAN: Starchy flesh and deep purple skin; All Blues often have a band of white under the skin, while the deep indigo of Peruvians goes all the way through.

AUSTRIAN CRESCENT: Yellow skinned fingerling with moist, dense yellow flesh.

CAROLA, SATINA, AND YUKON GOLD: Similar all-purpose yellow-fleshed potatoes; Yukon has distinctive pink "eyes."

FRENCH: Red skin and creamy, moist-fleshed fingerling, often with a pink "starburst."

GERMAN BUTTERBALL: All-purpose round with russeted, thick, netted skin; deep yellow, moist flesh (flakier than the Yukon); and rich, buttery taste.

KING EDWARD: Yellow skin with pink blush and white, starchy flesh; good for baking and mashing.

NORKOTAH RUSSET: A great baker, moister than a classic Russet Burbank.

ONAWAY: White skin, white flesh, and waxy enough to hold its shape in salads and gratins.

RED THUMB, ALL RED, AND CRANBERRY RED: All-purpose with red skin and red-pink flesh.

ROSE FINN APPLE: Pink-skinned, yellow-fleshed, waxy fingerling, also known as Ruby Crescent.

RUSSIAN BANANA: Also known as La Ratte, this tan-skinned, yellow-fleshed fingerling has a somewhat dry texture and a definite banana curve.

Smooth-as-Silk Parsnip Puree

Parsnips are sweet, sharp, citrusy, and pleasantly starchy—in other words, naturally complex—so if you have an onion and some parsnips on hand, you are well on the way to an interesting soup. Jerry Rutiz is among the few farmers who bring this oft-ignored relative of carrots and parsley to the Santa Monica Farmers' Market. Phil McGrath sells finger-sized baby parsnips, which are delicious sautéed whole in a little butter. Considered a cold-weather crop best handled by being "stored" in the ground until harvest, California parsnips grow sweetest where winter night temperatures drop below freezing. The hint of lemon here plays up the root vegetable's citrus notes.

MAKES 6 SERVINGS

Winter, Spring

1 large onion, chopped

3 tablespoons unsalted butter

Kosher or sea salt and freshly ground white pepper

3 pounds parsnips, peeled and cut into ½-inch-thick coins

8 cups Vegetable Stock (page 52), or 4 cups canned diluted with 4 cups water

½ lemon

Walnut or pistachio oil (optional)

Fleur de sel or other finishing salt

In a wide pot, gently cook the onion in the butter with a little salt over medium-low heat until translucent and soft, 5 to 7 minutes. Stir in the parsnips and season with salt and pepper. Cover and cook until partially tender but not browned, about 10 minutes. Add 2 cups of the stock, re-cover, and bring to a gentle boil. Reduce the heat to a simmer and cook for 15 minutes. Add 4 more cups stock and continue to simmer, covered, until the parsnips are very tender, about 15 minutes more.

Puree the soup with an immersion or stand blender. Parsnips are fibrous, so rub the soup through a fine-mesh sieve into a clean pot. You should have about 5 cups thick puree. Reheat the soup, thinning with the remaining 2 cups stock as needed to achieve the consistency of heavy cream. Add a couple squeezes of lemon—the soup shouldn't taste lemony, but the flavors should come alive. Top each serving with a swirl of oil and a little *fleur de sel*. The soup can be made up to a day ahead.

HOW TO CHOOSE PARSNIPS: Pick juicy-looking parsnips—avoid cracked ones—with the least tapered shape for more "meat." Although they aren't used in cooking, the attached greens are a good indicator of freshness. Discard the tops before storing the parsnips. They will keep for several weeks in an open plastic bag in the refrigerator crisper, especially if you slip in a paper towel to absorb moisture.

Classic Tomato Soup with a Goat Cheese Swirl

What gives old-fashioned tomato soup its comfort-food superstatus is its perfect sweet-acid balance. Sample tomatoes at the market and if they are too acid or too sweet, add a few of another variety to your shopping bag to adjust the flavors (especially important when using low-acid Japanese, orange, yellow, or white tomatoes). Chervil adds a delicate celerylike flavor that complements the tomatoes.

MAKES 8 SERVINGS

Summer, Autumn

1 leek, white part only (reserve green parts for making stock), finely chopped

1 small carrot, peeled and finely chopped

1 small onion, finely chopped

1 center rib celery with leaves, finely chopped

Kosher or sea salt and freshly ground black pepper

2 tablespoons unsalted butter

4 pounds ripe tomatoes, peeled, seeded (page 24), and chopped

2 sprigs parsley, 1 sprig thyme, and 1 bay leaf tied together in cheesecloth

5 cups Vegetable Stock (page 52), or 2½ cups canned diluted with 2½ cups water

2 ounces mild goat cheese such as Redwood Hill plain or herbed chèvre, at room temperature

Small handful of fresh chervil leaves, coarsely chopped

In a wide pot, cook the leek, carrot, onion, and celery with a little salt in the butter over medium-low heat until the vegetables are tender, 10 to 15 minutes, covering the pot halfway through the cooking time. Uncover, add the tomatoes and herb bundle, season with salt and pepper, and raise the heat to medium-high. Bring to a boil, reduce the heat as needed to maintain a gentle boil, and cook, uncovered, until the tomatoes break down and thicken slightly, about 10 minutes. Add 4 cups of the stock, bring to a boil, and cook for 20 minutes, reducing the heat if the soup becomes too thick.

Puree the soup with an immersion or stand blender. For a refined puree, pass the soup through a fine-mesh sieve into a clean pot to remove any stray seeds or lumps. If the soup is too thick, add the remaining 1 cup stock. If too thin, cook uncovered over medium heat to reduce. Season to taste with salt and pepper. Top each serving with a spoonful of goat cheese and chervil.

FARMER'S TIP: To enjoy good-tasting tomatoes long after the growing season has past, tomato grower Ed Munak recommends freezing whole ripe tomatoes on a baking sheet, and then storing them in resealable plastic bags. When you are ready to use them, rinse the frozen tomatoes briefly and the skins will slip right off. Ideal for winter soups and sauces.

Green Zebra Gazpacho

Perfect on a balmy summer evening, this ultrarefreshing gazpacho uses ripe heirloom green tomatoes, such as Green Zebra or the large Evergreens that Maryann and Paul Carpenter grow in Santa Paula, and thirst-quenching green grapes, cooling lime, and mint. Use the sweet, juicy (not watery) Persian cucumbers available from Beylik, Jaime, or Weiser farms or Munak Ranch. For more on tomatoes and cucumbers, see pages 84 and 87, respectively. If you don't have stale bread on hand, put torn fresh bread in a 250-degree oven until dry.

MAKES 8 TO 10 SERVINGS

Summer

2 pounds ripe Green Zebra or Evergreen tomatoes

2 Persian cucumbers (about 10 ounces total)

1 small white onion, coarsely chopped

1 cup seedless green grapes

2 cups torn, crust-free, stale French bread

Juice of 2 limes

½ to 1 small jalapeño chile, cut into small pieces

Leaves from 8 to 10 sprigs cilantro

Leaves from 8 to 10 sprigs mint

2 tablespoons canola or other mild cooking oil

Kosher or sea salt

1½ cups water

1 avocado, pitted, peeled, and cut into ¼- to ½-inch dice

Snipped fresh chives for garnish

Peel and seed tomatoes as directed on page 24, reserving the juices that collect in the bowl. Coarsely chop the tomatoes and add them to the bowl. Peel the cucumbers, cut them in half lengthwise, and use the tip of a spoon to scrape out the seeds. Cut the cucumbers into chunks and add them to the bowl. Stir in the cucumbers, onion, grapes, bread, juice of 1 lime, ½ chile, cilantro, mint, oil, 1 teaspoon salt, and water.

Puree the soup with a stand blender, leaving the texture a little chunky. Cover and chill for at least 2 hours or up to overnight. Taste and adjust the seasoning with salt. If the soup is not zesty enough, grind the remaining ½ chile with a little of the soup and stir it into the soup. Garnish each serving with the avocado, chives, and an extra sprinkling of salt.

HOW TO CHOOSE GRAPES: Look for small, round grapes that have not been "gibbed," treated with gibberalic acid to take in more water. Grapes left on the vine to ripen and sweeten, such as those from Balderama or Nicholas, will be more golden than green. Store unwashed in the cool part of the refrigerator for up to a week.

Once called alligator pears, avocados first appeared in California in the mid-nineteenth century, but they didn't become popular until the 1920s. The rich fruit has flourished here ever since, especially in northern San Diego County, where most of the U.S. crop is grown today. Vista avocados were pedigreed on fancy Los Angeles restaurant menus as early as the 1930s, and Fallbrook continues to label itself the world's avocado capital.

The subtropical Central American native pairs well with citrus on the plate and in the orchard and many local growers specialize in both. Avocados are harvested mature but hard from great drooping branches and ripen after picking. Although the different types vary in oil content, all possess less oil and lighter flavor early in the season. At the very end of the season, avocados can be stringy or have off flavors. Choose peak-season avocados with slight give when cupped in your hand. Ripe avocados can be refrigerated for several days.

There are dozens of varieties besides the familiar Hass and Fuerte. San Diego County farmers George Bamber of Holy Guaca-Moly, Armando Garcia of Garcia Organic Farm, Bob Polito of Polito Family Farms, and Peter Schaner of Schaner Farms, and San Bernardino County's Laura Ramirez of J.J.'s Lone Daughter Ranch have made a specialty of some of the best, listed here by peak season.

PINKERTON: Cross between Fuerte and Hass, with rough, green skin, a long, meaty neck, and a small seed. Easy to peel, it holds its shape and color when sliced and tastes more buttery than the Fuerte. The neck softens first, so check the body for true ripeness. Late winter through spring.

GWEN: An uncommon variety that is richer than the Hass. Brittle, dark green skin cracks and breaks easily in peeling, so it is best to scoop out the pulp from its shell. Winter through spring.

FUERTE: California's first avocado and the first commercial variety. Smooth green skin and a medium-rich nutty flavor with sweet overtones in early season; holds it shape and color when sliced. Spring.

HASS: Postman Rudolph Hass discovered and then grafted the eponymous variety at his La Habra Heights orchard in 1926. In the 1970s, the Hass replaced the Fuerte as the most important commercial variety. Available most of the year, but best in summer, it has rough black skin when ripe, very buttery flesh good for mashing, and discolors more easily than the Fuerte. Summer.

LAMB HASS: A new variety, this Hass "grandchild" was developed at the University of California at Davis from the Gwen. It is more block shaped than the Hass, and its darker, slightly smoother skin has some of the "chipping" tendencies of the Gwen. Late summer into fall.

REED: Large and as round as a cannonball, this green-skinned, tasty variety holds its shape and color well. Late summer into fall.

Cantaloupe Soup with Moscato d'Asti and Mint

Use a fragrant, intensely flavored cantaloupe for this refined summer first course that doubles as a dessert. The "broth"—simply the melon juices and Moscato d'Asti, a fizzy, low-alcohol Italian dessert wine—is created by hand chopping the fruit to release its juices and then seasoning with only lemon and delicate Persian mint. You won't get the same result using a blender! For dessert, serve the soup with Pistachio Shortbread Cookies (page 190).

MAKES 8 SERVINGS

Summer

1 large, ripe cantaloupe, 3½ to 4 pounds
2⅔ cups Moscato d'Asti
½ lemon

Handful of fresh mint leaves, preferably Persian, chopped

Peel and seed the cantaloupe (see Cook's Tip). Finely chop the fruit almost to a pulp. Pour the cantaloupe and its juices into a large bowl. Stir in ⅔ cup of the wine and a squeeze of lemon juice. Refrigerate until well chilled, at least 2 hours or up to 6 hours.

To serve, pour ½ cup of the melon mixture into each of 8 chilled soup bowls. Add ¼ cup wine to each bowl and scatter the mint over the top.

COOK'S TIP: To peel a cantaloupe efficiently, cut a thin slice off the top and bottom ends, and stand the melon upright. Tracing the curve of the melon with your knife, slice off the peel in thick strips. Cut the melon in half, scoop out the seeds, and then cut the fruit as desired.

Melon Mania

Melons range in taste from bitter to cucumber-like (Windrose Farm's long, striped cucumber is actually a snake melon) to honeyed and from inodorous to fragrant. The luscious summer fruit weighing down market tables and spilling over into great cartons basically divides into four groups: muskmelons, true cantaloupes, nonfragrant melons, and watermelons. Weiser, Rocky Canyon, and Munak bring exceptional and interesting summer melons to market. The entirely different nonsweet warm-weather melons—bitter melon and *donqua*, or Chinese winter melon—used in savory dishes are available from farmers specializing in Asian crops, such as Fresno Evergreen, Vang Thao, Phong Vang, and Briar Patch.

MUSKMELONS: Fragrant and ribbed with netted, or reticulated, rind, muskmelons are the most common grouping and include Persian melons and what we mistakenly call cantaloupes (I distinguish them here, but use the term *cantaloupe* as typically understood through the book). Look for delicately flavored and textured Ambrosia; Ananas (Sharlyn), which has a deep golden orange, netted rind and pale, juicy, sweet, soft flesh; green-fleshed, mild Rocky Sweet; and of course, "cantaloupes." Choose fragrant, heavy muskmelons with thick, developed netting. They should be slightly less than rock hard, with a bit of give at the blossom and stem ends. Store on the counter until ripe, then refrigerate.

TRUE CANTALOUPES: Fragrant, rounder than muskmelons, and prominently ribbed, true cantaloupes are sometimes "warty" but not netted. The small French Charentais, with gray-green rind and aromatic deep orange flesh, is the most famous cantaloupe. Ha-Ogen has yellow-green rind and green flesh (some experts group it with muskmelons). Choose melons that are fragrant and heavy for their size. True cantaloupes are more perishable than muskmelons and should be consumed within a couple of days.

INODOROUS (NONFRAGRANT) MELONS: Juicy honeydew, Crenshaw, and Casaba melons reveal little of their inner glory to the passing shopper. Instead, you must look for warm-colored rinds, such as honeydews that are ivory toned rather than icy green-white. Sugar scabs and small sugar cracks are also indicators of a good melon. Avoid melons that slosh when shaken, a sign they are overripe. Honeyloupe is one of my favorite varieties: its salmon-colored flesh has honeydew's smooth texture and deep honeyed flavor with the crispness of a "cantaloupe."

WATERMELONS: For centuries, watermelons have come in white, yellow, and red, with rinds ranging from almost black to gray, gold, green, variegated green-and-white, and yellow-starred. The only really "new" developments are the seedless, mini, and crisp-textured, less juicy varieties. Red-fleshed Moon and Stars, with its bright yellow spatters (stars) and splotches (moon) on black-green rind, is one of the best-known heirlooms (1926), but don't miss the incredibly flavorful Orange Glo, so delicate it practically breaks apart in your hands (both at Weiser). Look for hard, heavy watermelons that produce a resonant sound when slapped. They should have a bright rind, a buttery yellow belly, and a green, fresh-looking stem end. Store whole watermelons in a cool place for up to two weeks. Once cut, juicier varieties should be consumed within two days, but crispier seedless melons can last a week.

No-Cream Creamy Corn Soup with Chipotle-Lime Topping

The old-fashioned technique of grating raw corn to release its milk produces a creamy soup (and real creamed corn—see opposite) that can be enjoyed from summer's first pick to the last harvest at Thanksgiving time. The topping, made with chipotles (smoked dried jalapeños) from Windrose Farm, adds spicy contrast to the sweet corn and is also great as a dressing for corn salad or a condiment for grilled fish or chicken. The Tamais, who have been farming for three generations in coastal Oxnard and in the hot inland Imperial Valley, which extends their growing season, raise sweet white corn from mid-May through Thanksgiving. But my favorite is the more complexly flavored, yellow-and-white-speckled calico corn, available July through October.

MAKES 6 SERVINGS

Summer, Autumn

8 ears corn, shucked

1 onion, finely chopped

2 ribs celery with leaves, finely chopped

1 tablespoon olive oil

1 tablespoon unsalted butter

4 cups Chicken Stock (page 53) or
    Vegetable Stock (page 52), or 2 cups
    canned diluted with 2 cups water

Kosher or sea salt and freshly ground
    white pepper

FOR THE TOPPING

4 chipotle chiles

2 large cloves garlic

½ cup fresh cilantro leaves

¼ cup lime juice

1 teaspoon kosher or sea salt

½ cup olive oil

⅓ cup *crema* (Mexican crème fraîche),
    optional

Using the large holes of a box grater set in a deep bowl, grate the corn down to the cob. This will be messy but well worth it. You should have about 5 cups milky pulp. In a wide pot, sauté the onion and celery in the oil and butter over medium heat until translucent and soft, 5 to 7 minutes. Stir in the corn and stock and season with salt and pepper. Reduce the heat to medium-low, cover partially, and cook, stirring occasionally, until the corn is tender and the flavors are blended, about 15 minutes. Leave the soup as is or puree with an immersion or stand blender.

To make the topping, soften the chiles in water for 4 minutes in the microwave or 10 minutes simmering on the stove top, then discard the stems and some or all of the seeds (the heat is in the seeds). Using a food processor with the motor running, add the garlic cloves through the feed tube and process until chopped. Add the chiles, cilantro, lime juice, and salt and process until well blended. With the motor running, add the oil in a slow, steady stream until blended. You will have about ¾ cup. Alternatively, mince the topping ingredients by hand and whisk in the lime juice, salt, and oil.

Pour the hot soup into bowls. Lightly whisk the *crema* and drizzle each serving with an equal amount of the chile mixture and the *crema*.

REAL CREAMED CORN: Substitute 2 tablespoons butter for the butter and olive oil, and 1 cup stock or water for the stock. After sautéing the celery and onion, add the corn, season as directed, and cook over medium-low heat, stirring frequently, for 10 minutes. Stir in ½ cup stock or water and continue cooking until the corn mixture is thick and fluffy and has lost its raw starchy taste and texture, about 10 minutes more, adding the remaining ½ cup liquid as needed. Serve immediately, or let cool, cover, and refrigerate for up to 1 day, then reheat in a little butter. (You may notice some discoloration, but this will disappear on reheating.) Makes 6 to 8 servings.

HOW TO CHOOSE EARS OF CORN: Sisters-in-law Daisy and Gloria Tamai say, "There's no need to pull back the husk to check for quality." Look for plump ears with husks that are a nice fresh green (although in hot weather, outer husks may get dried and yellowed) and a dark-tipped silk, or tassel. Using both hands and starting from the stem end, work your way up, firmly squeezing the ear to check that it feels full with no gaps, which indicates the kernels are all fully developed, no rows of "teeth" are missing, and no worm damage is present. At most, take a peek near the silk, which is where a worm would go first (don't worry if there's evidence of one at the top; just cut it away when you get home). Kernels should look plump regardless of size or corn variety. Small kernels will be most tender but not necessarily the sweetest. That being said, sweeter white corn tends to have smaller kernels than calico. Shriveled or dry-looking kernels are signs of overly mature corn and will be starchier and have less milk. Yes, just-picked corn tastes best, but the Tamais get their corn to market within twenty-four hours, which is the best city folks can get. Although some of its sugar will turn to starch, unshucked corn will keep loose in your refrigerator crisper for about a week (remove the silk before storing). Use already-shucked corn within a couple of days.

Summery Zucchini-Lemon Soup

My daughter Rebecca taught me early on that a young child will eat just about any vegetable when it is turned into a delicious soup. Here, zucchini is paired subtly with Indian spices for a summer soup that is tasty cold or hot and can be made early in the day. But summer squash also marries well with other herbs and seasonings, so think of this easy soup as a master recipe and play with other flavor combinations, such as garlic, basil, and parsley, or hot Thai chiles, Thai basil, and lime.

MAKES 6 SERVINGS

Summer

2 pounds summer squash such as zucchini, marrow squash, pattypan, or scaloppini, cut into ½-inch-thick pieces

1 onion, chopped

1 tablespoon chopped fresh cilantro (optional), plus more for garnish

Kosher or sea salt

1 teaspoon curry powder, or ¼ teaspoon each ground coriander, cumin, ginger, and turmeric

½ teaspoon ground turmeric

1 tablespoon canola or other mild cooking oil

4 cups light chicken or vegetable stock (see Soup Basics, page 51)

½ to 1 lemon

Snipped fresh regular chives or garlic chives for garnish

In a deep, wide pot, sauté the squash, onion, cilantro, ½ teaspoon salt, curry powder, and turmeric in the oil over medium heat until the vegetables are golden, tender, and fragrant, 7 to 10 minutes. Add 2 cups of the stock and bring to a gentle boil. Reduce the heat and simmer, uncovered, for 10 minutes. Add the remaining 2 cups stock and continue to cook until the vegetables are very tender, about 5 minutes more.

Puree the soup with an immersion or stand blender. If the soup is too thick, add water (or ice cubes if serving it cold). Add the juice of ½ lemon. Taste and add more lemon juice and salt as needed until the soup has a refreshing tang. Serve hot, or chill well and serve cold. Garnish each serving with chives and cilantro.

HOW TO CHOOSE SUMMER SQUASH: Look for firm, shiny, not overly large squash with no soft or wrinkled spots. Store loose in the refrigerator crisper for up to a week.

COOK'S TIP: Valdivia Farms brings abundant squash blossoms, both female (with zucchini attached) and male (on a stem, and more flavorful), to the market. Discard the center stamen and sauté the blossoms with onion and garlic. Serve as a side dish, stir into risotto, or stuff into a quesadilla.

Elegant Borlotti Bean and Swiss Chard Soup with Red Carrots and Wild Mushrooms

Prepare the elements of this soup separately (most can be done a day ahead) and join them just before serving for a sparkling clear soup with a bright vegetable mosaic. Red and purple carrots are more fibrous than orange and taste better cooked than raw. They lose some color when peeled, but are still a vibrant red-orange inside. In fall, look for fresh borlotti, a kind of cranberry bean, in the pod from Two Peas in a Pod and Coleman Family Farm. They, along with Windrose Farm, offer them dried through the winter while the supply lasts. This soup is also beautiful with large Christmas limas from Two Peas that cook to a pale lavender. Use small golden chanterelles in the fall and yellow-footed chanterelles or hedgehogs in winter to early spring.

MAKES 8 SERVINGS

Autumn, Winter, Spring

1 bunch Swiss chard

1 bunch small red carrots, preferably the thickness of your little finger, unpeeled (about ½ pound after tops removed)

1 pound small chanterelles, hedgehogs, or yellow-footed chanterelles, brushed clean

Kosher or sea salt and freshly ground black pepper

2 to 3 teaspoons extra-virgin olive oil

8 cups Rich Poultry Stock (page 53)

2½ cups drained, cooked borlotti beans (from fresh or dried), page 25

Grated Parmigiano-Reggiano cheese for serving

Strip the stems from the chard leaves, discard the tough bottom parts, and cut the tender portions crosswise into ¼ inch wide slices. Cut the leaves into 1-inch-wide ribbons. Cook the stems and leaves in boiling salted water until the leaves are tender but still bright green, about 5 minutes. Drain and rinse the chard with ice water. Cook the whole carrots in boiling salted water until barely tender, 2 to 3 minutes (if using larger carrots, cut into 3- to 4-inch-long pieces before cooking). Drain and rinse the carrots in ice water, and then rub off their skins with your fingers. Slice lengthwise into ¼-inch-wide strips. The soup can be made to this point a day ahead; refrigerate the components separately.

To finish the soup, in a large skillet, sauté the mushrooms, seasoned with salt and pepper, in the oil over medium-high heat until all the liquid they release is reabsorbed and their edges are lightly browned, about 5 minutes. In a pot, bring the stock to a simmer. Add the beans, chard, and carrots, cover partially, and simmer for 10 minutes. Add the mushrooms and simmer to blend the flavors, about 5 minutes more. Season to taste with salt and pepper. Top each serving with a sprinkling of cheese.

Pumpkin Soup with Sage and Aged Cheese

This simple soup captures the essence of winter squash—subtle sweetness with vegetal notes—and achieves complexity through layered toppings of grated cheese, olive oil, sea salt, and fresh sage. It was inspired by a soup I ate on an autumn drive across northern Italy, where pumpkin dishes are a regional specialty. Nadia Santini, chef-owner of dal Pescatore near Milan, used a meaty, ribbed orange-and-green-mottled pumpkin that closely resembles the delicious La Estrella pumpkins Phil McGrath cultivates on the Ventura coast.

MAKES 6 TO 8 SERVINGS

Autumn, Winter

1 large onion, chopped

¾ cup chopped celery with leaves

5 fresh sage leaves, finely chopped, plus more for garnish

Kosher or sea salt and freshly ground white pepper

2 tablespoons extra-virgin olive oil, plus more for finishing

5 cups roasted pumpkin or other winter squash (page 25)

4 to 5 cups light vegetable or beef stock (see Soup Basics, page 51)

Grated cheese such as Winchester super-aged Gouda or Parmigiano-Reggiano for garnish

Fleur de sel or other finishing salt

In a wide pot, sauté the onion, celery, sage, and a little salt in the oil over medium heat until the vegetables soften, 5 to 7 minutes. Add the pumpkin, a little more salt, a few grinds of pepper, and 4 cups of the stock. Bring to a boil, reduce the heat to medium-low, cover partially, and simmer until the vegetables are very tender, about 20 minutes.

Puree the soup with an immersion or stand blender. If the soup is too thick, add the remaining 1 cup stock. Season to taste with salt and pepper. Top each serving with a healthy drizzle of oil and a little cheese, sage, and *fleur de sel*.

COOK'S TIP: To make this soup with raw squash, use 4 pounds small winter squash. Cut the raw squash in half, scoop out the seeds, peel, and cut into 1- to 2-inch pieces. Add the squash pieces to the pot when the onion is tender and sauté for 5 minutes. Add the stock and simmer the soup until the squash is very tender, 30 to 40 minutes.

CHEF'S TIP: Mix and match winter squash varieties to achieve the desired flavor and texture in the soup. Los Angeles chef Jason Travi uses kabocha or Hokkaido (Red Kuri) to thicken, butternut for pure sweetness, and Blue Hubbard for vegetal bass notes.

Are They Pumpkins or Winter Squash?

Pumpkins are winter squash. We often label classically shaped varieties pumpkins, but the terms are basically interchangeable. What is important is the taste. Avoid watery cultivars bred for jack-o'-lanterns, but even some heirloom beauties, such as Rouges Vif d'Etampes or Cheese pumpkins, are better gazed upon than eaten.

Sounds obvious, but winter squash grown in season are best. The cooler the weather, the slower they grow, which gives them time to develop flavor (rich La Estrella can take seven months on the vine). Time in the field and on the kitchen counter evaporates moisture and concentrates flavor; the squash that has been your table centerpiece for months is often the tastiest. That's a good thing, since they're so beautiful, with shapes from hatted to pear to serpentine and skins ranging from creamy white to buff to gray-blue-green to deepest red-orange.

Choose rock-hard squash (check the blossom end particularly) that are heavy for their size, with rather dull skin (a few exceptions are shiny when mature), a fat, dry stem still attached, and no nicks (indications that squash is fully mature, sealed from bacteria, and not watery). When shopping for elongated squash such as butternut, choose long necks and straight hips for more meat.

A large winter squash will keep for several months on the counter out of direct sun. Look for La Estrella, Tahitian, Moroccan, Jarrahdale, Queensland Blue, and Blue Hubbard.

Small varieties, such as butternut, will last several weeks. Use thinner-skinned small squash, like delicata, within a couple of weeks. Other interesting small squash include Sweet Dumpling, Carnival (acorn type), kabocha, Red Kuri or Hokkaido, Baby Pam, Prize Winner, Jack-Be-Little, and Black Futsu.

Golden Puree of Rutabagas with Their Greens

Rutabagas have an undeserved bad rap. This sunny-colored cousin to kale and turnips has a sweet nuttiness that is wonderfully heightened when accented by pistachios or hazelnuts. The nutrient-rich leaves echo the same nutlike quality and are delicious sautéed and used as a topping for texture and color. If you can't find rutabagas with their tops intact, substitute Swiss chard or kale for the leaves. James Birch of Flora Bella Farm in Three Rivers grows a rose-tinged elongated variety he harvests young, much different than the big, old globe-shaped specimens we're used to seeing.

MAKES 6 SERVINGS

Autumn, Winter

4 bunches small rutabagas with tops (about 3 pounds total)

Kosher or sea salt and freshly ground white pepper

2 tablespoons unsalted butter

1 carrot, peeled and cut into ¼-inch-inch thick coins

2 large leeks, white part only, chopped

6 cups light chicken stock (see Soup Basics, page 51)

1 to 2 tablespoons olive oil

2 large cloves garlic, sliced

¼ cup water

½ cup unsalted pistachios, toasted (page 25) and chopped

Trim leafy tops from the rutabagas and reserve, discarding any yellowed leaves. Peel the rutabagas and cut into ¼-inch-thick coins. In a wide pot, sauté the rutabagas and a little salt in 1 tablespoon of the butter over medium-low heat until partly tender and golden, about 15 minutes, covering the pot and turning the heat to low halfway through the cooking time. (If your rutabagas are on the old side, add a little water when you cover the pot to help them cook more quickly.)

Using a slotted spoon, remove the rutabagas from the pot, add the remaining 1 tablespoon butter, and sauté the carrot and leeks until soft, 5 to 7 minutes. Return the rutabagas to the pot, season with more salt and some pepper, and add 4 cups of the stock. Cover partially and simmer until the vegetables are very tender, 25 to 30 minutes.

While the soup is cooking, chop the rutabaga tops coarsely. In a large skillet, heat the oil over medium heat. Add the garlic and sauté for 1 minute, being careful not to let it brown. Add the greens and a generous sprinkling of salt and pepper and sauté until wilted, 2 to 3 minutes. Add the water and cook until the greens are tender, about 10 minutes, covering the pan halfway through cooking time and adding water if they begin to stick. Chop the greens finely and set aside.

Puree the soup with an immersion or stand blender. Add the remaining 2 cups stock as needed to achieve the consistency of heavy cream. Season to taste with salt and pepper. Top each serving with a spoonful of the greens and a sprinkling of pistachios.

HOW TO CHOOSE RUTABAGAS: Look for juicy-looking roots that are heavy for their size, without cracks or soft spots and with tops intact. Cut off the greens, leaving about 1 inch of stem, and store separately. The greens will keep for several days; the roots will keep in an open plastic bag in the coldest part of the fridge for up to 2 weeks.

CHEF'S TIP: Sweet-pungent celery root, or celeriac, is another knobby vegetable worth exploring autumn through winter. For the best texture, chef Alain Giraud of Four Stars Private Cuisine advises choosing pale beige roots no larger than an orange with fresh-looking greens. Julienned raw and marinated in a mustard-mayonnaise dressing, celery root becomes the classic French "coleslaw" appetizer, *céleri remoulade*. Alain also cooks celeriac with potatoes and leeks for an interesting vichyssoise, and turns the versatile root into "ravioli" by sautéing paper thin slices, folding them over seafood or vegetable filling, heating in a 350-degree oven, and then topping with black truffles, because "celeriac is a humble root that pairs well with expensive things."

Fresh Porcini and Potato Soup

Few soups are more decadent than a rich beef-and-mushroom broth voluptuous with thick slices of the prized fungi known as *cèpes* in France and porcini in Italy. In Florence, they are paired with *nepitella*, a strong-flavored, oregano-like wild mint available in late spring through fall from Coleman Family Farm (Bill Coleman grows *nepitella* because chef and Italian cooking expert Evan Kleiman asked him to). California has two short seasons—late spring and fall—when David West of Clearwater Farms receives as little as forty pounds of wild-harvested porcini a week from foragers. Use fresh porcini in season, or make a duskier version with the porcini David dries and sells year-round (see variation).

MAKES 6 SERVINGS

Spring, Autumn, Evergreen

½ ounce dried porcini

1 cup warm water

1 pound fresh porcini

1 pound waxy fingerling potatoes such as Rose Finn Apple, Russian Banana, or French, unpeeled, cut into ½-inch dice

2 ounces pancetta, cut into ¼-inch dice

4 tablespoons extra-virgin olive oil

½ red onion, finely chopped

2 tablespoons chopped fresh *nepitella*, or 4 teaspoons chopped fresh Italian oregano and 2 teaspoons chopped fresh spearmint

Kosher or sea salt and freshly ground black pepper

2 cloves garlic, minced

½ cup dry white wine

5 cups Simple Beef Stock (page 54) or light beef stock (see Stock Basics, page 51), heated

1 tablespoon chopped fresh Italian parsley or *nepitella*

Soak the dried porcini in the warm water until soft, about 25 minutes. Drain, gently squeezing the mushrooms, and reserve the liquid. Rinse the mushrooms and brush them clean using a mushroom brush or damp paper towel. Dry on paper towels and coarsely chop some of the larger pieces. Strain the soaking liquid through a fine-mesh sieve lined with a paper towel or coffee filter. Brush the fresh porcini clean, then cut into ¼-inch-thick slices and coarsely chop some of the larger pieces. Meanwhile, cook the potatoes in boiling salted water until just tender, about 10 minutes.

In a wide pot, sauté the pancetta in 1 tablespoon of the oil over medium heat until tender, about 5 minutes. Add the onion, *nepitella*, and 1 tablespoon of the oil to the pot. Continue cooking until the pancetta is browned and the onion is translucent and soft, 5 to 7 minutes more. Remove the pancetta-onion mixture from the pot. Add the remaining 2 tablespoons oil to the pot and the fresh porcini. Season with salt and pepper and sauté over medium heat until tender and the edges are browned, 10 to 15 minutes. Add the garlic, dried porcini, and pancetta-onion mixture, stir to combine, and cook for 3 minutes. Add the wine and cook until the liquid is absorbed, about 5 minutes. Add the reserved mushroom liquid and 2 cups of the stock, cover partially, and bring to a gentle boil. Reduce the heat and simmer for 10 minutes.

Add the remaining 3 cups stock and simmer for about 15 minutes to blend the flavors, adding the potatoes during the last 5 minutes of cooking time to heat through. Season to taste with salt and pepper. You should have a nice amount of broth, but if the soup needs thinning, add water. The soup can be made up to a day ahead; add the potatoes when reheating. Top each serving with parsley.

DRIED PORCINI VARIATION: Omit the fresh porcini and increase the dried porcini to 2 ounces. Reduce the amount of stock to 4 cups. Increase the warm water to 3 cups, and soak the dried porcini as directed, straining and reserving liquid. Do not remove the cooked pancetta onion mixture from the pot, but add all the dried mushrooms and garlic to it and cook for 3 minutes. Add the wine, cook until the liquid is absorbed, and then add 2 cups of the strained mushroom liquid and simmer for 10 minutes. Add the 4 cups stock and proceed as directed, adding the remaining mushroom liquid as needed for a good consistency.

The Great Porcino

It is no wonder Italians call their favorite woodsy wild mushroom a "piglet," given the porcino's stout white stem, rounded tan brown cap, and distinctive earthy aroma. California's *Boletus* species generally appear near pine and fir forests in the Sierras, along the north coast, and locally in the San Bernardino Mountains in May and again after early-autumn rains. They have a drier flavor and aroma than their European counterparts, which are typically found near chestnut trees.

Look for firm, dense porcini without pinholes. Keep them refrigerated in a brown paper bag and use within a day or two. Brush mushrooms clean with a damp brush before using and trim away any damaged spots you find as you slice them.

Young, firm porcini have sweet, creamy white "underhats" and can be sliced and used raw or pan-seared for salads and appetizers. Mature boletes have softer, stronger-tasting yellow and olive green underhats that mushroom purveyor David West calls "vegetarian foie gras." David likes to make a feast of slow-grilled "ripe" porcini: Remove the stems and split them lengthwise. Brush the stems and caps with olive oil. Place on a low, slow grill green side up. When the mushrooms start to sweat, season with salt so the salt melts into the flesh. Continue to grill the mushrooms slowly until the underhats are soft and plump, at least 10 to 15 minutes.

Salads

California is known for its innovative salads and microgreens, but these aren't recent inventions. In fourteenth-century England, cooks dressed tender cress, parsley, green garlic, and fennel with oil, vinegar, and salt. The Mayflower Pilgrims foraged mâche, and hip Los Angeles cooks were already adding peppery orange and gold nasturtiums to salads at the turn of the last century. So those aren't trendy greens at Maggie's Farm or Kenter Canyon Farms. They are merely rediscovered.

Who says salads require lettuce or tomatoes? That would mean half the year we would settle for a shadowy version of a great dish, because even lettuce has a prime time—spring to early summer. Think of the farmers' market as a wellspring of inspiration for salads that add seasonal sparkle to a menu, whetting the appetite, refreshing the palate, and providing a contrast in texture, flavor, and temperature. In this chapter, you'll find salads for every occasion— first course, main, and side; casual and dressy; new takes on old favorites— that use a wide array of fruits, vegetables, nuts, cheeses, and meats from the market. Some are easily dressed right in the bowl, while others call for easy make-ahead dressings.

About salad dressings: they aren't hard to make! Often times, a tablespoon of good olive oil and a generous pinch of kosher or sea salt are all that a pile of fine lettuces need, a dressing technique that is easy to master. Indeed, some of the best-dressed salads in town are scantily clad by chefs who know that when you start with the tastiest ingredients, less is more. Dress it, taste it, and adjust the amount of oil or salt. Soon you will be dressing and tossing like the pros.

Fava Bean and Pea Shoot Salad

Make this pretty spring salad, in shades of green, when young favas, pea shoots, and lettuces are at their peak. Fava, or broad, beans come double wrapped in cushiony pods and inner casings that must be removed (unless beans are particularly young) before you can enjoy their bittersweet flavor. Peeling the beans is a bit of a task, but one that offers its own pleasures. Farmer Bill Coleman compares shelling peas and beans to a family quilting bee, a time to catch up on news and gossip. In fact, he tests "future daughters-in-law by how willing they are to pitch in." Tender pea shoots, a favorite in Asian stir-fries, are the tips of pea plants that haven't developed pods or flowers, so all the sweetness goes into the leaves. Some farmers bring them trimmed to the tenderest top two or three inches. Others bring longer stalks, in which case you'll need to snap off the tender part where it breaks easily.

MAKES 6 SERVINGS

Spring

2 pounds young fava beans in the pod

1 bunch pea shoots, or ¼ pound pea shoot tips

1 large head butter lettuce, large leaves torn

¼ to ⅓ cup sprigs dill

¼ cup snipped fresh leek-chives or regular chives

About 1 tablespoon extra-virgin olive oil

About 1 tablespoon lemon juice

Kosher or sea salt and freshly ground black pepper

Shell the fava beans (you should have about 1 cup beans) and drop them into boiling salted water for 2 minutes. Drain, rinse with cold water, and slip off the skins. Trim the tender tops and leaves of the pea shoots (you should have 2 to 3 cups) and reserve the sturdier parts for soup or stock. Trim away any long tendrils that might be hard to chew (nibble one to find where the tender part begins).

Place the fava beans, pea shoots, lettuce, dill, and chives in a salad bowl. Drizzle with the oil and lemon juice to taste and season with salt and pepper. Toss and serve.

HOW TO CHOOSE FAVA BEANS: Young favas good for salads have bright green, firm, slightly fuzzy pods that are heavy for their size and show just a hint of the shape of the plump beans inside. The tender beans are also bright green beneath their inner casing. Mature fava pods are more flaccid and bumpy, with a tendency toward yellowing and translucence. Mature beans have a yellow or even darker cast and a harder, starchier texture that benefits from longer cooking in soups, stews, and for purees.

COOK'S TIP: Sauté pea shoots, seasoned with salt and white pepper, in a little butter for about a minute until wilted and a bright, shiny emerald green. Add a squeeze of Meyer lemon juice and serve.

Sorrel and Avocado Salad

Tart sorrel leaves make a lemony addition to green salads, but this is by no means a new idea. Eliza Acton offers a spring salad of sorrel, lettuce, and green onions in *Modern Cookery*, published in 1845, that she recommends serving with lamb. California avocados and pistachios are my market additions. This salad is also lovely with fish, smoked fish, or eggs. The Colemans have beautiful big-leaved garden sorrel in winter and spring, and Maggie's Farm has smaller leaved bunches nearly year-round.

MAKES 6 SERVINGS

Spring, Summer

1 large bunch sorrel

2 small heads Little Gem or Perella Red lettuce or 1 head butter lettuce, large leaves torn

3 green onions, including several inches of green, thinly sliced

1 Pinkerton or other avocado, pitted, peeled, and cubed

⅓ cup unsalted pistachios, chopped

About 1 tablespoon pistachio or fruity extra-virgin olive oil

About 1 tablespoon lemon juice

Kosher or sea salt and freshly ground black pepper

Stem the sorrel. If the leaves are small, tear them into bite-sized pieces. If larger, cut crosswise into thin ribbons. Put the sorrel, lettuce, onions, avocado, and pistachios in a salad bowl. Drizzle with the oil and lemon juice to taste and season with salt and pepper. Toss and serve.

Lots of Lettuce

Lettuces are divided into four basic types: butterhead or Bibb, softly compact heads with buttery textured and flavored leaves; crisphead, known for their solid heft (iceberg is the familiar example); romaine or Cos, crisp, tall, hardy heads that stand up to summer heat in the field, making them a good seasonal choice; and looseleaf, floppier open bouquets, such as Black-Seeded Simpson or any of the oak-leaf types. The term *mesclun* is used for salad mixes that are grown together in the field and can include baby lettuces, herbs, chicories, cresses, and mâche.

Some "new" lettuce varieties we see at such farms as Coastal and Coleman have graced salad bowls for centuries. A type of iceberg was already on seed lists in the 1820s. Light green, frilly Black-Seeded Simpson was introduced in the United States in the 1870s, oak leaf in the 1880s (earlier in Europe), and maroon-splashed Speckled dates from the late 1700s. Look also for maroon-and-green Forellenschuss, an Austrian heirloom; smallish heads of red-speckled Freckles romaine; bright green, compact Little Gems with dense, sweet leaves; and meaty Perella Red.

Roasted Beet and Blood Orange Salad with Arugula Flowers

A riot of color and taste, this salad uses golden and candy-striped Chioggia beets. Berry-toned blood oranges from Polito, Schaner, or Garcia farms brighten the beets' sweet earthiness. In spring, sweet-spicy arugula flowers from Maggie's, McGrath, Coleman, or Flora Bella are a beautiful addition to the salad. The delicate, little whiskered blossoms also make a pretty kitchen counter bouquet.

MAKES 6 SERVINGS

Winter, Spring

4 blood oranges

3 bunches golden and Chioggia beets (about 1½ pounds total without tops), roasted and sliced (page 104)

1 cup packed pepper cress (about 1 ounce)

1 head red butter or Vulcan lettuce, large leaves torn, or ¼ pound baby lettuces

1 Pinkerton or Fuerte avocado, pitted, peeled, and cubed

1 to 2 tablespoons extra-virgin olive oil

Kosher or sea salt and freshly ground black pepper

½ cup arugula flowers (optional)

Peel and segment the oranges into a salad bowl, reserving the membranes (page 24). Add the beets, pepper cress, lettuce, and avocado to the bowl. Drizzle with 1 tablespoon oil, and squeeze the membranes over the top, releasing their juice. Sprinkle the salad with salt and pepper and toss, then taste and adjust with more oil if needed. Scatter the arugula flowers over the top and serve.

CHEF'S TIP: Brooke Williamson and Nick Roberts, chef-owners of Beechwood Restaurant in Venice, add complexity to their beet salads by marinating the roasted beets for at least 24 hours in a mixture of honey, olive oil, shallots, thyme, salt, and a splash of sherry vinegar.

The Best Beets

Beets love sunny days and cool nights. In California, the sweetest and richest-colored beets are available in late spring and again in late fall from such farms as Coastal, Flora Bella, McGrath, Jaime, Tamai, Nakamura, and Fairview Gardens. The popular hybrid Red Ace with tender red-veined tops, deep-hued Bull's Blood with matching burgundy leaves, dark torpedo beets, rose-skinned Chioggia with candy-striped interiors, and orange-shouldered golden, pale yellow, and white varieties are all on display. Many chefs and farmers consider red beets more minerally, yellows and whites sweet and mild, and Chioggias sweet-tart, but flavor differences are slight. Whichever color you choose, earthy beets go well with citrus and peppery cresses and arugula; apples and horseradish; green beans and whole-grain mustard; and prosciutto or smoked fish. They make a classic filling for ravioli and, of course, a beautiful borscht.

Novelist Tom Robbins calls beets the most intense vegetable, but some folks don't think that's a good thing. Here's the dirt on beets from master plant breeder and beet specialist Dr. John Navazio: "Beets contain the flavor component geosmin that is also manufactured by microbes present in soil. Geosmin levels increase with stress, making poorly stored old beets more pungent." So if you think beets taste like dirt, perhaps you've only eaten stressed-out beets.

Happy, fresh beets with their perky, leafy tops still attached are a twofer. The nutrient-rich greens, milder than the root, taste similar to their close relative, Swiss chard. Red beet tops have the nicest texture for cooking and are lovely sautéed on their own, as farmer Maryann Carpenter suggests, or in dishes calling for a hearty green, such as Farro Penne with Winter Greens, Potatoes, and Cheese (page 135) or Garganelli with Pumpkin, Sausage, and Swiss Chard (page 153). Use beet greens within a couple of days; the beets will keep refrigerated for up to three weeks.

Cherry and Almond Salad

Cherries are the first stone fruits to arrive in the market, announcing summer's approach with a crackle of sweet-tart juices. Their peak season lasts only about a month, beginning in late May, so focus on their pleasures while you can. I got the idea of using cherries and nuts in a savory salad from a recipe in the 1911 *Los Angeles Times Cook Book Number Four*. Use several kinds of cherries for flavor, color, and texture contrast. This salad goes well with grilled sausages, pork, or duck.

MAKES 4 SERVINGS

Summer

½ head escarole, or 2 heads frisée
¾ pound (1½ cups) mixed cherries such as sweet Bing, Rainier, Garnet, Black, and Tartarian and sour Montmorency, pitted and halved
¼ cup dried cherries
½ cup almonds, toasted (page 25) and coarsely chopped

1 lemon
2 tablespoons grape seed or almond oil
Kosher or sea salt and freshly ground black pepper
¼ pound blue cheese or aged goat cheese such as Redwood Hill crottin or boucheret, at room temperature, cut into 4 equal pieces

If using escarole, cut leaves into thin ribbons (chiffonade); you should have 3 to 4 cups. If using frisée, use only the tender, light-colored hearts and tear them into bite-sized pieces. In a salad bowl, toss together the greens, fresh and dried cherries, and almonds. Grate the zest of the lemon directly onto the salad. Add the oil, a squeeze of lemon juice, and salt and pepper to taste and toss again. To serve, divide the salad among 4 plates and place a piece of cheese on each plate.

California's Cherry Jubilee

Most California cherry production centers around Stockton, Linden, and Lodi, where temperatures stay cool enough to set beautiful fruit. Brooks, Tulare, and Early Burlat are first to arrive in the market. With a softer texture and decent flavor, they are harbingers for the midseason main event: plump, winy, almost-black Bings that fairly snap in your mouth and big, yellow, supersweet Rainiers. The Barbagelata and Bautista families grow both in Linden and nearby Stockton, and Harry Nicholas brings dark red Garnets from around Fresno that are not to be missed in a good cherry year. Occasionally, the small and slightly soft Black Tartarian, once the red cherry of choice, and the delicate Royal Ann, once the most popular yellow variety, are spotted at a stand. Late season brings Lamberts from Tenerelli Orchards. If you spot bright red Montmorencies, classic sour pie cherries, grab some to make a special crisp (page 166). They require cold winters, and only a few California farmers at higher altitudes attempt them.

Peas and Potato Salad

Snap peas are, as the French say, *mange tout*, "eat all" peas with juicy, crisp pods that contain fully developed sweet peas. When market supervisor Laura Avery gives a school tour, she teaches kids to recognize the difference between a dolphin snout–shaped snap pea and a domed whale–shaped English pea. Although snap peas are delicious raw, their color and flavor brighten with brief steaming or sautéing. Snap peas are available spring through summer at Two Peas in a Pod, Tutti Frutti, Coleman, Rutiz, and other market farm stands. When English pea season is over, make this dish with all snap peas. It is lovely with cold poached salmon or chicken and travels well on a picnic.

MAKES 6 TO 8 SERVINGS

Spring

1 shallot (about 1 ounce), quartered

3 tablespoons white wine vinegar

2 teaspoons Dijon mustard

Kosher or sea salt and freshly ground black pepper

⅓ cup plus 1 tablespoon grape seed or canola oil

4 tablespoons chopped fresh tarragon or dill

2 pounds waxy potatoes such as Rose Finn Apple, French Fingerling, or Onaway, unpeeled, cut into 1-inch cubes

½ pound sugar snap peas, strings removed and cut into ½-inch pieces

1 cup shelled English peas (about 1 pound in the pod)

2 tablespoons water

⅓ cup long-snipped fresh chives (½-inch lengths)

To make the dressing, put the shallot, vinegar, mustard, 1 teaspoon salt, and a few grinds of pepper in a blender and process until smooth. With the blender running, slowly add the ⅓ cup oil. Add half of the tarragon and process briefly. Set aside. Cook the potatoes in boiling generously salted water until just tender, 10 to 15 minutes. Drain, place in a bowl, and immediately toss with the dressing.

While the potatoes are cooking, heat the remaining 1 tablespoon oil in a skillet over medium-high heat. Add the snap peas and sauté until bright green, 1 to 2 minutes. Add the English peas, a little salt, and the water, cover, and cook until all the peas are crisp-tender, about 2 minutes. Uncover, remove from the heat, and let cool. Add the peas, chives, and remaining 2 tablespoons tarragon to the potatoes and mix well. Taste and adjust the seasoning. Serve warm or at room temperature.

Potato, Romano Bean, and Olive Salad

Like many responsible farmers, Molly and Rick Gean of Harry's Berries include legumes in their crop rotation to replenish nutrients in the soil. Primarily known for premium strawberries, they also grow protein-rich *edamame* (soy beans), flat wax romanos (yellow Italian beans), juicy Blue Lakes, old-fashioned wax beans, and elegant, thin haricots verts (or fillet beans). This robust summertime potato salad goes well with grilled meats and sausages.

**MAKES 8 TO 10
SERVINGS**

Summer

3 pounds waxy potatoes such as Rose Finn Apple, French Fingerling, or Onaway, unpeeled, cut into 1-inch cubes

1 pound romano beans, trimmed and cut into ½-inch pieces

6 tablespoons extra-virgin olive oil

2 large cloves garlic, finely chopped

3 bay leaves, preferably fresh, broken in half

⅛ to ¼ teaspoon red pepper flakes

6 anchovy fillets (optional)

2 tablespoons red wine vinegar

½ cup Kalamata olives, pitted and halved

¼ cup chopped fresh Italian parsley

2 tablespoons capers

Kosher or sea salt

Cook the potatoes and beans in boiling salted water until just tender, 10 to 15 minutes for the potatoes and 5 to 7 minutes for the beans. Drain the potatoes and beans and place in a large bowl.

While the potatoes and beans are cooking, heat the oil, garlic, bay leaves, and pepper flakes together in a small pot over medium-low heat. When the oil is hot, remove from heat and add the anchovies, mashing them with a fork until they are completely dissolved. As soon as the potatoes and green beans are cooked, toss them with half of the anchovy-oil mixture. Stir the vinegar into the remaining anchovy-oil mixture. Add the olives, parsley, and capers to the potatoes and beans, drizzle with the remaining anchovy-oil mixture, and toss. Taste and adjust with more salt, vinegar, or oil, if needed. Serve at room temperature. The salad can be made several hours ahead and kept at room temperature; taste again just before serving and adjust the seasoning if necessary.

FARMER'S TIP: Molly Gean speed-snaps beans. She takes a handful, turns them all the same direction, and plucks off the stem ends with her fingertips. You will be amazed how much faster it goes.

Summer Snaps

Snap beans are immature bush beans whose pods are still tender and whose beans haven't fully developed. Molly Gean says the best green beans are picked at just the right moment when they are juicy and bright: "Even one day can make a difference, especially in the hot summer. You know when you've gotten an overly mature one; it's tough and fibrous." She says really fresh beans will stick to your clothes like Velcro, because the little hairs on the pods haven't rubbed off in a packing crate.

Formerly known as string beans, green beans today are mostly string free. A good fresh bean will produce a nice snap when broken in half. Excellent Blue Lake and wax beans, green and wax romanos, dramatic Dragon's Tongue beans (although they lose much of their red mottling when cooked), and pricey haricots verts (they are very time-consuming to pick) are available at Coastal, Harry's Berries, Weiser, and Tamai farms into fall. Molly steams cut-up Blue Lakes, tosses them with a little soy sauce, a pinch of sugar, and some toasted sesame seeds, and serves them warm or cold. Summer snaps are wonderful quick-roasted (page 103), which concentrates and caramelizes their natural sugars.

Chinese long beans, which are not snap beans but a subspecies of southern peas popular in Asia, are available at Briar Patch, Vang Thao, and other stands specializing in Asian vegetables. Sang Yoon, chef-owner of Father's Office, showcases their meaty crunch, creamy interior, ridged texture, and length by coiling them into three-inch rings, tucking the ends in to hold the shape, and quickly deep-frying them in a beer batter seasoned with garam masala. A squeeze of lemon and crunchy salt is all you need, but Sang serves them with a blender sauce of red chile sambal, honey, ginger, garlic, soy sauce, rice vinegar, and vegetable and sesame oils.

How to Build a Tomato Salad

There's no substitute for truly vine-ripened (but not necessarily still attached to the vine), sun-drenched, picked-at-peak tomatoes, and they don't need anything except a bit of great olive oil and crunchy salt to become a delicious salad. But since you'll want a tomato salad just about every day during the season, there are lots of "add-ins" besides the familiar basil. Choose judiciously, as you want to highlight the tomato flavor, not mask it. First, some general guidelines: Figure on ⅓ to ½ pound tomatoes per person. Use a variety of colors and sizes, including cherry tomatoes, and cut them into a mix of chunks, wedges, and slices for interesting texture. Thick slices showcase taste and texture better than thin. Mound the tomatoes on a platter, instead of in a bowl, to show off your summer bounty at its best. Use excellent-quality fruity green or peppery olive oil and kosher salt, Maldon sea salt, or *fleur de sel*. Serve as is, or dress your salad with one or more of the following suggestions.

SEASONINGS: freshly ground black pepper, a splash of red wine or black currant vinegar or a few drops of artisanal balsamic vinegar or balsamic reduction (page 88).
FRESH HERBS OR GREENS (about 1 tablespoon chopped or torn): arugula, basil, chives, garlic chives, Italian parsley, mint, onion tops or flowers, oregano, thyme.
CHEESE AND HERB PAIRINGS (2 to 8 ounces of cheese, depending on whether used as accent or equal partner): sliced or cubed fresh mozzarella with basil, parsley, or arugula; crumbled feta or goat's milk feta with mint or oregano; sliced or crumbled mild goat cheese with thyme.

Tomato Time

When premier tomato grower Maryann Carpenter hangs out her Tomato Time sign, she both braces and prays for an onslaught of customers. "It's the one crop of the year where we actually make money," says the owner of Coastal Farms, "and every year I worry 'will the plants produce, will I be able to keep up with the glut, will customers come again to buy, especially if it's a late year?'" (In 2006, the crop didn't show up at the market until August.) Maryann's husband, Paul, plants fifty thousand tomato plants each spring and early summer. "When you think of all the tomatoes they'll yield, it's mind-boggling," says Maryann.

Field-ripe tomatoes are the one savory farmers' market crop no one can get enough of. Chefs buy them by the case, home shoppers by the bagful. They may seem pricey, but premium thin-skinned heirlooms must be handled, sorted, and packed with care, and tiny cherry tomatoes are the devil to pick and sort. It can take a farmer two days to get ready for a market. Plus, customers seldom realize this summer crop occupies farmland most of the year, making it impossible for a farmer to earn money from another crop off the same land.

Like other farmers who love the taste of a great tomato—the Geans of Harry's Berries, Ed Munak of Munak Ranch, and the Spencers of Windrose Farm (who bring tomato plants to the Santa Monica

Farmers' Market)—the Carpenters started growing them because "a good one was just so hard to come by," and they have never grown tired of their voluptuous flavors. Besides slicing them on toast for breakfast and making soups and salads, Maryann slow-roasts plenty of Early Girls, covers them in olive oil, and stores them in the refrigerator to enjoy later in the year. Mark Carpenter, who farms and works the markets with his mom, makes sauce by the caseload from their Costoluto Genovese harvest to give to family and friends. Nicknamed Evan's Tomatoes, Costolutos were introduced to the Santa Monica market by chef Evan Kleiman, who brought the seeds from Italy to the Carpenters.

Climate dictates which varieties are grown and when they show up at the market. The Wong family, who farm in hot Imperial County, have outdoor hydroponic tomatoes in early spring, but by May their "summer" is over. The harvests at Coastal Farms start later but end earlier than Munak Ranch in Paso Robles, where tasty tomatoes are picked as late as Thanksgiving. Then there are the hydroponically grown tomatoes from Beylik Farms in Fillmore that defy season and terroir. Consistent, perfect looking, but less complex tasting than their counterparts cultivated in soil, they grow on beanstalklike plants eight to twenty feet high.

There are juicy slicing tomatoes and fleshy varieties for roasting and sauces, delicate century-old heirlooms and sturdy, delicious hybrids. There are low acid, acid, fruity, and candy-sweet tomatoes. And there is a seasonal arc of flavor. Early-season fruit is tarter yet milder and simpler than sun-soaked midseason harvests, and late-season tomatoes have a deep richness. Look for well-colored tomatoes with a little to a lot of give but no bruising. Ripe tomatoes that haven't quite reached maximum color will "color up" on your counter in a day or two. Never refrigerate tomatoes—they will permanently lose flavor and texture—until they are so soft they'd go bad otherwise, and then use them in soups or sauces.

HYBRIDS
RED SLICING: Celebrity, Early Girl, Carmello, Big Beef, Momotaro
ELONGATED OR SAUCE: San Remo
RED CHERRY OR SALAD: Sweet 100, Sweet Chelsea, Juliet (grape shaped)
ORANGE CHERRY OR SALAD: Sun Gold

OPEN-POLLINATED AND HEIRLOOMS
SLICING: Beefsteak, Black Krim (Russian reddish brown heirloom), Brandywine and Black Brandywine (exceptionally rich-tasting heirlooms), Cherokee Purple (purple-pink-green heirloom thought to have been grown by the Cherokee), Evergreen (large, mild, emerald green), Green Zebra (small, fruity, green and yellow striated), Old German (sweet, large, yellow with red center Mennonite heirloom), Persimmon (deep-flavored, orange, oblong heirloom), Pineapple (large, meaty, sweet, red-dappled, yellow-orange heirloom)
SAUCE: Roma, Costoluto Genovese (flat, round, lobed), Sicilian Stripe
CHERRY: Yellow Pear (mild, noteworthy for shape and texture)

Heirloom Tomato Aspic

When made with succulent ripe heirloom tomatoes, aspic is summer in suspension, a rainbow of pure tomato flavor and, when called *gelée*, a favorite with chefs. So forget what you remember about ladies who lunch in department-store tearooms, and charm your guests with this do-ahead salad in several colors. Working with gelatin is simple, no more than a matter of dissolving it completely and rinsing the molds before filling them so the aspic will release easily.

MAKES 8 SERVINGS

Summer

2 pounds ripe, juicy tomatoes such as Pineapple, Green Zebra, or Brandywine, coarsely chopped with juices (about 5 cups)

2 tablespoons grated onion

⅓ cup minced celery with leaves

1 large bay leaf, preferably fresh

1 cup water

2 envelopes unflavored gelatin

1 tablespoon lemon juice

1 to 2 teaspoons kosher or sea salt

Butter lettuce

Mayonnaise

Prepared horseradish or hot-pepper sauce such as Tabasco (optional)

Put the tomatoes, onion, celery, bay leaf, and ½ cup of the water in a pot and place over medium-high heat. Bring to a boil, reduce the heat to medium, and simmer for 10 minutes. Meanwhile, stir the gelatin into the remaining ½ cup water to soften and set aside. Remove and discard the bay leaf and put the tomato mixture through a food mill fitted with a fine disk or through a sieve. Return the thin puree to the pan and add the lemon juice and salt (be generous with the salt). Bring to a simmer, remove from the heat, add the softened gelatin, and stir until thoroughly dissolved.

Rinse eight ½-cup molds with cold water and pour the aspic into them, filling them almost to the top. Or, pour the mixture into a rinsed 1-quart ring mold. Chill until firm, at least 4 hours or up to overnight. To unmold, run a sharp knife around the inside edge of each mold, dip the bottom briefly in hot water, and invert onto a salad plate. Garnish with lettuce leaves and a dollop of mayonnaise (homemade if possible) spiked with horseradish.

TO MAKE ASPIC IN TWO COLORS: Use 1 pound tomatoes of each color, and put the colors in separate pots. Divide the remaining ingredients between the pans and proceed as directed. Fill 4 molds with each color. For a striped effect, prepare the first color, fill 8 molds half full, and chill until firm, 2 to 3 hours. Prepare the second color and cool until thickened to about the consistency of egg white. Pour the second color on top of the first and chill for at least 4 hours or up to overnight.

Tomato and Cucumber Bread Salad

This lettuce-less salad is perfect in high summer when it's too hot for delicate greens to survive in the field but ideal weather for cucumbers. It is a kind of *panzanella*, a do-ahead Italian tomato-bread salad that gets better as it stands. Japanese and Persian cucumbers look similar, but the former have a spiky skin and crunchy texture and the latter are smooth-skinned, sweeter, and softer.

MAKES 8 SERVINGS

Summer

½ loaf stale country bread (not sourdough), torn into bite-sized pieces

3 pounds assorted ripe tomatoes, including cherry

2 or 3 Japanese or Persian cucumbers (about 10 ounces total)

⅓ cup black olives such as Adams Olive Ranch Kalamata or oil-cured

2 to 3 tablespoons extra-virgin olive oil

½ to 1 tablespoon red wine vinegar

Kosher or sea salt and freshly ground black pepper

½ cup torn fresh basil leaves

Preheat oven to 250 degrees. Dry the bread chunks on a baking sheet in the oven, about 20 minutes. Cut the tomatoes into wedges, chunks, and thick slices, and place them and whole cherry tomatoes in a large bowl. Peel the cucumbers, cut them in half lengthwise, and use the tip of a spoon to scrape out the seeds. Cut the cucumbers crosswise into ½-inch-thick slices. Add the cucumbers, olives, and bread to the bowl. Drizzle with the oil and vinegar, using the smaller amounts to start, and sprinkle with salt and pepper. Toss well and add more oil and vinegar to taste. Add the basil and toss again. Let stand for 1 to 2 hours before serving.

HOW TO CHOOSE CUCUMBERS: Look for firm cucumbers with no soft spots, shriveling, or yellowing. Bitterness occurs during cold weather and plant stress, and shows up first at the stem end and close to the skin. Cucumbers are a summer crop, so if you are buying just-picked, good-looking cucumbers in season, you should be fine. Because their high water content makes them perishable, buy only what you will use within a few days and wrap in paper towels to refrigerate.

Grilled Fig and Market Ham Salad

Soft, voluptuous, and honeyed, ripe figs are difficult to find anywhere but at a farmers' market or on a backyard tree because they are so fragile. If picked too early "they'll be like cotton inside," says grower P.Y. Pudwill. But ripe high-summer Black Mission figs (named for the padres who brought them to California in 1769) are rich and jammy and near-strawberry color inside. Look for them from Pudwill, Avila, or Garcia Organic, who also grows the unusual sweet, white, seedless Garnsey fig and green-skinned White Genoas. Avila also grows Kadotas; brownish red, creamy Texas honey figs; and Calimyrnas, considered by many to be the best light-skinned California fig for drying. Carl Fetzner grows uncommon pink-tinged Osborns and greenish Conadrias. A caveat about Brown Turkeys: they can be tough skinned with insipid flavor.

This rustic composed salad can serve as a main dish on a warm summer evening with a glass of rosé. Prepare the components a couple of hours ahead—don't forget to bring the cheese to room temperature—and assemble the salad just before serving. Grilled figs are also a lovely complement to grilled poultry or pork or a cheese course.

MAKES 6 TO 8 SERVINGS

Summer

⅓ cup good-quality balsamic vinegar

1 pint basket ripe figs

About 2 tablespoons extra-virgin olive oil

Kosher or sea salt and freshly ground
   black pepper

¼ pound ham steak or thickly
   sliced pancetta

⅓ cup whole raw almonds

6 to 8 cups young dandelion greens,
   frisée, or arugula

½ lemon (optional)

¼ pound Camembert-style cheese
   such as Redwood Hill Camellia or
   Cowgirl Creamery Mt. Tam, cut
   into 6 to 8 wedges

In a small pot, bring the vinegar to a gentle boil over medium heat. Cook until it thickens and reduces to about 1½ tablespoons, about 8 minutes, watching carefully to prevent scorching. Immediately pour into a small dish to cool.

Heat a grill to medium-high, or place a grill pan over medium heat. Cut the figs in half lengthwise, brush on both sides with 2 to 3 teaspoons oil, and season with salt and pepper. Grill cut side down until the surface is caramelized, about 2 minutes. Turn and grill on the second side for 1 to 2 minutes. Place cut side up on a plate to cool. If using ham steak, cut on the diagonal into ⅛-inch-thick slices and grill on both sides until nicely crisped, 2 to 4 minutes. Cut into julienne strips and set aside. If using pancetta, cut into ½-inch dice, cook in a skillet over medium heat until crisp, and set aside.

Wipe out the skillet and heat 1 teaspoon oil over medium heat. Add the almonds and a sprinkle of salt and toast, shaking the pan often, until the almonds are golden brown and fragrant, about 3 minutes. Remove from the heat, let cool, and chop coarsely.

To serve, toss the greens with about 2 teaspoons olive oil, salt, pepper, and a tiny squeeze of lemon juice—do not make this a lemony salad. Scatter the ham and almonds over the greens, top with the figs, and drizzle with the balsamic syrup. Serve with the cheese wedges.

HOW TO CHOOSE FIGS: Look for fruits that are plump and heavy for their size, with some give when cupped in your hand. Their skins should be slightly shriveled rather than taut. Some cracking from their natural sugars is okay, but avoid bruised fruits. Keep them in the warmer part of the refrigerator and use within 2 days. Bring to room temperature to serve.

FARMER'S TIP: Jeff Rieger of Penryn Orchard freezes dead-ripe Black Mission figs on small wooden skewers for a simple summertime dessert. The fig's high sugar content and low moisture keeps the fruit pops from freezing rock solid.

COOK'S TIP: The balsamic reduction, a poor man's version of *aceto balsamico tradizionale*, the long-aged true balsamic of Modena, is a handy condiment for roasted vegetables and many cheeses and keeps indefinitely (gently reheat to soften). If you have a $150 bottle of the real stuff, drizzle about 2 teaspoons over your salad.

Melon, Cucumber, and Mint Salad

At first glance, melon and cucumber seem an unlikely pairing, but they are cousins that go well together in a refreshing sweet-salty salad that is a variation on an Israeli summer favorite made with watermelon. Don't pass up those prickly, pale yellow lemon cucumbers at Munak Ranch, Tutti Frutti, or Windrose Farm. Named for their looks, not their flavor, the best ones are the pale color of lemon sorbet and firm. Inside, they are icy green with tender seeds that mimic the texture of citrus juice sacs. Lemon cucumbers keep longer than green varieties.

MAKES 6 SERVINGS

Summer

1 cantaloupe or other melon (about 3 pounds), cut into bite-sized chunks (see Cook's Tip, page 62)

4 cucumbers, preferably a mix of lemon and Persian or Japanese (about 1 pound total)

½ white onion, sliced paper-thin

½ cup fresh mint leaves, torn into pieces

2 to 3 tablespoons lemon juice

1 tablespoon honey

2 ounces feta cheese, crumbled

Kosher or sea salt and freshly ground black pepper

Place the melon chunks in a large bowl. If using lemon cucumbers, peel them, cut into wedges, and cut each wedge in half crosswise. If using Persian or Japanese cucumbers, peel them and cut in half lengthwise. Use the tip of a spoon to scrape out the seeds, then cut the cucumbers crosswise into ½-inch-thick slices and add them to the bowl. Rinse the onion slices in water to remove a bit of their bite, and add them to the bowl. Add the mint, lemon juice, honey, feta, and salt and pepper to taste and toss gently. Taste and adjust the seasoning. Chill for 1 hour before serving.

CHEF'S TIP: Chef Scooter Kanfer serves watermelon and feta for dessert. Arrange thin slices of salty cheese and sweet watermelon (use more than one color!) on dessert plates. Drizzle a little warmed honey (add a bit of honeycomb, too) over and season with *fleur de sel* and crushed black pepper. Delicious with an ice-cold Pinot Gris or Riesling.

Roasted Vegetable and Chicken Salad
with Lemon-Mustard Vinaigrette

Roast plenty of summer vegetables early in the day to have on hand for this convenient hot-weather main-dish salad. Use the mix suggested, or see Roasted Seasonal Vegetable Primer (pages 102 to 105) for more ideas. Harry's Berries grows *edamame* (soybeans) from seed propagated at the farm. For a nourishing vegetarian salad, increase the amount of protein-rich soybeans and skip the meat.

MAKES 6 SERVINGS

Summer

1 large onion, preferably ultramild Maui or Vidalia type, cut crosswise into thick slices

1 pound green beans, trimmed

1 pound wax romano beans, trimmed and cut crosswise into thirds

1 pint basket cherry tomatoes, stemmed

1 to 2 tablespoons olive oil

Kosher or sea salt

¼ teaspoon red pepper flakes

1 large head sturdy lettuce such as romaine, or several heads Little Gem, large leaves torn

1 pound grilled or roasted chicken breast, sliced

½ pound *edamame*, boiled and shelled (see Cook's Tip)

5 large fresh basil leaves, torn

¼ cup chopped fresh Italian parsley

FOR THE VINAIGRETTE

1 tablespoon Dijon mustard

1 tablespoon lemon juice

1 teaspoon kosher salt

Freshly ground black pepper

⅓ cup extra-virgin olive oil

Preheat oven to 450 degrees. In separate bowls, toss the onion, green and wax beans, and tomatoes each with 1 to 2 teaspoons oil and season with salt; add the red pepper flakes to the tomatoes. Roast the vegetables on separate baking sheets as directed in the Roasted Seasonal Vegetable Primer (pages 102 to 105). Let all the vegetables cool to room temperature.

Place the onion and beans, lettuce, chicken, *edamame*, basil, and parsley in a salad bowl. To make the vinaigrette, whisk together the mustard, lemon juice, salt, and pepper to taste, then whisk in the oil. Drizzle over the salad and toss well. Add the tomatoes, toss again gently, and serve.

FARMER'S TIP: Raw *edamame* are difficult to shell. Molly Gean of Harry's Berries recommends boiling them whole in generously salted water until the beans are just tender, about 5 minutes. Drain and let stand until cool enough to handle, then squeeze along the outside curve of each pod and the beans will easily pop out of the inner curve. One-half pound in the pod yields about 1 cup shelled.

Bacon and Deviled Egg Salad

This salad is nice for breakfast or brunch, and these no-mayo deviled eggs are great on their own for snacks or picnics. Follow the directions below for green ring–free hard-boiled eggs. Greg Nauta of Rocky Canyon Produce smokes superlean shoulder and belly bacon from the Hampshire and Duroc pigs he raises in Atascadero. Look for locally grown peppery watercress from Tsugio "Frank" Imamoto, one of the market's original farmers or arugula from Maggie's Farm. In summer when plants are seeding, you will find pretty light purple flowers in chive bunches and white ones in garlic chive bunches. Either will add sweet-spicy beauty to the salad.

MAKES 6 SERVINGS

Summer

6 eggs

3 ounces bacon, cut into ¼-inch dice

¼ pound arugula or stemmed watercress

1½ teaspoons Dijon mustard

1½ teaspoons white wine vinegar, plus
   more for salad

Kosher or sea salt and freshly ground
   black pepper

4 tablespoons olive oil

3½ tablespoons snipped fresh chives

Handful of chive or garlic chive flowers
   (optional)

1 pint basket cherry tomatoes, stemmed
   and slow roasted (page 103)

Put the eggs in a pot with salted water to cover. Cover and bring to a boil over medium heat. Turn off the heat and allow the eggs to sit for 7 minutes. Rinse the eggs in cool water and refrigerate briefly in the water before peeling. Cook the bacon over medium heat until crisp, 2 to 3 minutes. Transfer to paper towels to drain. Finely shred enough of the arugula to measure 2 tablespoons.

Peel the eggs, cut in half lengthwise, and place the yolks in a small bowl. Gently rinse the whites and turn upside down on paper towels to dry. In a small bowl, whisk together the mustard, 1½ teaspoons vinegar, ½ teaspoon salt, and a couple of grinds of pepper. Whisk in 3 tablespoons of the oil. Mash the yolks with a fork, stir in the dressing, the shredded arugula, 1 tablespoon of the chives, and 2 tablespoons of the bacon. Season the egg whites with salt and pepper and spoon some of the yolk mixture into each white.

To serve, toss together the whole arugula leaves, 2 tablespoons of the chives, the chive flowers, a little oil and vinegar, and ½ teaspoon salt. Spoon the greens onto a serving platter, and nestle the eggs and tomatoes in the greens. Sprinkle the remaining bacon and chives over the eggs.

Shrimp, Mango, and Avocado Salad

For two to four weeks in September or October, the Wong family brings marvelous Keitt mangoes from the Coachella Valley. A rare crop at California farmers' markets, these juicy, nearly fiberless mangoes are big (about two pounds), remain green when ripe, and have a terrific sweet-tart flavor. Not only that, the "bone," or pit, is nearly flat, which means more meat per fruit. This salad is also delicious with low-acid yellow nectarines, such as Fitz Kelly's mangolike Carmen Mirandas.

MAKES 6 SERVINGS

Summer, Autumn

1 large mango, cut into ½-inch dice (see Cook's Tip)

2 tablespoons canola or other mild cooking oil

2 tablespoons seasoned rice vinegar

Grated zest and juice of 2 limes,

1 tablespoon fish sauce

½ to 1 teaspoon Thai chile paste

1 pound shrimp, grilled or boiled and peeled

1 large head butter lettuce, torn

1 cup sugar snap peas, strings removed and cut into bite-sized pieces

3 green onions, including several inches of green, thinly sliced

1 Reed or other avocado, cut into 1-inch cubes

1 cup small cherry tomatoes, preferably Sun Gold, stemmed

½ cup each fresh mint and basil (preferably Thai or opal) leaves, torn

¼ cup fresh cilantro leaves, torn

To make the dressing, put one-fourth of the mango, the oil, vinegar, lime juice, fish sauce, and chile paste in a blender and process until smooth. You should have 1 cup; set aside.

Place the shrimp, lettuce, peas, green onions, avocado, tomatoes, remaining mango, lime zest, basil, mint, and cilantro leaves in a large bowl. Toss the salad with just enough of the dressing to coat well. Reserve the rest for another use; it will keep refrigerated for up to 1 week.

HOW TO CHOOSE MANGOES: Seek out fragrant, smooth-skinned fruits that give a little (like a ripe avocado) when cupped in your hand. Ripe mangoes will keep on the counter for up to 1 week, and in the refrigerator for up to 1 month with some dehydration (skin will start to shrivel).

COOK'S TIP: To peel and cut a mango, stand the fruit on one end and, using a serrated knife, cut from top to bottom, running the blade close to the large, flat pit. Turn the mango and repeat on the opposite side. With the tip of your knife, cut a ½- to 1-inch crosshatch pattern into the flesh without cutting through the skin. Push the skin side upward to expose the cubes and cut them away from the skin. Use a spoon to scoop out any remaining flesh, and cut away any usable flesh attached to the pit.

94 California Salad Rolls with Almond Dipping Sauce

The multiple varieties of golden and crimson Asian pears, particularly Ichiban Nashi, Hosui, and Shinko, at Briar Patch and Penryn Orchard lend crunch, sweetness, and juiciness to salads summer through fall. My son, Adam, who has lived in Vietnam and Cambodia, told me about an unusual salad roll filled with grilled marinated meat and tropical star fruit, which resembles an Asian pear in taste and texture. Here, the fruit, meat, green onions, and aromatic herbs are rolled up in tender lettuce leaves and dipped in a California almond sauce spiked with Thai chiles. Paso Almonds brings freshly ground almond butter to the market after the fall harvest.

MAKES 6 SERVINGS

Summer, Autumn

3 cloves garlic, pressed

2 tablespoons plus 2 teaspoons fish sauce

Juice of 1 lime

½ pound boneless, skinless chicken breast, pork tenderloin, or strip steak

½ cup almond butter

½ cup chicken stock

1 Thai or serrano chile

2 Asian pears (about ¾ pound total), unpeeled, halved and cored

1 large Persian or Japanese cucumber (about ½ pound), peeled or unpeeled, halved and seeded

1 bunch green onions

1 large head looseleaf lettuce such as Black-Seeded Simpson or Vulcan, leaves separated

1 small bunch each cilantro, Thai basil, and mint

In a bowl, mix together the garlic, 2 tablespoons of the fish sauce, and half of the lime juice. Add the meat, turn to coat with the garlic mixture, and marinate for 30 minutes. Heat a grill to medium-high, or preheat a broiler with the rack close to the heat source. Grill or broil the meat, turning once, until the chicken or pork is just opaque throughout or the steak is done to your liking. Cut the meat into thin 3-inch-long strips and place in a serving bowl.

Stir together the almond butter, stock, the remaining 2 teaspoons fish sauce, and the remaining lime juice, mixing well. Mince the chile, crushing a few pieces to release their heat, and add to the almond sauce to taste. Cut the pears and cucumber into batons about ½ inch by 2 or 3 inches. Sliver the green onions, including several inches of green, lengthwise into 3-inch-long pieces.

Arrange the pears, cucumber, green onions, lettuce, and whole cilantro, basil, and mint sprigs on a platter. Have guests fill the lettuce leaves with a little meat, herbs, onions, pears, and cucumbers, roll up, and dip into the almond sauce.

Persimmon, Pomegranate, and Pecan Salad

The autumn colors and bright flavors of this salad are a refreshing counterpoint to rich holiday foods. Sweet-spicy, tomato-shaped Fuyu persimmons are eaten firm, and when sliced, their seed markings create a pretty sand-dollar design. Pomegranates add jeweled tang to salads and traditional Mexican dishes. In addition to ruby-red Wonderfuls, look for the more exotic low-acid Spanish Sweet pomegranates, with a yellowish rind and pale pink kernels from J.J.'s Lone Daughter. Laura Spensley of Cal-Pecan in Clovis brings several varieties of fresh pecans after the late-fall harvest through winter, and cold-storage pecans the rest of the year.

MAKES 8 SERVINGS

Autumn

1 pomegranate

4 ribs celery, preferably inner whiter ribs
    with leaves

2 small or 1 large Fuyu persimmon

½ cup pecan or walnut pieces, toasted
    (page 25)

½ pound mixed baby salad greens

About 1 tablespoon extra-virgin olive oil
    or nut oil

1 lemon

Kosher or sea salt and freshly ground
    black pepper

½ cup crumbled feta cheese (optional)

To remove the pomegranate kernels, make a cut near the blossom end of the fruit, submerge the pomegranate in a bowl of water, and break the fruit into large pieces. Use your fingers to loosen all the kernels, then drain and reserve them. They will keep refrigerated for up to 3 days.

Use a vegetable peeler to peel the celery, then slice paper-thin on the diagonal. Place in a salad bowl along with the leaves. Core the persimmon, cut it vertically into quarters, and then crosswise into thin slices. Add to the bowl along with the nuts, greens, and as many pomegranate kernels as you like. Grate the zest from the lemon in long, thin strands into the bowl. Drizzle on the oil, squeeze in some lemon juice, and season with salt and pepper. Toss well and sprinkle with the cheese.

HOW TO CHOOSE FUYU PERSIMMONS: The deeper the color, the sweeter and riper the fruit. The persimmon should be firm, but not rock hard. Store them on the counter for up to 3 weeks (they will soften gradually). Fuyus are the most common nonastringent persimmon, but look for the elusive Chocolate persimmon, with a brown-flecked interior and haunting chocolate notes from Penryn.

HOW TO CHOOSE POMEGRANATES: The best pomegranates are large and heavy for their size and have a fresh-looking rind. Some splitting is okay (thought to be an indicator they are ripe and bursting with juice), but avoid fruits with cracks that show signs of mold. Store in the refrigerator for up to 1 month.

Pummelo, Fennel, and Radish Salad

Closely related to grapefruits, pummelos are one of the oldest and largest citrus fruits (though much of the girth consists of thick pith). Revered in their native Asia, where they are often paired with seafood, pummelos can be quite sweet, with pleasantly crunchy juice vesicles (the juice sacs inside a segment) that hold their shape in a salad and release a burst of juice with every bite. Armando Garcia and Peter Schaner grow the popular pink-fleshed, sweet-acid Chandler variety. Grapefruit or Oro Blanco, a pummelo-grapefruit cross, may be substituted. Briar Patch, Flora Bella, and Coleman farms grow interesting radishes, from multicolor Easter Egg to elongated French Breakfast. Use flavorful winter salad greens such as velvety mâche, slightly bitter mizuna, or cabbagelike tatsoi (related to bok choy). This frosty winter salad is a nice contrast to winter stews and braises and goes well with smoked fish for brunch.

MAKES 6 SERVINGS

Winter

2 fennel bulbs (about 1 pound)
½ bunch radishes
1 pummelo, Oro Blanco, or grapefruit
1 to 2 tablespoons snipped fennel fronds
½ cup oil-cured black olives
2 tablespoons snipped fresh chives

2 handfuls (about 2 ounces total) of
    mâche, mizuna, or tatsoi
About 1 tablespoon extra-virgin olive oil
½ lemon
Kosher or sea salt and freshly ground
    white pepper

Trim the fennel bulbs and radishes, thinly slice them with a sharp knife or mandoline and place in ice water while you prepare the remaining ingredients. Peel, seed, and segment the pummelo, Oro Blanco, or grapefruit (page 24). If using a pummelo, use your fingers to separate the vesicles into little clumps. If using an Oro Blanco or grapefruit, cut the segments crosswise into small bite-sized pieces.

Drain the fennel and radishes and place in a bowl with the fennel fronds, citrus, olives, chives, and greens. Drizzle with the oil and a squeeze of lemon juice and sprinkle with salt and pepper. Toss, then taste and adjust the seasoning before serving.

HOW TO CHOOSE FENNEL BULBS: Look for white, juicy bulbs with fresh-looking fronds. The rounder bulbs (Italians call these "female") are often sweetest, and the flatter ("male") bulbs stronger tasting. The bulbs will keep refrigerated in a plastic bag for up to 1 week. Use the feathery tops for grilling or roasting fish (page 148).

CHEF'S TIP: Paul Shoemaker, chef de cuisine of Providence Restaurant, rings paper-thin slices of brilliant watermelon radishes around a crab, sugar snap pea, and blood orange salad.

Arugula Salad with Dates and Mandarins

If you think you don't like dates, it's probably because you haven't tasted a good one. Commercial dates, almost all of which are grown near Palm Springs and Indio, are often harvested when they are too dry and stored too long. They also typically come in only one variety, Deglet Noor—a fine variety, but not the whole story. Aficionados enjoy dates at several stages of ripeness, from pale gold and astringently crunchy to meltingly soft to chewy (but not dried out!). Different cultivars have taste and textural nuances. Caramel-like Empress, creamy Honey, and chewy Teddy Roosevelt from Davall Date Gardens, and tangy Zahidi, supersweet Khadrawy, Halawy, and Deglet Noor from Bautista Family Organic Date Ranch are all good choices for this salad because they will keep their shape. But for an exquisite dessert, don't miss large, plump organic Medjools, the king of dates, from Four Apostles Ranch and Bautista, or Robert Lower's spicy, round, almost-liquid Barhis from Flying Disc Ranch (and pick up a couple of otherworldly frondlike female date blossoms—inflorescences—for an exotic centerpiece).

MAKES 6 SERVINGS

Winter, Spring

½ cup (about 2 ounces) dates such as Honey, Halawy, or Teddy Roosevelt

5 mandarin oranges such as satsuma, clementine, Page, or Perfection

4 cups (about ¼ pound) arugula

About 1 tablespoon extra-virgin olive oil

Kosher or sea salt and freshly ground black pepper

2 ounces aged, salty cheese such as Winchester super-aged Gouda

Remove any hard caps at the stem ends of the dates, and use your fingers to pull out the pits. Use kitchen scissors to cut the dates into quarters lengthwise and place in a salad bowl. Peel and section 4 of the mandarins, peeling away any webbing clinging to the segment membranes. Add the mandarin segments and arugula to the dates. Drizzle with the oil and the juice of the remaining mandarin and sprinkle with salt and pepper. Toss the salad and shave the cheese over the top to serve.

Citrus

Beginning in 1841, when the first commercial orange grove was planted in Los Angeles, citrus has been the agricultural icon of California sunshine and promise of riches. Today, citrus sets Southern California farmers' markets apart from markets in the rest of the country, offering golden pleasures in the dead of winter. The subtropical climate and cool nights of the state's southern half allow mature fruit to hang long on the trees to color and sweeten deeply and develop complexity. The Santa Monica Farmers' Market features some of California's best citrus from Polito Family Farms, Garcia Organic Farm, Schaner Farms, J.J.'s Lone Daughter Ranch, Betty B's, Regier Farms, and Friend's Ranch.

The most important criterion in choosing citrus is taste, according to grower Bob Polito. Fragrance, rich color, smooth skin, a little give, and good heft in the hand generally mean a fruit is juicy and flavorful. Heavily pebbled, loose skins often indicate fruits left on trees too long and an insipid flavor. Of course, inconsistencies exist, depending on differences among varieties, the age of the trees, where the trees are grown, and when the fruits are harvested. For example, Armando Garcia leaves his late-season tangelos on the tree until the last moment before decline begins, and the fruits are incredibly sweet and as puffy as pillows. To avoid confusion, ask the farmer and taste the fruit. Citrus lasts two to three weeks in the refrigerator; eventually the skins harden and discolor, although the pulp stays tasty for a while. Bring citrus to room temperature to restore juiciness.

ORANGES
NAVEL: Washington, the most important seedless California variety, was first planted in Riverside in 1873. Easy to peel and section; at peak winter through spring. Distinctive Cara Cara navels are pink fleshed with a sweet "fruity" taste; at Garcia Organic and J.J.'s Lone Daughter in late spring.
VALENCIA: Sweet-tart, seeded, originally from Iberia, and regarded as the best juice orange. Rind may be green tinged. At peak spring through summer.
BLOOD: Seeded, red-streaked to almost-black pulp, skin with a little to a lot of deep red blush, and complex flavors. This Sicilian native is the standard European juice orange; Moro is the most common variety, but also look for Tarocco at Bernard Ranches. Winter through spring; best from mid- to late season.

MANDARINS (A.K.A TANGERINES)
SATSUMA: Japanese type, sweet, seedless, easy to peel, light orange skin. Early season.
CLEMENTINE: Seeded, complex sweet-acid flavor, darker orange skin and harder to peel than satsuma. Peter Schaner's Algerians are a kind of clementine. Early to midseason.
HONEY: Golden, difficult-to-peel skin, very sweet, appropriately named. Midseason.
TOM'S TERRIFIC: Name coined by Bob Polito for his son, though actually a Tahoe Gold. Midseason.
TANGELO: A mandarin-grapefruit cross, Minneola is the California variety; deep red-orange, relatively easy-to-peel skin, complex sweet-tart flavor, usually slightly oval with a noticeable "neck." Midseason.

PAGE: Tangelo-clementine cross with deep orange flesh and rich flavor. Midseason.

PIXIE: Small, seedless, very sweet with thin, bright orange skin. Ojai considered best region; a Friend's Ranch specialty. Late season.

W. MURCOTT AFOURER: Juicy, honeyed flavors and aroma. Late season.

GOLD NUGGET: Excellent seedless Pixie-type mandarin. Late season.

LEMONS

EUREKA: Standard tart, seeded lemon originated in California, nearly year-round. Coastal crops peak late winter to early spring, inland orchards have two crop cycles.

MEYER: Lemon-orange cross, extremely fragrant, with floral, delicate flavors. Winter through spring but best mid- to late season.

PERSIAN: Very low acid, almost bland, used as a table fruit. Best late fall through summer.

VARIEGATED PINK EUREKA: Yellow-and-green-striped Eureka type with mottled leaves, pink flesh. At J.J.'s Lone Daughter Ranch winter through spring.

BUDDHA'S HAND: Fingered citron highly regarded for its fragrance and ornamental qualities; almost no pulp. Primarily available in fall.

GRAPEFRUITS

STAR RUBY: Dark rosy, sweet pulp, yellow rind, and low to no seeds. Mid- to late season.

MARSH: Classic white variety, with sweetest grown in the desert. Davall Date Gardens brings exceptional Marsh grapefruits in winter.

PUMMELO: Ancient relative of the grapefruit, with thick pith, crunchy juice vesicles, sweet pink flesh; Chandler, with no hint of grapefruit bitterness, is most popular variety. Winter through spring.

ORO BLANCO: Sweet cross between pummelo and grapefruit. Winter through spring.

COCKTAIL: A fragrant, deep gold mandarin-pummelo cross. Winter through spring.

KUMQUATS

NAGAMI: Oval, acidic pulp, sweet, edible skin; most common variety. Available late winter through summer.

MEIWA: Round, sweet. At Garcia winter through spring.

LIMEQUAT AND ORANGEQUAT: George Schnurer of Betty B's specializes in unusual hybrids with haunting flavors and fragrances. Limequat fall through winter; orangequat winter through spring.

LIMES

BEARSS: Large, oval, nearly seedless, not as fragrant or as flavorful as Key lime. Choose fruit somewhere between green and yellow. Called Persian lime in Florida. Late summer through spring.

KEY (MEXICAN): Small, round, seeded, very aromatic, yellow when mature. Summer through fall.

Sides

Even the simplest side dishes—steamed or boiled carrots, broccoli, or potatoes—sing when prepared with produce grown for flavor and picked at its peak. Steamed German Butterball or peewee Russian Banana Fingerling potatoes rolled in a little soft butter and sea salt bear no relation to generic long-stored spuds. Roasted crazy-sweet Nantes carrots or custard-centered summer squash hardly resemble their carelessly under- or overboiled counterparts. Quality of produce alone can save you from indifference when it comes to cooking and eating your vegetables.

Dinner is so much more satisfying and polished when all the components on the plate share traits that make sense together, and it is easier to do than you may think. A moment's thought at the market about the ingredients' main attributes will guide you to pleasing combinations: bitter-edged rapini to cut the richness of a grilled cheese sandwich, or sweet fennel to go with briny fish.

This chapter offers easy ways to showcase the natural goodness of vegetables, from roasting and grilling to new ideas for old standbys to recipes for ingredients you may have overlooked. Never tried rutabagas? Not too sure about beets or okra? The fresh, carefully grown specimens at farmers' markets will surprise you.

Despite falling under the banner of accompaniments, many of these recipes, such as Pan-Roasted Baby Cauliflower, Fresh Black-eyed Peas with Tomatoes and Onions, and Rustic Eggplant-Tomato Bake, can stand in as main dishes. Others, like Romanesco with Green Olives and Capers can shrink to starter size, while still others, like Melted Cabbage and Green Garlic can grow into a soup.

Roasted Seasonal Vegetable Primer

As much as I like grilled vegetables, I find roasting accentuates their unique characteristics in a gentler way. It concentrates flavors, develops and caramelizes natural sugars, and gives vegetables that appetizing bubbled and crisped look. Roast plenty of them, as they're delicious hot from the oven or at room temperature. Leftovers can be marinated, layered into sandwiches, chopped into salads (page 91), stuffed into omelets or frittatas, and more. Roasted vegetables with Jessica's Aioli (page 46) make a special starter or a satisfying main dish.

Here's a selected how-to, roughly divided into seasons. Experiment with your own market finds. Mix and match vegetables with similar cooking times and temperatures: carrots, parsnips, and leeks, or mushrooms, eggplants, and summer squash. Follow the basics given below; variables such as cooking time, temperature, and additional seasonings are covered under each vegetable. Amounts given will average six servings.

THE BASICS

1. Roasting causes evaporation (shrinkage), so you need a good measure of raw vegetable to start.
2. Keep vegetables or vegetable pieces a uniform size for even cooking.
3. Toss cleaned, trimmed vegetables with 1 to 2 tablespoons olive oil (usually 1 tablespoon per pan), kosher or sea salt, and freshly ground black pepper. For convenience, do this directly in the pan.
4. Always preheat the oven.
5. Don't crowd the pan, or your vegetables will steam rather than brown. Large baking sheets (half sheet pans) and heatproof-glass dishes are ideal for roasting.
6. Roast vegetables uncovered in the upper third of the oven for better browning.
7. Halfway through the cooking time, remove the pan from the oven and give it a shake or use a spatula to loosen and turn the vegetables.
8. When the vegetables are browned and tender, season again with salt (try a finishing salt such as *fleur de sel* or Maldon sea salt) and pepper.
9. If serving the vegetables at room temperature, allow them to cool completely before piling them onto a serving dish. Room-temperature vegetables may need extra seasoning.

SPRING AND SUMMER

ASPARAGUS: Preheat oven to 450 degrees. Use 1½ pounds (3 bunches) finger-thick asparagus spears, woody ends snapped off, and a handful of thyme sprigs if desired. Roast until slightly shriveled and browned in spots, 10 to 12 minutes.

EGGPLANTS: Preheat oven to 400 degrees. Cut 2 globe eggplants crosswise into ½-inch-thick slices, or cut 6 Japanese eggplants in half lengthwise or thick diagonal slices. Use extra olive oil. Roast until browned, about 30 minutes. Season with chopped fresh Italian parsley and garlic and with lemon juice or red wine vinegar. To marinate, add more vinegar, oil, and garlic, and refrigerate overnight.

SNAP BEANS: Preheat oven to 450 degrees. Use 2 to 2½ pounds Blue Lake, wax, or green or wax romano beans. Snap off stem ends; leave Blue Lake and wax beans whole and cut romanos into thirds. Roast until slightly shriveled and browned in spots, 10 to 12 minutes.

SUMMER SQUASH, LONG: Choose medium-sized zucchini, marrow, or similar squash (3 or 4 to a pound), and use 1½ to 2 pounds total. Preheat oven to 425 degrees. Cut squash into thick diagonal slices. For baby zucchini, use whole or halve lengthwise. Roast until cut surfaces are browned and squash are tender, about 15 minutes.

SUMMER SQUASH, ROUND: Choose squash such as Flying Saucer Pattypan or Ronde de Nice. Preheat oven to 425 degrees. Use 1½ to 2 pounds squash, each 2 to 3 inches in diameter. Cut squash in half crosswise and place cut side down on pan after tossing with olive oil, salt, and pepper. Roast without turning until cut surface is nicely browned when you lift an edge to peek and flesh is tender and custardlike, about 15 minutes. If using 1-inch squash, roast about 12 minutes; 4-inch or larger squash can take up to 20 minutes. Turn cut side up to serve or to cool. If desired, top with chopped fresh Italian parsley and a squeeze of lemon. For larger cannonball-shaped squash, cut into ½-inch-thick slices and turn once halfway through cooking time. See page 25 for winter squash.

TOMATOES, CHERRY, QUICK ROASTED (good for sauce): Preheat oven to 450 degrees. Use 2 pint baskets. If desired, add a generous pinch of red pepper flakes. Roast until collapsing and browned in places, 5 to 10 minutes. If you like, after roasting, add 1 tablespoon chopped fresh Italian parsley, basil, thyme, or tarragon. For an easy pasta sauce, toss roasted tomatoes and their juices straight from the oven with 1 pound pasta, cooked and drained; fresh herbs; and additional salt and olive oil.

TOMATOES, CHERRY, SLOW ROASTED (good for salads or chopping): Preheat oven to 300 degrees. Use 1 pint basket if using as a condiment, 2 baskets if serving as a side. If desired, add 1 teaspoon red wine vinegar for each pint basket with the salt and pepper. Use nonreactive pan(s) and roast until browned and jammy, about 1½ hours.

TOMATOES, ROMA, SLOW ROASTED (good with grilled or roasted meats or in Roasted Tomato–Olive Salsa, page 147): Preheat oven to 300 degrees. Use 2 pounds Roma or other meaty tomatoes. Cut in half lengthwise. Use nonreactive pan(s) and roast tomatoes cut side up without turning until deeply caramelized and shrunken (sort of like sun-dried tomatoes), 2 to 3 hours.

AUTUMN, WINTER, AND EVERGREEN

BEETS: Preheat oven to 400 degrees. Use 4 bunches beets. Cut off tops, leaving 1 inch of stems; reserve tops for another use. Leave golf ball–sized beets whole; halve or quarter larger beets; cut torpedo beets in half lengthwise. Cover and roast, shaking the pan halfway through cooking, until almost tender when pierced with a knife, about 30 minutes. Uncover, shake the beets again, and roast uncovered until tender, about 15 minutes longer. When cool, peel beets using a paring knife (skins should come off easily). Serve with olive oil, salt, pepper, and a little vinegar or lemon juice, or use in recipes calling for roasted beets.

CARROTS OR PARSNIPS: Preheat oven to 425 degrees. Use 3 pounds parsnips or carrots, such as Nantes or Chardonnay. Peel and leave whole or cut into 3-inch-long pieces. If more than ½-inch thick, cut in half lengthwise. Use white pepper and season with several thyme sprigs, if desired. Roast until shiny, browned, and tender, 30 to 40 minutes. Top with chopped fresh Italian parsley and lemon juice or balsamic reduction (page 88).

CAULIFLOWER: Preheat oven to 425 degrees. Use 2 large heads white or orange cauliflower, about 2 pounds each, broken into bite-sized or smaller florets (the tinier they are, the more popcornlike they will be). Boil florets in, or steam over, salted water for 2 to 3 minutes, then drain and pat dry. Roast until crusty brown in places, about 25 minutes. Top with grated lemon zest and/or a squeeze of lemon juice and chopped fresh Italian parsley, if desired.

FENNEL: Preheat oven to 425 degrees. Use 6 to 8 fennel bulbs (about 3 pounds total) with fronds still attached. Cut off fronds and stalks where the bulb ends. Discard tough outer leaves from each bulb, cut away any bruised areas, and trim the root end, but leave the bulb intact. Quarter each bulb lengthwise, then steam fennel over boiling salted water for 10 minutes. Use white pepper. Roast until tender and caramelized, 25 to 30 minutes.

LEEKS: Preheat oven to 425 degrees. Use 24 baby leeks (about the size of green onions) or 5 or 6 large leeks. Leave baby leeks whole (including tops), but trim away roots. For large leeks, trim off dark leaves, cut white part in half lengthwise, then cut crosswise into 3-inch lengths. Season with thyme sprigs. Roast until tender and the edges are crisp, 30 to 40 minutes.

MUSHROOMS, CRIMINI: Preheat oven to 425 degrees. Use 2 pounds. Leave 1-inch mushrooms whole; halve or quarter larger ones. Roast until browned and shriveled, about 20 minutes. Top with chopped fresh Italian parsley and a squeeze of lemon juice. Good as a first course with wedge of Winchester mild Gouda or young pecorino cheese.

ONIONS: Preheat oven to 450 degrees. Use 2 large onions, cut crosswise into thick slices. Roast until tender and browned, about 20 minutes.

POTATOES: Preheat oven to 400 degrees. Use 2 pounds tiny unpeeled fingerlings, larger fingerlings halved, or larger potatoes cut into 1-inch pieces, and a handful of rosemary or thyme sprigs. Roast until tender and browned in spots, about 40 minutes. For extraspecial roasted potatoes, first cook in boiling salted water for 10 minutes. Drain well, toss with olive oil and seasonings, and roast until slightly puffed and golden brown, 20 to 30 minutes.

RUTABAGAS: Preheat oven to 400 degrees. Use 2 pounds small, young rutabagas. Save greens for another use. Cut small rutabagas into halves or quarters, or larger rutabagas into bite-sized pieces. Place cut side down, cover, and roast for 25 minutes. Uncover, loosen the rutabagas from the pan, and continue roasting, uncovered, until very tender and golden brown, 20 to 30 minutes longer. Toss roasted rutabagas with 2 to 3 tablespoons softened butter and *fleur de sel*.

SHALLOTS OR CIPOLLINE (SMALL, FLAT ITALIAN ONIONS): Preheat oven to 400 degrees. Use 16 golf ball–sized shallots or cipolline (about 1½ pounds), unpeeled, and season with a small handful of thyme sprigs. Roast until browned, tender when pierced with a knife, and some of the papery skins have split, about 40 minutes. Serve in their skins, like little surprise packages.

TURNIPS: Preheat oven to 400 degrees. Use 4 bunches baby turnips (about 2 pounds), preferably all-white Tokyo variety, or 2 pounds large purple and white turnips. Save greens for another use, or sauté and mix with roasted turnips. Cut small turnips in half, larger turnips into thick slices or batons. Roast cut side down until tender and browned, 20 to 30 minutes.

Melted Cabbage and Green Garlic

This is a fondue in the literal French sense: the vegetables cook slowly until they melt to luxurious creaminess. Cabbage can be surprisingly sweet, and a quick boil before sautéing will take care of any hidden sharpness (a good technique for many brassicas, such as Brussels sprouts, cauliflower, broccoli, or kale). Use round, mild, bumpy-leaved Savoy cabbage or Bill Coleman's conical, heirloom Early Jersey Wakefield. (Green garlic is discussed on page 56.) This dish is delicious with roasted salmon or poultry, can be thinned into a soup, stirred into risotto or pasta, and enhanced with crisped ham or bacon. To make a similar dish when green garlic isn't in season, substitute leeks and mature garlic.

MAKES 6 SERVINGS

Spring

1 large head green cabbage (2 to 3 pounds), cored and cut into narrow wedges

3 or 4 bunches green garlic (1 to 1 ⅓ pounds), or 3 large leeks, white part only, and 4 cloves garlic

4 tablespoons unsalted butter

1 onion, chopped

Kosher or sea salt and freshly ground white pepper

½ cup chicken or vegetable stock, or as needed

Bring a large pot of salted water to a boil, add the cabbage, and boil for 3 minutes. Drain well, chop finely, and set aside. Trim the root end and tops off the garlic so that you have the white part and about 4 inches of the green (save the trimmings for garlicky soup stock). Discard any yellowed or old-looking leaves, then chop the garlic. If using leeks and garlic cloves, chop the leeks and mince the garlic. You should have about 3 cups.

In a deep, wide pot, melt the butter over medium-low heat. Add the onion, green garlic (or leeks and garlic), and a little salt and cook gently, stirring occasionally, until translucent and soft, 5 to 7 minutes. Add the cabbage and 1 teaspoon salt and cook, uncovered, for 5 to 10 minutes. Cover, reduce the heat to low, and cook slowly until the vegetables are reduced and very creamy, about 1 hour. Stir occasionally and add the stock after 30 minutes. If there is a lot of liquid the next time you check the pan, leave the lid off for a while. If the mixture is dry or sticking, add a bit more stock or water. Season to taste with salt and pepper. This dish can be made a day ahead and reheated over low heat.

Smashed Potatoes with Long-Cooked Leeks

A riff on the Irish potato dish champ, this is true comfort food. Roasting instead of boiling the potatoes yields extra flavor and texture. For a multicolor variation, take advantage of the different colors of potatoes Alex Weiser grows, such as indigo Purple Peruvians and All Reds (see page 57 for more about potatoes). This dish is also delicious made with green garlic or spring onions.

MAKES 8 SERVINGS

Winter, Spring

3 pounds moderately starchy potatoes such as Yukon Gold or Satina
6 to 8 tablespoons extra-virgin olive oil
Kosher or sea salt and freshly ground white pepper

3 bunches leeks (about 10 leeks), white part only
¼ to ½ cup chicken stock or water

Preheat oven to 400 degrees. Cut potatoes in half if medium sized or into quarters if large, and place in a single layer in a shallow baking pan(s). Toss with 2 tablespoons of the oil and season with salt and pepper. Cover the pan(s) with aluminum foil and roast for 30 minutes. Uncover, toss the potatoes to loosen, and continue roasting, uncovered, until tender and lightly browned, about 20 minutes more.

Meanwhile, quarter the leeks lengthwise and thinly slice them. In a wide pot, heat 4 tablespoons of the oil over medium-low heat. Add the leeks, season with salt and pepper, reduce the heat to low, and cook gently, stirring occasionally, until the leeks are almost dissolving, about 30 minutes. Stir occasionally and add a little stock toward the end of cooking if the leeks seem dry or are sticking to the pan.

Smash the potatoes in the pan(s) with a fork or potato masher and scrape up any browned bits. Stir in the cooked leeks and add a little more oil or stock to moisten as needed. This dish can be made earlier in the day and reheated in a 350-degree oven.

THREE-COLOR VARIATION: Use 1 pound potatoes each of 3 colors, such as Purple Peruvian, Red Thumb, and Satina, and use a separate pan for each color. Smash them separately, divide the leeks among the 3 colors, and stir. Then gently fold the 3 batches together so the different colors remain visible.

Braised Tiny Artichokes

Baby artichokes aren't young artichokes, but instead the small offshoots away from the main thistle. Although you must still strip away tough outer leaves, these "babies" are choke free and can be used whole, halved, or shaved raw in salads. A member of the aster family, artichokes flourish in cool coastal climates. Green Farms and Suncoast Farms in Lompoc on the Santa Barbara coast grow excellent specimens. Try their green Big Hearts for this dish, or purple Fiesole or Campania varieties that keep a pretty lavender blush after cooking. Available year-round, small and large artichokes are at their peak in spring.

MAKES 6 SERVINGS

Winter, Spring

2 lemons

2½ pounds tiny artichokes, ½ to 1½ ounces each and 2 to 3 inches long

3 to 4 tablespoons extra-virgin olive oil

Kosher or sea salt and freshly ground black pepper

2 cloves garlic, finely chopped

3 tablespoons chopped fresh Italian parsley

½ cup chicken stock

Using a zester, grate the zest from the lemons in long, thin strands and reserve. Squeeze the juice of 1 lemon into a large bowl of water. Trim the artichokes (see following directions), cut into halves or quarters (if they're a little big), and drop into the lemon water to keep them from discoloring (they will a bit anyway, but this disappears when they cook).

In a large skillet, heat 2 tablespoons of the oil over medium-high heat. Drain the artichokes well, add them to the pan with a little salt, and sauté until shiny bright green and browned in places, about 5 minutes (do this in batches if necessary, adding more oil as needed).

Add the garlic and 2 tablespoons of the parsley and stir until fragrant, 30 to 60 seconds. Add the juice from half of the remaining lemon, the stock, and a little salt and pepper. Bring to a boil, scraping up any browned bits. Reduce the heat to low, cover, and cook until the artichokes are tender, the liquid is absorbed, and the artichokes are glazed. If the artichokes are tender after 10 minutes but liquid remains in the pan, uncover the pan, raise the heat to medium, and cook until the liquid is gone. Season to taste with salt, pepper, and lemon juice. Stir in the remaining 1 tablespoon parsley and the reserved lemon zest just before serving. The artichokes can be served hot, or they can be made up to several hours ahead and served at room temperature.

HOW TO CHOOSE ARTICHOKES: Large or small, some varieties are elongated and tulip shaped with slightly flared outer leaves, while others are globe shaped with leaves that curl inward. Choose firm, closed artichokes. A few dusty frost marks are okay, but avoid blackened artichokes. Large artichokes should be heavy for their size with fat stalks, an indicator of a large heart. When peeled, the stalk is a continuation of the prized heart, or crown. Store artichokes loose in the coldest part of the refrigerator (usually the back of the lowest shelf), and ideally use them within a few days, though they will keep a couple of weeks.

HOW TO TRIM ARTICHOKES: Be ruthless about peeling away outer tough leaves from an artichoke of any size, large to tiny, as they are fibrous even when cooked. Bend back the darker green or purple leaves to the point at which they snap off. Continue until you get to leaves that are pale green or pale purple and green. Use a paring knife to shave away the dark remnants at the base. Cut off the tops of the artichokes to remove prickly tips. Cut tiny artichokes in half or quarters. There shouldn't be any choke (the inedible fuzzy core), but if there is, dig it and any hidden prickly parts out with the tip of a knife or grapefruit spoon. The larger the artichoke, the more you will need to trim. To remove the choke from a large whole artichoke, knock a whole trimmed artichoke on a counter edge to loosen the leaves. Pry open and use a paring knife or grapefruit spoon to scoop out the choke and prickly inner leaves. Or, quarter large artichokes and cut out the choke.

CHEF'S TIP: Cardoons, which, like artichokes, belong to the aster family, look like flattened celery stalks but taste like artichoke hearts. They are a favorite of chef-owner Salvatore Marino of Il Grano, and he is a standing customer for Bill Coleman's late-winter crop. To prepare them, Salvatore suggests washing them well, soaking them overnight in very lightly salted water, peeling them as you would celery, and then steaming or boiling them until just tender. Then use them sliced in salads with grated hard-boiled egg, marinated anchovies, and capers, or sautéed with garlic on fusilli with grated ricotta salata and black truffles. Raw young cardoons are a traditional dipper for *bagna cauda*.

Elegant Spring Hash

Use some or all of a rhapsody of grassy greens and yellows—asparagus, fiddlehead ferns, ramps, fava beans, English peas, yellow-fleshed potatoes—with delicate spring morel mushrooms in this company dish that complements wild salmon or roast chicken. Use one pan, but cook the vegetables separately, one after the other, to keep their color, texture, and flavor intact. Suncoast Farms and Green Farms in Lompoc specialize in asparagus as well as artichokes, but you will also find wild and cultivated spring asparagus at Flora Bella, Jerry Rutiz, Harry's Berries, and Fairview Gardens. Fiddleheads are coiled young fern fronds with an asparagus-like quality, and ramps are small native wild leeks with tender, broad tops. Both grow wild in northern climes. Look for them, along with conical, honeycombed morels, at David West's Clearwater Farms.

MAKES 8 TO 10 SERVINGS

Spring

1½ pounds waxy or all-purpose yellow-fleshed potatoes such as Yukon Gold, Russian Banana Fingerling, or French Fingerling

½ pound morel mushrooms

About 1 pound finger-thick asparagus

¼ pound fiddlehead ferns

Handful of ramps, or 3 tablespoons snipped fresh chives

3 tablespoons unsalted butter

Kosher or sea salt and freshly ground black pepper

1 cup shelled English peas (about 1 pound in the pod)

2 tablespoons chopped fresh tarragon

½ cup peeled shelled fava beans (about 1 pound in the pod), page 76

2 to 3 tablespoons water

½ lemon

Peel the potatoes if desired, cut into ½-inch dice, and reserve in a bowl of water. Cut the morels in half lengthwise and clean well (see following directions). Cut larger halves in half again lengthwise. Snap off woody asparagus stems and discard or save for stock. Cut the asparagus crosswise into ½-inch pieces, reserving tips separately. Drop the fiddleheads into boiling salted water and boil for 2 minutes. A lot of "fern debris" will come loose. Drain the fiddleheads and rinse well in ice water. Trim the ends off and rub away any remaining brown film clinging to the ferns. Clean the ramps, discard the roots, and cut the bulbs and leaves crosswise into thin slices.

In a sauté pan or wide pot, heat 1 tablespoon of the butter over medium heat. Add the morels, season with salt and pepper, and sauté until tender and any liquid they release evaporates, about 5 minutes. Remove to a large, flat dish. Add 1 tablespoon of the butter to the pan and add the asparagus pieces (but not the tips), ramps, fiddleheads, peas, 1 tablespoon of the tarragon, and salt and pepper. Sauté until the colors brighten, about 2 minutes. Cover the pan to steam the vegetables until just tender, 2 minutes more. Add the vegetables to the mushrooms and spread them out on the plate so they cool quickly. Add the remaining 1 tablespoon butter to the pan, drain the potatoes, and add them to the pan with a little salt and pepper. Cover, reduce the heat to medium-low, and cook the potatoes until tender, about 10 minutes, adding the 2 tablespoons of water and stirring halfway through the cooking time. The dish can be made up to this point 2 hours in advance.

To finish the dish, stir the vegetable-mushroom mixture, fava beans, and raw asparagus tips into the potatoes, and heat gently until the asparagus tips are tender, about 2 minutes. Stir in the remaining 1 tablespoon tarragon, a squeeze of lemon juice, and salt and pepper if needed.

HOW TO CHOOSE ASPARAGUS: Look for firm stalks with tight heads. Pencil-thin spears are best quickly steamed or boiled and served with butter or chilled and served with a lemon vinaigrette. Fatter spears are delicious roasted (page 102); I find them to be sweeter and meaty. Asparagus do fine loosely wrapped in plastic in the crisper and are best used within a few days.

HOW TO CHOOSE MOREL MUSHROOMS: Select firm, tan morels and store in a brown paper bag in the refrigerator crisper for no more than a few days. Check with the forager or vendor about their cleanliness; they could need anywhere from a dry brushing to several rinses.

CHEF'S TIP: For Suzanne Goin, chef-owner of A.O.C. and Lucques restaurants, the ramp's delicate leaves are one of its best features, but they cook more quickly than the bulb end. To preserve the plant's natural shape, Suzanne loosely wraps the tops together in foil and lowers the bulb ends into boiling salted water, draping the leaves outside the pot. In a few minutes when the bulbs are tender, she unwraps the leaves and dips them in the water to wilt. The ramps are now ready to be brushed with olive oil and grilled or sautéed in butter.

About Purple and White Asparagus

In the late nineteenth century, Jules Arthur Harder, chef de cuisine of San Francisco's Palace Hotel, wrote that purple asparagus is the one "preferred by all gourmets" for its exceptional sweetness. Today, we might dispute the grandeur of his claim, but the fat spears (available from Zuckerman), which turn deep green when cooked, are indeed particularly sweet.

Temperamental white asparagus are grown in the dark to prevent any greening. More brittle than green asparagus, the spears quickly turn fibrous and bitter if not kept chilled and used soon after harvest. Christopher Blobaum, chef-partner of Wilshire Restaurant, looks for pearly, finger-thick spears at Fairview Gardens. They must be completely peeled and take longer to cook than green or purple asparagus. To bring out their mild nutty flavor, the chef (and Iowa farm boy) blanches the spears in a skillet of boiling salted water with lemon juice, and then sautés them in butter until tender, 10 to 12 minutes. Serve with lots of butter, salt, and pepper.

Blood Orange–Glazed Roasted Beets

Here's a simple, elegant way to serve beets that is especially beautiful when tiny whole beets are used (think Easter and Passover). For convenience, roast the beets a day ahead and glaze just before serving. Blood oranges add a berry complexity to traditional beets with orange. In the fall, when the first round of California beets shows up in markets but blood oranges haven't yet arrived, make this dish with seasonal Valencia oranges and pomegranate juice from Sherrill Orchards (see variation).

MAKES 6 SERVINGS

Winter, Spring

4 to 5 blood oranges

24 small beets, 1 to 2 inches in diameter, or 3 pounds larger beets, quartered, roasted (page 104)

Kosher or sea salt and freshly ground black pepper or crushed toasted black peppercorns (page 34)

1 tablespoon unsalted butter, softened

2 to 3 tablespoons chopped toasted pistachios (page 25), optional

Using a zester, grate the zest from 1 orange in long, thin strands and reserve. Juice the oranges to yield 1¼ cups. Pour the juice into a large skillet, set over medium-high heat, and cook until reduced by half and slightly syrupy, about 10 minutes.

Add the roasted beets, zest, and a little salt and pepper to the skillet, reduce the heat to medium, and cook the beets, frequently spooning the juice over them, until the juice becomes a thick syrup, 6 to 7 minutes. Stir in the butter, reduce the heat as needed to keep the glaze from browning, and stir constantly until the beets are richly coated and the juices are a thick glaze, 1 to 2 minutes. Season with salt and pepper and sprinkle with the pistachios.

POMEGRANATE-ORANGE VARIATION: Substitute ¾ cup orange juice and ⅓ cup pomegranate juice for the blood orange juice and proceed as directed.

Charred Rapini

Rapini, also called broccoli raab, broccoli rabe, *cime di rapa*, and *broccoli di rapa*, is a cool-weather Italian favorite harvested in spring or fall. It has tender stems (check that they don't look fibrous), small florets, and ruffled leaves that distinguish it from sweeter Chinese broccoli, with its large, leathery leaves, and from sprouting, or "baby," broccoli, which has small, oblong leaves. A quick toss on the grill adds sweet smokiness to its pleasing bitter edge. In addition to being a great accompaniment to lamb, pork, and game birds, it is wonderful as an appetizer on bruschetta, in a grilled cheese sandwich, or mixed with cannellini beans.

MAKES 6 SERVINGS

Spring, Autumn

4 bunches rapini (about 2 pounds total)

4 tablespoons extra-virgin olive oil

Kosher or sea salt and freshly ground black pepper

Trim away about 1 inch of the tough stem from the rapini stalks and discard. Cook in a large pot of rapidly boiling salted water for 3 minutes. Drain the rapini and rinse (shock) in ice water to retain the color and stop the cooking. Drain again and toss with 3 tablespoons of the oil and salt and pepper.

Heat a grill to medium-high. Spread the rapini over the grill. It will be kind of a tangle, which is fine, just get as much rapini as possible touching the hot rack directly. Grill, turning once, until the rapini leaves are charred, 2 to 3 minutes total. Remove to a cutting surface and chop coarsely. Drizzle with the remaining 1 tablespoon oil and season to taste with salt and pepper.

TREVISO VARIATION: Torpedo-shaped Treviso radicchio has a more delicate flavor than the more common round Chioggia variety. Use 2 large or 4 small heads Treviso. Don't precook them. Leave them whole if the heads are small, or cut larger heads lengthwise into halves or quarters. Soak in ice water for 20 minutes, then drain, pat dry, and toss with the oil, salt, and pepper as for rapini. Grill as directed, fanning out the leaves so as many as possible touch the rack. Chop to serve.

CHEF'S TIP: Brian Wolff, chef de cuisine at Lucques Restaurant, grills tart wild summer purslane after the steaks come off the barbecue, which adds extra flavor—"like deglazing the grill with the wild green." Flora Bella and Rutiz farms forage this California native plant to bring to market. Slightly succulent and tangy, it is also delicious sautéed, or used raw in salads when its leaves are tiny.

Roasted Baby Broccoli with Chiles and Crispy Garlic

Available at such farms as Coastal, Coleman, and Flora Bella, baby, or sprouting, broccoli are actually mature but tender side shoots cut from central stalks (like Brussels sprouts on a stalk). Their few tiny leaves and small stems help distinguish them visually from rapini and Chinese broccoli. When roasted, those little leaves turn crisp, and the stalks and buds develop a rich, nutty flavor.

MAKES 6 TO 8 SERVINGS

Spring, Autumn

2 pounds baby broccoli
5 tablespoons extra-virgin olive oil
Kosher or sea salt and freshly ground
   black pepper

3 dried árbol chiles
4 large cloves garlic, thinly sliced
½ to 1 tablespoon red wine vinegar

Preheat oven to 425 degrees. On a baking sheet, toss the broccoli with 1 tablespoon of the oil and salt and pepper, and then spread it out on the pan. Roast for 10 minutes, shake the pan, and return it to the oven. Continue roasting until the stalks are crisp-tender and the leaves and tops are crisped, about 10 minutes more.

Meanwhile, pour the remaining 4 tablespoons oil into a small skillet over medium-low heat. Break the chiles into pieces over the pan and drop them and their seeds into the oil. Cook until fragrant and beginning to color, about 2 minutes. Add the garlic and cook, stirring, until the garlic is golden, about 2 minutes more. Remove from the heat and, using a slotted spoon, transfer the garlic to paper towels to drain. The chiles will continue to infuse the oil.

Toss the hot broccoli with the crisped garlic and the chile-infused oil and vinegar to taste. Taste and adjust with salt, then serve hot or at room temperature.

FARMER'S TIP: Alex Weiser is proud of his spring treats, heirloom sprouting Red Arrow and Purple Sprouting broccoli. Although they lose much of their red when cooked, their sweet flavor is what is important. They are delicious boiled briefly, then sautéed with sliced garlic in a little olive oil, salt, and pepper.

Romanesco with Green Olives and Capers

Green, spiky-spired romanesco is a cross between cauliflower and broccoli. Growers Richard Sager of Two Peas in a Pod and Alex Weiser of Weiser Family Farms like its nutty taste that sweetens with cold growing nights. Boiling the garlic with the romanesco flavors the florets and tames the garlic for the dressing (which is also great over steamed or boiled potatoes). This dish is good hot or at room temperature, as a side or as part of an antipasto platter (add more lemon and garlic and marinate for a couple of hours or overnight). I like to use brined green olives from Adams Olive Ranch here.

MAKES 6 SERVINGS

Spring

1 large or 2 medium heads romanesco or cauliflower (about 2 pounds)

⅔ cup brine-cured green olives, pitted

2 tablespoons capers

4 tablespoons fresh Italian parsley leaves

Grated zest of 1 lemon

⅓ cup extra-virgin olive oil

¼ teaspoon red pepper flakes

Kosher or sea salt

1 tablespoon lemon juice

4 large cloves garlic, peeled

Cut the romanesco into small florets and soak in ice water to cover for 20 minutes. Meanwhile, chop together the olives, capers, 3 tablespoons of the parsley, and the lemon zest. In a small pot, heat the oil and red pepper flakes over medium-low heat until hot. Remove from the heat and stir in the olive mixture, ½ teaspoon salt, and the lemon juice. Set aside.

Bring a large pot of salted water to a boil. Drain the romanesco, drop it into the boiling water with the garlic cloves, and cook the florets until just tender, 3 to 5 minutes. Drain well. Chop the cooked garlic with the remaining 1 tablespoon parsley, place in a large bowl, add the florets and olive-caper dressing, and toss well. Taste and adjust with salt, red pepper flakes, and lemon juice. If serving at room temperature, adjust seasoning again before serving.

Rustic Eggplant-Tomato Bake

Like southern France, California produces sumptuous summer eggplants and tomatoes. Inspired by a Patricia Wells recipe from Provence, this casserole is great hot or cold (when it cuts neatly into squares), delightful for a midsummer or early-autumn buffet when eggplants are at their peak, and hearty enough to be the center of the plate in a vegetarian meal. Make this with Scott Peacock's striped, creamy Rosa Bianca eggplants, or succulent Japanese or Neon eggplants from Elmer Lehman, one of the market's first farmers.

MAKES 6 TO 8 SERVINGS

Summer, Autumn

2 or 3 globe eggplants (about 2 pounds total), preferably Rosa Bianca, or 2 pounds Japanese eggplants
6 tablespoons extra-virgin olive oil
Kosher or sea salt and freshly ground black pepper
2 cloves garlic, peeled

¼ cup mixed chopped fresh herbs such as Italian parsley, rosemary, basil, and thyme
6 to 8 small ripe, red tomatoes such as Early Girl or Celebrity (about 1½ pounds total)

Preheat oven to 450 degrees. If eggplants are large, cut in half lengthwise. Cut eggplant halves or whole Japanese eggplants crosswise into ½-inch-thick slices. Drizzle 2 tablespoons of the oil over the bottom of a shallow 2-quart baking dish. Arrange the eggplant slices, overlapping them, in a single layer in the prepared dish, and season with salt and pepper. Put the garlic cloves through a garlic press directly into a small bowl. Add the herbs, ½ teaspoon salt, and enough oil to make a stiff paste. Dot the eggplant with the garlic-herb mixture. Core the tomatoes, cut them in half crosswise, and salt the cut sides. Place the tomato halves cut side down spaced evenly over the eggplant. Drizzle the remaining oil evenly over all, and sprinkle the tomatoes with a little salt.

Bake in the upper third of the oven, basting occasionally with the juices that collect in the dish, until the eggplant is tender and the tomatoes are soft and blackened on top, about 1 hour. Serve warm or at room temperature.

Tangy White Beans

In Argentina, this dish is considered a staple with any grilled meat and this recipe comes from my son-in-law Rodolfo's family. Make it in late summer or early fall with fresh white cannellini beans or light green flageolets, or through the winter with dried beans. You can use canned beans for this simple recipe, but the dish is dramatically better when made with good beans.

MAKES 8 SERVINGS

Evergreen, Summer, Autumn

6 cups drained, cooked cannellini beans (from fresh or dried), page 25

2 cloves garlic, minced

2 tablespoons finely chopped fresh Italian parsley

2 tablespoons extra-virgin olive oil

3 tablespoons cider vinegar

Kosher or sea salt

In a serving bowl, stir together the beans, garlic, parsley, oil, and vinegar. Season to taste with salt. Make at least 1 hour ahead, or up to 1 day ahead and refrigerate, then bring to room temperature. Taste and adjust the seasoning with salt and vinegar before serving.

Fresh and Dried Beans at the Market

Technically speaking, late summer and fall shell beans are developmentally halfway between summer snaps with barely formed seeds and mature dry beans. These moist, flavorful, fully formed seeds of every hue and stripe encased in leathery, inedible pods have a "greener," younger taste and texture and cook more quickly than dried beans.

This is not to say that summer green beans have the genetic makeup to turn into plump-seeded beans worth cooking, but most shelling varieties do make first-rate dried beans (though not all dried bean varieties make good shell beans). Often identified by how they grow—runner, pole, bush— "shellies" include limas (noteworthy at McGrath Farms), red-mottled cranberries, borlotti (a cranberry type), scarlet runners, creamy white cannellini, black- and pink-eyed peas, and pale green flageolets (excellent at Fairview Gardens). Richard Sager of Two Peas in a Pod grows lots of jewel-toned shell beans, and when some of his open-pollinated varieties cross in the field, they yield gorgeous surprises that range from iridescent bronze to lilac to navy speckled. The colors mute when cooked, but no matter. A mix of types and sizes makes a delicious quick-cooking ragout over polenta or rice.

Beans left longer on the bush dry naturally as fall progresses. The pods turn brown, then the plant, "looking neglected, like green beans someone forgot to pick," says Barbara Spencer, who specializes in dried beans at Windrose Farm in Paso Robles. "There's a peak moment when each variety is ready for harvest [when the beans have hardened and turned starchy], and we've learned when that is."

The Spencers' heirloom varieties are often too small for commercial sorters, so they are harvested and sorted by hand. The beans aren't kept for more than one season, which means they don't need to be soaked before cooking. It also means that when the supply runs out, customers must wait for Barbara and Bill Spencer to bring the next year's crop.

Like potatoes, different kinds of beans differ in texture, from waxy types that hold their shape when cooked to starchy ones that turn creamy and dissolve with long cooking. Windrose's Southwest varieties include small, dense Midnight Turtle black beans; nutty, firm Indian Woman Yellow, smooth, cream-colored Peruano (can be substituted for cannellini; high-protein ancient tepary and white tepary; sweet, meaty maroon-and-white Anasazi; black-and-white Appaloosa; and black-and-gray-striated Dos Mesas, whose markings evoke desert land formations. The Spencers' dramatic French Coco Rubicos, creamy pink with bright rose markings, are similar to pintos but richer.

Fresh Black-eyed Peas with Tomatoes and Onions

We usually think of earthy black-eyed peas cooked with smoky ham hocks or bacon, but tender, young peas available in early fall have a more delicate flavor and texture that deserve to star on their own. Here, these shelling peas are cooked with late-summer tomatoes in a quick ragout, delicious with meat or on their own over white or brown rice. The dish tastes richer if made with stock, but water will do, and will be even better made a day ahead. Black-eyed shelling peas are harvested by Flora Bella Farm in Three Rivers, Coastal Farms in Santa Paula, Kanji Yasutomi in nearby Pico Rivera, and Weiser Family Farms in Tehachapi. The Weisers also grow pink-eyed peas.

MAKES 8 SERVINGS

Autumn

6 small ripe, red tomatoes such as Celebrity (1½ pounds)

2 tablespoons olive or canola or other mild cooking oil

1 small onion, finely chopped

2 teaspoons kosher or sea salt

1 clove garlic, minced

1 tablespoon chopped fresh Italian parsley

2 to 3 cups Vegetable, Chicken, or Beef Stock (page 52 to 54); 1 to 1½ cups canned diluted with 1 to 1½ cups water; or water

2 pounds fresh black- or pink-eyed peas in the pod, shelled (about 4 cups)

Freshly ground black pepper (optional)

Core the tomatoes and cut in half crosswise. Scoop or gently squeeze out the seeds. Using a box grater set in a deep bowl, grate each tomato half on the cut side, rubbing it over the large holes until you reach the skin. Discard the skins. You should have about 1½ cups tomato pulp.

In a wide pot, combine the oil, onion, and ½ teaspoon of the salt over medium-low heat and cook, stirring occasionally, until the onion is translucent and quite soft but not browned, 7 to 10 minutes. Add the garlic and parsley and cook for 1 minute. Stir in the tomato pulp, 2 cups stock, and 1 teaspoon salt. Raise the heat to medium and cook for 5 minutes, reducing the heat a little once the tomato mixture is simmering. Stir in the peas, cover, reduce the heat to medium-low or low, and simmer until the peas are tender, about 25 minutes. There should be ample sauce, so add the remaining 1 cup stock if the mixture seems dry. Season with the remaining ½ teaspoon salt and pepper.

HOW TO CHOOSE YOUNG BLACK-EYED PEAS: Look for pods that are still greenish but starting to yellow and are dry. The peas inside should range from glossy pale green to cream and have the familiar "black eye." Dark green pods are more difficult to open and the peas are often too tiny. Fully brown dry pods contain the more familiar mature matte beige bean with a hearty texture and flavor.

Roasted Okra with Fresh Peanuts

Aficionados find the slippery quality of okra to be one of its charms, but I prefer to focus on its pearly seeds, tender ribbed flesh, and asparagus-like flavor. Roasting finger-sized okra pods whole prevents the release of viscous juices that occurs when the pods are cut. A member of the mallow family, as are hibiscus and cotton, okra is a favorite in the Middle East, Africa, Asia, and the American South. From late summer through fall, you will find red and green okra at the Weiser, Flora Bella, and Windrose stands, and at Vang Thao, Phong Vang, and Yee Her's Fresno Evergreen, all of whom also grow peanuts. Fresh peanuts have moist shells that are easily removed with a light tap of a mallet.

MAKES 6 SERVINGS

Summer, Autumn

1 pound small red or green okra pods, 2 to 3 inches long

1 cup shelled fresh peanuts (about ½ pound in the shell), coarsely chopped

1 tablespoon extra-virgin olive oil

Kosher or sea salt

Togarashi or *nanami togarashi* (page 28) or red pepper flakes

1 lemon

Preheat oven to 425 degrees. Rinse the okra and rub dry with paper towels to remove sticky fuzz. Trim the stem ends but do not cut away the caps. Scatter the okra and peanuts on a large baking sheet and toss with the oil and some salt and *togarashi*. Roast in the upper third of the oven, giving the pan a shake halfway through the cooking time, until the okra is tender and its edges are browned and crisped and the peanuts are crunchy, about 20 minutes. Place on a serving dish, squeeze the juice from the lemon over all, and season to taste with salt and additional *togarashi*.

Slow-Grilled Butternut Squash

When the season changes but the weather is still nice for outdoor dining, grill squash slowly until the outside is crisped but not burnt and the inside is tender and tinged with smoke and spice. It is great with chicken, pork, or sausages that can be prepared while the squash are cooking. Try this same method with quicker-cooking delicata squash.

MAKES 8 TO 10 SERVINGS

Autumn, Winter

3 butternut squash, about 1½ pounds each

½ cup extra-virgin olive oil

1 tablespoon each fresh rosemary, thyme, and summer savory leaves, minced

1 teaspoon kosher or sea salt

⅛ teaspoon red pepper flakes

Freshly ground white pepper

Maldon sea salt or other finishing salt

Heat a grill to medium-low. In a small pot, heat the oil, herbs, kosher salt, red pepper flakes, and a little white pepper over medium-low heat until the oil is hot and the herbs just begin to sizzle. Remove from the heat and let stand while preparing the squash. Cut the squash in half lengthwise and scoop out and discard the seeds and strings. Brush the cut surfaces with some of the olive oil mixture.

Place the squash halves cut side down on the grill. After 15 minutes, turn cut side up; some dark grill markings should be visible. Brush with some of the olive oil mixture, being sure to include some of the herbs. Grill cut side up for 20 minutes, brush again, turn cut side down, and grill for 10 minutes. Turn and brush again, and continue grilling until the squash halves are tender. They will take a total of 50 to 60 minutes. (Delicatas will be done in 40 to 45 minutes.) Brush once more with the oil mixture and finish with a little Maldon sea salt. Cut squash crosswise into thirds to serve.

TO ROAST IN THE OVEN: Preheat oven to 400 degrees. Brush the cut side of the squash halves generously with some of the olive oil mixture, and place cut side down in a shallow pan. Roast without turning until tender, about 40 minutes. They will have some caramelization and be moister than the grilled version. If desired, run the under the broiler for a few minutes to color further. Brush with the remaining olive oil mixture before serving.

Roasted Sweet Potatoes, Two Ways

I love the way sweet potatoes contrast with spicy chiles and tangy citrus. Here are two different flavor profiles that draw their character from seasonings available at the market. The first uses bumpy-skinned kaffir limes and leaves and fruity, deep green poblano chiles. Kaffir limes, which are popular in Southeast Asian cooking, have a dusky undertone, and their double leaves are highly aromatic when fresh and shiny green. Look for them at Coleman, Betty B's, and Schaner farms. Bearss or Mexican (Key) limes and their zest may be substituted.

In the second version, sweet potatoes are contrasted with pungent garlic, chipotles (smoked dried jalapeños), and smoked dried tomatoes from Windrose Farm in Paso Robles. Bill Spencer built a smoker at his farm, the perfect way for farmers—and cooks—to extend an abundant pepper and tomato season. Keep a supply of these condiments in your freezer.

With Kaffir Lime and Roasted Chiles

MAKES 6 SERVINGS

Autumn, Winter

2 poblano chiles, roasted and peeled (page 25)

3 pounds sweet potatoes, unpeeled, cut into 1-inch pieces

3 tablespoons canola or other mild cooking oil

Juice of 1 kaffir lime

Kosher or sea salt

Generous pinch of red pepper flakes (optional)

8 fresh kaffir lime leaves (4 sets double leaves)

Small handful of fresh cilantro or Thai basil leaves or a mixture

Preheat oven to 375 degrees. Seed the roasted peppers. Taste the peppers for heat; if very mild and you want more heat, reserve some of the seeds. Cut the peppers into ½-inch pieces and set aside. On a large baking sheet or in a bowl, toss the sweet potato pieces with the oil, 1 tablespoon of the lime juice, a generous sprinkling of salt, and the red pepper flakes. Crush or tear 4 lime leaves and scatter among the potatoes. Spread the potatoes evenly over 1 or 2 baking sheets; the pieces of potato should be no more than 2 deep.

Roast the potatoes for 15 minutes. Add the roasted peppers and any reserved seeds, toss with the potatoes, and continue roasting until the potatoes are tender and their edges are browned, about 15 minutes more. Transfer the potatoes to a serving bowl. Remove the central stems and ribs from the remaining lime leaves. Stack the leaves, roll up lengthwise, and cut crosswise into thin shreds. Season the potatoes with salt and the remaining lime juice to taste and toss with the shredded lime leaves and the cilantro, then serve.

With Garlic, Smoked Tomatoes, and Chipotles

MAKES 6 SERVINGS

Autumn, Winter

4 smoked dried tomatoes

3 chipotle chiles

1 head garlic

3 pounds sweet potatoes, unpeeled,
   cut into 1-inch pieces

3 tablespoons olive oil

Kosher or sea salt

Small handful of fresh cilantro leaves

Preheat oven to 375 degrees. In separate bowls, soak the tomatoes and chiles in boiling water to soften, 20 to 30 minutes. Drain the tomatoes and use scissors to snip them into ¼-inch pieces. Drain the chiles and remove the stem and seeds (keep some seeds if you want a spicier dish), then snip into ¼-inch pieces. Break apart the head of garlic and remove the outer loose papery skins but do not peel the cloves. On a large baking pan or in a bowl, toss the potato pieces with the garlic cloves, oil, and a generous sprinkling of salt. Spread the potatoes evenly over 1 or 2 baking sheets; the pieces of potato should be no more than 2 deep.

Roast the potatoes for 15 minutes. Add the smoked tomatoes and chiles, toss with the potatoes, and continue roasting until the potatoes and garlic are tender and the edges of the potatoes are browned, 15 to 20 minutes more. Peel the chewy, sweet garlic cloves before serving or have diners peel their own. Transfer the potatoes and garlic to a large bowl. Season the potatoes with salt and toss with the cilantro, then serve.

When Is a Sweet Potato Not a Yam?

Always. And it's not a potato either. The idea of calling it a yam likely grew out of a 1930s marketing campaign by Louisiana growers who wanted to distinguish their sweet, moist-fleshed tubers from the floury, mildly sweet ones grown in Virginia. But both dry- and moist-textured sweet potatoes (*Ipomoea batatas*) are native to South America. They were introduced to Europe by Columbus following early voyages to the New World and were being cultivated in the American South by the seventeenth century. True yams (*Dioscorea* species), which are native to Southeast Asia and Africa, are starchy and rarely sweet. The mucilaginous Japanese yam (*yamaimo*), sometimes called Japanese mountain yam, is the type most Americans know. Regular potatoes belong to the altogether different *Solanum* (nightshade) genus, along with tomatoes, eggplants, and peppers, and didn't become popular in Europe or the United States until the eighteenth and nineteenth centuries. So when Falstaff implored the heavens to rain potatoes in *The Merry Wives of Windsor*, he meant sweet potatoes.

Come fall and winter, you will find Garnets with reddish purple skin and deep orange, sweet, moist flesh; copper-skinned Jewels with deep orange, soft flesh; sweet, dense, moist, and knobby Satsuma-Imos with reddish orange skin and greenish yellow to creamy flesh. Rocky Canyon Produce grows Diane, a Garnet-Beauregard cross, and Satsuma-Imos. Look for Windrose Farm's magnificent mystery tuber, a tan-skinned sweet potato that grower Barbara Spencer doesn't know the name of. It has buttery yellow to pale apricot flesh, a mildly sweet, nutty flavor, and a creamy texture akin to a great russet potato.

Some types of sweet potatoes are grown specifically for their greens (not to be confused with toxic potato leaves!), which are stir-fried, steamed, or added to soups and stews in Asian cooking. Vang Thao, Phong Vang, and Fresno Evergreen bring sweet potato leaves to the market in spring.

Tromboncino Trifolati

Come October, you will find coiled Tromboncino, a snakelike, buff-colored squash begging to be a Halloween centerpiece. It is actually a beautiful lime-and-white heirloom summer squash that is left on the vine to mature to an orange-fleshed vegetable that peels and cooks more easily and quickly than a true winter squash. Farmer Alex Weiser says that if you train this hearty climbing vine over a trellis instead of leaving it loose along the ground like he does, the squash grows straight and long. But where's the fun in that? The long neck is all meat; save the more fibrous bulb end for Pumpkin Soup with Sage and Aged Cheese (page 68).

A few years ago, I had the good fortune to walk through the market with Italian cooking teacher and author Marcella Hazan when we spotted a tangle of Tromboncino squash at Alex's stand. Marcella immediately suggested preparing it *trifolati*: with garlic, olive oil, and parsley, the holy trinity of Italian seasoning. This recipe also works well with the green summer Tromboncino.

MAKES 6 TO 8 SERVINGS

Summer, Autumn

1 or 2 Tromboncino squash (about 5 pounds total)
3 to 4 tablespoons extra-virgin olive oil
Kosher or sea salt and freshly ground black pepper
2 cloves garlic, minced
2 to 3 tablespoons chopped fresh Italian parsley
½ lemon (optional)

Cut off the bulb end of the squash and reserve for another use. Cut the neck crosswise into several pieces, and use a vegetable peeler to remove the skin, peeling deeply enough to reach the orange flesh. Cut the squash into ½-inch dice. You should have about 8 cups. This can be done a day ahead, covered, and refrigerated.

In a large sauté pan, heat the oil over medium heat. Add the squash, being careful not to crowd the pan (you may need to do this in 2 batches for good browning), and season with salt and pepper. Sauté, stirring occasionally, for 5 minutes. Cover, reduce the heat to medium-low, and cook until the squash is browned at the edges and cooked through, about 5 minutes more, stirring in the garlic and parsley after 2 minutes. Taste and adjust with salt and with a squeeze of lemon juice, if needed.

COOK'S TIP: Look for Italian parsley, also known as flat-leaf parsley, which tastes similar to curly parsley, the familiar garnish, but has a markedly different and more pleasing texture. Parsley is one of the richest sources of vitamins A and C.

Glazed Brussels Sprouts

Even nonfans like Brussels sprouts when they are roasted. Glazed with either Italian balsamic or Japanese rice vinegar, they also make a nice cocktail snack. As with most brassicas (cauliflower, broccoli, and the like), using very fresh, young sprouts and giving them a quick boil first eliminates any cabbagelike offense. Although a bit labor-intensive to clean, marble shooter–sized Brussels sprouts, a Coastal Farms specialty, are the best choice for this recipe.

MAKES 6 TO 8 SERVINGS

Autumn, Winter

1½ pounds tiny Brussels sprouts, left whole, or regular-sized sprouts, halved or quartered lengthwise

1 to 2 tablespoons extra-virgin olive oil

6 tablespoons balsamic vinegar

Kosher or sea salt and freshly ground black pepper

Preheat oven to 375 degrees. Boil the Brussels sprouts in salted water or steam over salted water until crisp-tender, about 3 minutes. Drain and dry thoroughly on paper towels or dish towels. On a large baking sheet, toss the Brussels sprouts with the oil, 3 tablespoons of the vinegar, and a little salt and pepper. Spread the sprouts evenly over the baking sheet.

Roast the Brussels sprouts in the upper third of the oven for 20 minutes. Remove from the oven, toss with the remaining 3 tablespoons vinegar, and return to the oven. Continue to roast the sprouts until they are completely glazed and browned in places and any loose leaves are crisped, 20 to 25 minutes more. Taste and adjust the seasoning with salt, pepper, and vinegar, then serve.

RICE VINEGAR AND TOASTED SESAME SEEDS VARIATION: Substitute canola, grape seed or other mild cooking oil for the olive oil, 6 tablespoons seasoned rice vinegar for the balsamic vinegar, and *togarashi* (page 28) for the black pepper. Prepare as directed and toss with 2 to 3 tablespoons toasted sesame seeds just before serving.

Braised Winter Greens
with Chipotle Chiles and Market Bacon

Make this cold-weather side with Swiss chard, collards, beet greens, or a kale, such as dusky *cavolo nero*, from the Carpenters or the Colemans. Bill Coleman also grows *spigarello*, an ancient leafing Italian broccoli with no heads, that is delicious in this recipe. Turn this into a main dish by adding 3 or 4 cups of southwestern beans, such as Indian Woman Yellow, cooked with extra chipotles and a couple of smoked tomatoes from Windrose.

MAKES 6 TO 8 SERVINGS

Autumn, Winter

2 bunches winter greens, such as kale or *spigarello*, leaves only, coarsely chopped

½ cup water

2 chipotle chiles

6 ounces bacon, cut into 1-inch pieces

1 onion, chopped

2 large cloves garlic, sliced

Kosher or sea salt

1 cup stock, any kind (page 52 to 54), or ½ cup canned diluted with ½ cup water

Cook the greens in a large pot of boiling salted water until just tender, 5 to 10 minutes, and drain. Bring the water to a boil in a small pot, drop in the chiles, and simmer for 10 minutes to soften (or combine in a bowl and microwave for 4 minutes). Drain, reserving the water. Remove the stems and seeds from the chiles (keep some seeds for a spicier dish), then use scissors to snip into ¼-inch pieces.

In a large sauté pan, fry the bacon over medium heat, stirring occasionally, until moderately crisp, about 5 minutes. Drain off all but 1 tablespoon of the fat from the pan, and return the pan with the bacon to medium heat. Add the onion, stir to scrape up any browned bits, and cook, stirring often, until the onion is translucent and soft, 5 to 7 minutes. Add the garlic and chiles and cook, stirring, for 1 minute more. Add the greens, season with salt, and sauté for about 5 minutes. Reduce the heat to low, pour in the stock and reserved chile water, cover, and simmer gently until the greens are tender and the flavors are blended, 10 minutes to 20 minutes (or much longer in true southern style).

CHEF'S TIP: Louisiana-born Steven Roberts, chef-owner of Café Boogaloo in Hermosa Beach, uses smoked onions he prepares himself to give extra depth to vegetarian braised collard and mustard greens. To efficiently cut collards or other broad-leaved greens for cooking, Steven stacks the leaves after stripping out the stems, rolls them up into a bundle, and then cuts the bundle crosswise into strips.

Kohlrabi and Its Greens with Brown Butter

Kohlrabi, a mild brassica with a bulblike stem, looks like an alien spaceship. Light green or purple skinned and from greenish white to creamy white inside, its crisp texture reminds me of water chestnuts with a sweet, nutty flavor. Sautéing sliced kohlrabi in a little browned butter accentuates this appealing characteristic. At farmers' markets, kohlrabi is sold with its leaves still attached; the tender ones are delicious added to this dish. Kolhrabi is also good raw in salads or in an assortment of crudités. Very young specimens don't require peeling.

MAKES 6 SERVINGS

Winter

1 large bunch kohlrabies with leaves
(2 to 2¼ pounds total)
3 tablespoons unsalted butter

Kosher or sea salt
¼ to ½ cup water

Trim stems and leaves from kohlrabi bulbs, reserving any good-looking leaves. Discard the stems and chop the leaves. Cut the end off each bulb and then peel deeply enough to remove the fibrous outer layer, exposing the smoother flesh. Cut the bulbs in half, turn cut side down, and cut crosswise into thin slices. You should have about 4 cups.

In a large skillet, melt the butter over medium heat. When it starts to turn brown, after about 2 minutes, add the kohlrabi slices and leaves and season with salt. Sauté, stirring occasionally, until the slices are browned in places and the leaves are wilted, 7 to 8 minutes. Reduce the heat to low, add ¼ cup water, stir, cover, and cook, stirring occasionally, until slices and leaves are tender, 15 to 20 minutes, adding the remaining ¼ cup water if the pan seems dry.

FARMER'S TIP: Alex Weiser has started growing crosnes, spiral-shaped tiny tubers (another kind of swollen stem) that are a European chef favorite. Also called Chinese artichokes (but a member of the mint family), they absorb flavors easily, making them a nice accompaniment with sauced dishes. Scrub the crosnes and sauté in butter until they are tender with a little crunch, 10 to 15 minutes.

This is a farmers' market treat and a special side dish: tiny white or orange cauliflowers harvested very young and still enrobed in their greens, cooked in stock for richness, crisped in a skillet, and dusted with Parmigiano-Reggiano cheese. Use slightly larger cauliflowers for a beautiful vegetarian main course. Look for baby cauliflowers at Weiser Family Farms, Green Farms, and Suncoast Farms.

MAKES 6 SERVINGS

Winter

2 pounds baby cauliflowers (2- to 4-ounce heads), left whole, or regular-sized cauliflowers

8 cups Vegetable Stock (page 52) or light chicken stock (see Soup Basics, page 51), or 4 cups canned diluted with 4 cups water

4 to 6 tablespoons extra-virgin olive oil

2 large cloves garlic, peeled

¼ cup flour

Kosher or sea salt and freshly ground black pepper

2 to 3 tablespoons chopped fresh Italian parsley

2 to 4 tablespoons grated Parmigiano-Reggiano cheese

Finely shredded zest of 1 lemon

Preheat oven to 375 degrees. If using baby cauliflowers, trim the bottom of each, keeping most of the leaves still attached. If using large cauliflowers, discard the leaves, and break into florets. Set aside ½ cup of the stock and the pour the remainder into a large pot. Bring to a boil, add the cauliflowers, and cook until slightly resistant when pierced with a knife, about 5 minutes. Drain and dry well. This step can be done 1 day ahead. Bring to room temperature before continuing.

In an ovenproof skillet large enough to accommodate all the cauliflowers, heat 3 tablespoons of the oil with the garlic over medium heat. Lightly dust the cauliflowers with the flour and season with salt and pepper. Working in batches to avoid crowding, add the cauliflowers, head side down, and sauté until golden brown, about 3 minutes. Turn and cook until the bottoms are golden brown, about 3 minutes more, adjusting the heat and adding more of the oil as needed to prevent scorching. Turn the garlic from time to time as you cook the cauliflowers, and discard the cloves when they become deep golden brown. This step can be done a few hours ahead.

When all the cauliflowers have been browned, return them to the pan, head side up, with 1 tablespoon of the parsley and the ½ cup stock. Cover tightly, transfer to the oven, and bake until the cauliflowers are tender, 15 to 20 minutes. Uncover, baste with the pan juices, and sprinkle with the cheese. Return the uncovered pan to the oven and continue baking until the cheese melts, about 10 minutes more (or place in a preheated broiler several inches from the heat source to brown). Season to taste with salt and pepper and top with the lemon zest and the remaining parsley.

Mains

MEATS

Good farmers' markets offer a wealth of first-rate ingredients for making main dishes, from locally farmed eggs to milk and cream, cheeses, fish, and meat. Many of us already know the difference field-to-market produce makes in quality, freshness, and flavor. It is reassuring to get the same excellence in our meats, fish, and dairy. And it is wonderful to be able to meet the growers of all we feed our families.

You may be surprised how many ingredients in these recipes are found at the farmers' market. With a few well-chosen items stocked in your pantry (suggestions on pages 27 and 28), your market becomes a practical "one-stop shop."

Nettle and Potato Frittata

The stuff of fairy tales and home remedies, nutritious stinging nettles grow wild and are often dismissed as a weed. Their delicate spinachlike flavor lends itself to egg dishes and to emerald green soups, and their sting disappears the moment the nettles hit the heat. Schaner and Flora Bella bring armloads of nettles to market in winter and spring. Serve the frittata warm or at room temperature for breakfast, brunch, or light supper, or slice thinly and offer as part of a tapas menu.

MAKES 6 SERVINGS

Winter, Spring

1 bunch stinging nettles (about ½ pound)
1 onion, finely chopped
Kosher or sea salt and freshly ground
    black pepper
3 tablespoons extra-virgin olive oil
8 eggs

¼ cup water
¼ cup grated Parmigiano-Reggiano
    cheese
½ pound potatoes such as fingerling or
    Yukon Gold, peeled, cut into ½-inch
    cubes, and boiled until just tender

Preheat oven to 350 degrees. Wear gloves to trim the nettles, stripping away the leaves and small stems by pulling them downward from the top of the stalk. Or, hold the bunch in a gloved hand and trim with scissors. Discard the woody stems and chop the nettles.

In a well-seasoned 10- or 12-inch ovenproof skillet, cook the onion with a little salt and pepper over medium-low heat until translucent and very soft, 7 to 10 minutes. While the onion is cooking, lightly beat together the eggs, water, and a little salt and pepper. Stir in the cheese and set aside.

Add the nettles to the onion, raise the heat to medium, season with salt and pepper, and cook, stirring until the nettles are wilted and bright deep green, about 3 minutes. (If using a 10-inch skillet, add them in batches.) Stir in the remaining 2 tablespoons oil and the potatoes and spread over the bottom of the skillet. Pour the egg-cheese mixture over the cooked vegetables. Cook the frittata until the bottom is set and the edges look dry, about 5 minutes. Transfer the skillet to the oven and bake until the top is set, about 10 minutes more in a 12-inch pan or 15 to 20 minutes more in a 10-inch pan.

To serve, run a spatula or knife around the edge of the frittata to loosen it and slide it onto a large plate. Top with another plate, and flip the frittata so the nicely browned bottom is on top. Serve warm or room temperature. The frittata will keep at room temperature for up to 2 hours.

COOK'S TIP: Farmers forage other greens worth seeking out. In summer, James and Dawn Birch bring lamb's quarters, nutritious, nutty wild spinach once gathered by local Indians and often used in *quelites*, Mexican stewed greens. Lamb's quarters are delicious in this frittata.

Quick Pasta with Spinach, Tomatoes, and Aged Goat Cheese

One day, David Schack of Redwood Hill suggested setting a round of his family's California crottin on the counter to age for a week or two to make a sharp grating cheese. What a great idea! Just set the wrapped cheese out of direct sun until it gets almost hard and then grate it, rind and all, into pasta or a salad. Here it adds pizzazz to a quick pasta sauce prepared in the time it takes to cook the penne. Ricotta salata (pressed and salted ricotta cheese) is also a good choice here.

MAKES 4 SERVINGS

Summer, Autumn

- ¼ pound spinach, preferably Bloomsdale or other Savoy type
- 3 ripe tomatoes (about ½ pound)
- ¾ pound penne or similar pasta shape
- 4 tablespoons extra-virgin olive oil
- 2 tablespoons chopped fresh Italian parsley
- 2 cloves garlic, minced
- ⅛ to ¼ teaspoon red pepper flakes
- Kosher or sea salt
- 2 ounces aged Redwood Hill California crottin or ricotta salata, grated on large holes of a box grater

Trim and discard any tough spinach stems. Roughly chop the spinach. Use a vegetable peeler to skin the tomatoes, or don't worry about peeling at all. Core and seed the tomatoes (page 24), and cut into ½-inch pieces. You should have about 1 cup. Cook the pasta in a generous amount of boiling salted water until just al dente.

Meanwhile, in a deep skillet or wide pot large enough to accommodate the pasta, heat 2 tablespoons of the oil over medium-high heat. Add the parsley, garlic, and red pepper flakes to taste and cook, stirring, until the garlic is fragrant but not browned, 30 to 60 seconds. Add the spinach and a little salt, stir once, and cook until the spinach turns dark green, wilts, and the stems are becoming tender, about 2 minutes. Add the remaining 2 tablespoons oil, the tomatoes, and salt to taste, stir once, and cook just until the tomatoes start releasing their juices but still retain their shape, 2 to 3 minutes.

When the pasta is ready, drain, reserving 1 cup of the cooking water. Return the skillet to medium-high heat, add ½ cup of the pasta water, and cook for 1 to 2 minutes. Add the pasta, reduce the heat slightly, and cook until the noodles are well coated and glossy, about 3 minutes, adding more pasta water if the mixture seems too dry. Serve with the cheese.

Farfalle with Five Herbs and Cherry Tomatoes

Years ago, at a tasting of cheeses and cured meats in his sixteenth-century apartment in Florence, Italian cooking teacher and author Giuliano Bugialli prepared a palate-refreshing pasta to counterbalance the richness of the offerings. In the mix of fragrant herbs, he included nonbulbing wild fennel, the anise-scented Tuscan favorite that also grows abundantly on the hillsides and along the roadways of California. Farmer Peter Schaner will bring you an armload if you can't find your own hillside clump to harvest (avoid plants immediately next to the street), or you can substitute dill. This pasta also makes a satisfying first course for eight.

MAKES 4 SERVINGS

Summer

1 pound farfalle, fusilli, or other pasta shape that will trap the herbs

½ cup extra-virgin olive oil

4 cloves garlic, slivered

⅛ to ¼ teaspoon red pepper flakes, or ½ jalapeño chile, minced

1 teaspoon kosher or sea salt

1 pint basket small, ripe red cherry tomatoes, stemmed

½ cup lightly packed fresh Italian parsley leaves

½ cup lightly packed fresh basil leaves

½ cup lightly packed fresh spearmint leaves

3 tablespoons snipped wild fennel fronds, or 2 tablespoons snipped fresh dill

⅓ cup snipped fresh chives

Cook the pasta in a generous amount of boiling salted water until just al dente. When the pasta is about half cooked, heat the oil in a small pot over medium-low heat for a minute or two until it is hot, but not so hot that the ingredients sizzle when they are added to it. Remove from the heat, stir in the garlic, red pepper flakes, and salt, and let stand for 5 minutes.

When the pasta is ready, drain and place in a warmed serving bowl with the tomatoes and all the herbs. Pour the warm oil mixture over all, toss well, and serve.

COOK'S TIP: For another quick summer tomato sauce, cook 2 pounds ripe tomatoes, peeled, seeded, and chopped, in a little olive oil with some sautéed onion and garlic until the tomatoes break down, about 10 minutes. Stir in some fresh basil or Italian parsley and a tablespoon of softened unsalted butter.

Farro Penne with Winter Greens, Potatoes, and Cheese

This is enticing, fast, and nutritious winter comfort food. Use quick-cooking winter greens such as beet tops, escarole, Swiss chard, or Windrose Farm's braising mix. *Farro*, also known as emmer, is an ancient wheat with more complex flavor than common whole wheat, but either one adds texture and color to this rustic dish, which is rounded out with a creamy melting cheese. Part of comfort food is having fewer pots to wash, so cut the potatoes into small pieces that will cook in the same amount of time as the pasta. Serve with a simple green salad tossed with oil, vinegar, and salt.

MAKES 6 SERVINGS

Autumn, Winter

1 onion, chopped

¼ cup olive oil

1 head escarole or 2 bunches Swiss chard, beet tops, or other quick-cooking green

2 large cloves garlic, minced

Kosher or sea salt and freshly ground black pepper

½ pound *farro* or whole-wheat penne

1 pound waxy potatoes such as French Fingerling, peeled and cut into 1-inch cubes

¼ pound Fontina or Gouda cheese such as Winchester mild, cut into ½-inch cubes

Bring a large pot of salted water to a boil. In a deep skillet or wide pot large enough to accommodate the pasta, sauté the onion in the oil over medium heat until translucent and soft, 5 to 7 minutes. While the onion is cooking, wash but don't dry the greens and roughly chop them, discarding any tough stem ends. You should have about 8 cups. Add the garlic to the onion, stir, and cook until fragrant, 30 to 60 seconds. Add the greens, a little salt, and a few grinds of pepper. Stir a few times to help wilt the greens, then reduce the heat to medium-low, cover, and cook until the greens are tender, about 10 minutes. Stir a couple of times during cooking and add a bit of water if the pan seems dry.

Meanwhile, add the pasta and potatoes to the boiling water and cook until the pasta is al dente and the potatoes are tender, about 10 minutes. Drain the pasta so it is still dripping, reserving about 1 cup of the cooking water. Stir the pasta and potatoes into the cooked greens, adding a little of the pasta water if the mixture seems dry or stiff. Season to taste with salt and generously with pepper. Remove from the heat, stir in the cheese until melted and creamy, and serve.

Farmers' Market Risotto

Risotto is delicious on its own or as an elegant way to showcase market produce. Many of the recipes in this book, such as Sfranta (page 38), Winter Squash Puree with Shaved Parmesan (page 41), Sautéed Escarole (page 43), Melted Cabbage and Green Garlic (page 106), Braised Tiny Artichokes (page 108), or simple tomato sauce (see Cook's Tip, page 134), make wonderful flavoring bases. Think of this as a master recipe to try with your own market purchases. You will need to use an Italian rice variety, such as Arborio, Carnaroli, or Vialone Nano. As the grains cook, their center remains firm, while their translucent exterior turns creamy with the gradual addition of hot liquid. The rice and base are joined in the first moments of cooking so their flavors and textures meld completely.

MAKES 4 SERVINGS

Evergreen

2 tablespoons unsalted butter
1 tablespoon extra-virgin olive oil
1 small onion, finely chopped
2 cups braised vegetables or vegetable
   puree or sauce
1 cup Arborio or other Italian rice

6 cups light chicken, beef, or vegetable
   stock (see Soup Basics, page 51), at a
   gentle simmer
½ cup grated Parmigiano-Reggiano cheese
Kosher or sea salt and freshly ground
   white pepper

In a pot, melt 1 tablespoon of the butter with the oil over medium-low heat. Add the onion and sauté until translucent and soft, 5 to 7 minutes. Stir in the braised vegetables and add the rice. Raise the heat to medium-high and cook, stirring constantly, until the grains whiten but do not brown and are coated with the onion mixture.

Add 1 ladleful of the simmering stock, reduce the heat to medium-low, and stir until the liquid has been completely absorbed. Continue adding the stock 1 ladleful at a time, always cooking and stirring until completely absorbed before adding more, until the rice is tender but still a bit firm at the center of each grain and creamy, about 20 minutes total. You may not need all of the stock. Or, if you see that you will need more liquid as you near the end of the stock, add a little boiling water to the stock remaining in the pan. When the rice is cooked, remove from the heat and stir in the remaining 1 tablespoon butter and the cheese. Season with salt and pepper and serve.

Chanterelle and Camembert Sandwiches

Maggie and David Schack, who celebrated their sixtieth wedding anniversary in 2003, sell their family's Redwood Hill goat cheeses, including their award-winning Camembert-style Camellia, at the Santa Monica Farmers' Market. David West of Clearwater Farms brings big, meaty chanterelles beginning in autumn, with Louie Mello following in early winter. Instead of using lettuce, give this sandwich zip with young, hot and spicy Osaka mustard greens from Maggie's Farm or Kenter Canyon, or onion sprouts from Sproutime. Toss a little mesclun with olive oil and lemon juice, pour some Sauvignon Blanc, and you'll have a cozy, sophisticated meal for two.

MAKES 2 SERVINGS

Autumn, Winter

5 ounces large chanterelle mushrooms
1 tablespoon extra-virgin olive oil
4 tablespoons unsalted butter
1 small red onion, thinly sliced
Kosher or sea salt and freshly ground
    black pepper
½ lemon

4 slices country bread
2 ounces Camembert or Camembert-style
    cheese such as Redwood Hill Camellia,
    cut into 6 slices
Handful of tender mustard greens such as
    Osaka or onion sprouts

Brush the mushrooms clean and slice lengthwise into as many ¼-inch-thick slices as you can. Finely chop any small pieces. In a large skillet, heat the oil with 1 tablespoon of the butter over medium heat. Add the onion and a little salt and pepper and sauté until translucent and soft, 5 to 7 minutes. Add the mushrooms and sauté, stirring occasionally and seasoning with salt, pepper, and a squeeze of lemon juice, until tender and crisped at the edges, about 10 minutes. Remove from the heat.

    Preheat a griddle or grill pan over medium heat. Meanwhile, in a small pan, melt the remaining 3 tablespoons butter. Brush 1 side of each bread slice with the butter and lay buttered side down on a work surface. Divide the mushroom mixture evenly between 2 of the bread slices, and top the mushrooms with the cheese slices. Place these and the remaining 2 bread slices buttered side down on the griddle and toast until the undersides are golden and the cheese has softened slightly. Remove from the griddle, arrange the mustard leaves on the cheese, and top with the remaining toast, buttered side up. (If using a panini press, assemble the sandwiches completely, including the greens, before putting in the press.) Cut in half to serve.

Mixed Mushroom Ragout with Polenta

Use a mix of wild and cultivated mushrooms, depending on what is in season, for this versatile sauce that is lovely over roasted meats, pasta, or rice, or diluted with stock for a soup. Keep some sun-dried tomatoes from Betty Kennedy or Ed Munak in your freezer as a handy substitute for tomato paste (no half-used cans!) to add depth and a hint of sweetness to winter dishes.

MAKES 6 SERVINGS

Autumn, Winter

¼ pound dried porcini

3 cups warm water

2 pounds mixed fresh mushrooms such as crimini, portobello, black trumpet, shiitake, chanterelle, and hedgehog, brushed clean

¼ cup extra-virgin olive oil

1 small red onion, chopped

1 carrot, peeled and finely chopped

1 rib celery with leaves, finely chopped

2 cloves garlic, finely chopped

¼ cup fresh Italian parsley leaves, chopped, plus more for garnish

Grated zest and juice of 1 lemon

Kosher or sea salt and freshly ground black pepper

1 cup dry white wine

About 2 cups Vegetable Stock (page 52), or 1 cup canned diluted with 1 cup water

3 sun-dried tomatoes, cut into ¼-inch pieces

1 bay leaf, preferably fresh

Few sprigs thyme

7 cups cold water

1 cup polenta

1 cup grated or finely cubed cheese such as Parmigiano-Reggiano, pecorino romano, or mozzarella

In a bowl, soak the dried mushrooms in the warm water until soft, about 25 minutes. Drain, gently squeezing the mushrooms and reserving the liquid. Rinse the mushrooms, brush clean or wipe with a damp paper towel, then pat dry on paper towels and chop. Strain the soaking liquid through a sieve lined with a coffee filter or paper towel and set aside. Trim the stems of the fresh mushrooms. Leave the small mushrooms whole, slice the larger mushrooms, and finely chop some of the slices.

In a wide pot, heat the oil over medium heat. Add the onion, carrot, celery, garlic, parsley, lemon zest, and a little salt and pepper and sauté until the vegetables are tender, about 10 minutes. Stir in the dried and fresh mushrooms, season with salt and pepper, and cook, stirring occasionally, until the mushrooms give up and then reabsorb their moisture, about 15 minutes. Add the wine, raise heat to medium-high, and cook until most of the wine has evaporated, about 10 minutes more. Stir in 1 cup of the stock, the reserved mushroom soaking liquid, sun-dried tomatoes, bay leaf, and thyme. Reduce the heat to medium-low and simmer, uncovered, until the sauce is thick and fragrant, about 30 minutes, adding more stock if the pan begins to get dry. Season to taste with salt, pepper, and lemon juice, and discard the bay leaf and thyme sprigs. The ragout can be made a day ahead and gently reheated just before serving.

In a pot, bring the cold water to a boil over high heat, season with salt, and reduce the heat to medium-low. Add the polenta in a slow, steady stream, stirring constantly. Keep the polenta at an occasional bubble and cook, stirring frequently, until the polenta comes cleanly away from the side of the pan and no longer tastes gritty, about 40 minutes. Remove from the heat and stir in the cheese until it melts. Divide the ragout among warmed bowls and top with a generous dollop of polenta and a scattering of parsley leaves.

Pan-Crisped Fillet of Sole with Green Garlic Topping

Caught off the nearby Channel Islands hours before it reaches the market, the rex sole from Anjin II is firm yet delicate, sweet, and quick cooking. This native Pacific flatfish (others include flounder, halibut, turbot, and sanddab) is indeed the king of sole and lends itself to many presentations. Fisherman Dennis Tsunoda catches it year-round, but here it is dressed up for spring with a crunchy topping of green garlic (excellent on chicken and hearty soups, too). In summer, top sole with roasted cherry tomatoes (page 103), or try one of the chefs' suggestions opposite. Dennis also catches sanddabs, that Mark Peel, chef-owner of Campanile restaurant, sautés whole with brown butter, lemon, and capers.

MAKES 4 TO 6 SERVINGS

Evergreen, Spring

2 bunches green garlic (about ⅔ pound), or 3 leeks, white part only, and 2 cloves garlic

3 to 4 tablespoons extra-virgin olive oil

1 cup fresh bread crumbs

Kosher or sea salt and freshly ground black pepper

⅓ cup white wine

2 lemons

½ cup coarsely chopped fresh Italian parsley

2 pounds fillet of sole

½ cup flour

Trim the root end and tops off the garlic leaving the white part and about 4 inches of the green. Discard yellowed leaves, then chop the garlic. If using leeks and garlic, chop the leeks and mince the garlic.

In a large skillet, heat 1 tablespoon of the oil over medium heat. Add the bread crumbs and toast, stirring often, until deep golden brown, 4 to 5 minutes. Be careful they do not burn. Pour the crumbs into a bowl and set aside. Wipe out the pan, return to medium heat, and add 1 tablespoon of the oil. Add the green garlic (or leeks and garlic), season with salt and pepper, and sauté until beginning to soften, about 3 minutes. Add the wine and continue cooking until the wine evaporates and the garlic is tender, 3 to 5 minutes longer. Meanwhile, grate the zest of 1 lemon. When the garlic is ready, stir in the lemon zest and parsley, pour into a shallow dish, and set aside. Wipe out the skillet. The garlic mixture and crumbs can be prepared up to a couple hours ahead and held at room temperature.

Dry the fish fillets, season with salt and pepper, and dust lightly with the flour, shaking off the excess. Heat 1 tablespoon of the oil in the skillet over medium–high heat. Working in batches if necessary to avoid crowding (or use 2 pans), cook the fish fillets until golden brown on the underside, about 3 minutes. Turn the fish, add more oil if needed to prevent sticking, and cook until opaque at the center when tested with a knife tip, 2 to 3 minutes longer. Transfer to a platter and squeeze a little juice from the zested lemon over the fish. Stir the bread crumbs into the garlic mixture, and spoon over the fish. Cut the remaining lemon into wedges and serve with the fish.

TOMATILLOS: In early autumn, Mary Sue Milliken, chef-owner of Border Grill, uses the tart husk-wrapped relative of the gooseberry, "diced like little jewels in a pan sauce for fish or sautéed softshell crabs." Use 4 or 5 small tomatillos that are full to bursting from their husks. Discard the husks, wash the tomatillos well in warm water to remove their sticky coating, and give them a "quick shuffle" in the fish cooking pan that you've deglazed with a little lime juice and butter.

SHISO: Sang Yoon, chef-owner of Father's Office, makes shiso (a kind of perilla) vinaigrette to serve with raw fish. "Most people don't eat the shiso leaf they find on their sushi because they don't know what it is, but its perfume and basil-mint flavors are great with raw fish." Puree a bundle of saw-toothed shiso leaves with a little shallot, young ginger, sugar, yuzu (Japanese citrus fruit) or lime juice, wasabi, and oil. For cooked fish, Sang makes a similar blender topping using *agretti*, a briny green also known as monk's beard that he gets from Bill Coleman.

NASTURTIUMS: In summer and fall, Suzanne Goin, chef-owner of A.O.C. and Lucques restaurants, uses spicy yellow and orange nasturtiums in a beautiful compound butter. Blend softened butter with diced shallots stewed with thyme, "tons and tons" of chopped nasturtiums, and chopped parsley.

GREEN ALMONDS: In spring, Suzanne sautés green (immature) almonds in brown butter to serve with fish. Available for a short time around the end of April into early May, the almonds have a mild grassy flavor and a jellylike center that becomes firmer as the nut matures. Use your fingers or a paring knife to open the hulls and extract the "nutlets."

Spring Vegetable and Fish Ragout

Mix and match your favorite spring vegetables, using all or some of those listed below. Early-season cherry tomatoes from Wong Farms in the Coachella Valley are especially good in the colorful soup base that is ready in just fifteen minutes. Drop in fish, shrimp, or scallops about five minutes before serving, and they will be perfectly poached. You can use this same base for a chicken stew made with cut-up boneless chicken breasts (chicken will take a few minutes longer to cook).

MAKES 4 TO 6 SERVINGS

Spring

1 bunch small spring or green onions, including several inches of green, chopped

½ bunch green garlic, white part and 4 inches of green, chopped, or 1 large clove garlic, minced

8 young carrots or 3 large carrots, peeled and sliced

½ pound fennel bulbs, trimmed, with a few fronds reserved, and sliced

1 tablespoon olive oil

Kosher or sea salt and freshly ground black pepper

1 pound potatoes, preferably new French Fingerling, LaRatte, or Russian Banana, left whole if tiny or cut into 1-inch cubes if larger

4 sprigs thyme

2 cups Vegetable Stock (page 52), or 1 cup canned diluted with 1 cup water

3 sun-dried tomatoes, cut into ¼-inch pieces, or 1 cup small red cherry tomatoes, stemmed

1¼ pounds skinned fish fillets such as halibut, sea bass, or salmon, cut into 2-inch pieces; 1¼ pounds peeled shrimp or scallops; or a mixture

1 cup shelled English peas (about 1 pound in the pod)

2 tablespoons chopped fresh Italian parsley

Grated zest and juice of 1 lemon

In a wide pot, sauté the onions, green garlic, carrots, and sliced fennel with a little salt in the oil over medium heat until soft, 5 to 7 minutes. Add the potatoes, thyme, fennel fronds, stock, and sun-dried tomatoes (if using fresh tomatoes, add these later), and season with salt and pepper. Cover and bring to a boil, then reduce the heat to medium-low, cover partially, and simmer until the potatoes are almost tender, about 10 minutes.

Season the fish or shellfish with salt and pepper. Add the peas, fresh tomatoes (if using), and fish or shellfish to the pan. Spoon some of the liquid over the seafood, cover, and poach the fish just until opaque at the center when tested with a knife tip, about 5 minutes, or less for shrimp or scallops. Stir in the parsley and lemon zest, and season to taste with salt, pepper, and lemon juice.

Spot Prawns with Peas, Almonds, and Olives

Santa Barbara spot prawns aren't true prawns, but a kind of sweet pink shrimp ("sweet shrimp" at sushi restaurants) with four distinctive white spots. Available in spring, they are often sold live and rarely need deveining. Cathy Tsunoda of Anjin II recommends refrigerating them on trays at home until ready to cook, and since they are already pink, cook them just until you see the shells start to look dry. In this tapas-inspired dish, toasted Spanish paprika and salty black olives complement the sweetness of the peas and shrimp. Cooking shrimp with their shells on adds flavor to the finished dish, even though you have to do some peeling at the table. To double this recipe, use two large skillets rather than overloading one pan. This dish also makes a good first course for four to six.

MAKES 2 TO 3 SERVINGS

Spring

1 pound spot prawns or large shrimp in the shell

2 tablespoons olive oil

⅓ cup whole raw almonds, chopped

Kosher or sea salt and freshly ground black pepper

1 tablespoon Spanish smoked paprika

2 cloves garlic, minced

⅓ cup oil-cured olives such as Adams Olive Ranch oil-cured olives with Celtic sea salt, pitted and chopped

1 cup shelled English peas (about 1 pound in the pod)

1 ripe, red tomato, chopped

Sherry vinegar

Pat the prawns dry. If the "veins" appear large, use kitchen scissors to snip along the curved part of the shell and then ease out the vein with the tip of a knife. In a large, heavy skillet, heat the oil over medium heat. Add the almonds and a little salt and sauté for 2 minutes. Stir in the paprika and cook, stirring, until browned and fragrant, about 1 minute. Stir in the garlic and olives and cook, stirring, for 1 minute more. Add the peas, tomato, and a little salt and pepper and sauté, stirring frequently, until the peas brighten and start to soften, about 2 minutes. Add the prawns, pushing the peas aside as needed so all the prawns lay flat on the surface of the pan. Cook, stirring occasionally, just until the prawn shells start to dry (or the shrimp turn pink) and are lightly browned on both sides, 3 to 5 minutes. Season to taste with vinegar.

Black Cod with Green Tomatoes

Everyone has heard of fried green tomatoes, but on a visit to the Coleman farm, I had a revelation about cooking with unripe tomatoes. Bill, an excellent cook, prepared fish using tangy green tomatoes for the sauce. Brilliant! Drawing culinary inspiration from his Filipina wife, Delia, Bill uses *patis* (Philippine fish sauce) and tamarind sauce to flavor the dish. I experimented using Bill's suggested seasonings with various fish available at the farmers' market, and succulent, sweet black cod (sablefish) was the hands-down winner. Look for green tomatoes that have started to take on a little pink, or leave completely green tomatoes on your counter for a couple of days so they start ripening. Either way they will be juicier and more flavorful than if you used fully green tomatoes, but still firm enough to skin with a vegetable peeler. Bearss limes add fruity tartness. Serve the fish with steamed rice.

MAKES 4 SERVINGS

Spring, Summer

1½ pounds unripe green tomatoes with a blush of color

1 onion, chopped

2 tablespoons canola or other mild cooking oil

2 tablespoons plus 2 teaspoons fish sauce

2 cloves garlic, finely chopped

1 lime, preferably Bearss or kaffir, halved

½ cup chicken stock or water

1 pound skinned black cod fillet, ½ to ¾ inch thick, cut into 4 equal pieces

Kosher or sea salt and freshly ground black pepper

Handful of fresh whole cilantro or Thai basil leaves or finely slivered kaffir lime leaves

Peel the tomatoes with a vegetable peeler, core, and cut into ½-inch pieces. In a wide pot, sauté the onion in the oil over medium-low heat with 2 teaspoons of the fish sauce until translucent and soft, 5 to 7 minutes. Stir in the garlic and cook for 1 minute more. Add the tomatoes and the remaining 2 tablespoons fish sauce. Raise the heat to medium and cook uncovered until the tomatoes lose their bright color and start to break down, about 5 minutes. Add the juice of ½ lime and the stock, cover, reduce the heat to low, and simmer, stirring occasionally, until the tomatoes completely break down, about 15 minutes. The sauce can be made up to 6 hours ahead and reheated.

Just before serving, season the fish pieces with salt and pepper and place on top of the hot sauce in the pan. Spoon a little of the sauce over the fish, squeeze the juice of the remaining lime half over all, cover, and simmer over medium-low heat until the fish is opaque at the center when tested with a knife tip, about 5 minutes. Scatter the cilantro over the fish.

Salmon with Creamy Watercress Sauce

Whether cultivated or wild, watercress grows with its "feet" dangling in water. Tsugio Imamoto, a grower in the Los Angeles area, says the peppery green he grows year-round is best from winter through early spring. Land cresses—pepper, upland, crinkled, and curly—are spicier and can be used interchangeably; you'll find one or another throughout the year at Maggie's Farm or Kenter Canyon Farms. This versatile, European-style sauce spiked with Moessner Orchard garlic-dill pickles, uses both watercress and land cress and is beautiful on cold or hot salmon as well as chicken.

MAKES 6 SERVINGS

Spring, Summer

1 clove garlic, peeled

1 small shallot, quartered

1 bunch watercress, large stems removed (about 2 cups packed)

¼ cup packed pepper, curly, wrinkled, or upland cress

¼ cup packed fresh Italian parsley leaves

2 tablespoons capers

2 tablespoons chopped dill pickle

1 hard-boiled egg

1 cup sour cream, whole-milk plain yogurt, or crème fraîche

Kosher or sea salt

1 lemon, halved

1½ pounds salmon fillet, 1 inch thick and with or without skin, cut into 6 pieces, or 3 large salmon steaks

Extra-Virgin Olive oil

To make the sauce, turn on a food processor and drop in the garlic clove and shallot to mince. Stop the processor, add the watercress, pepper cress, parsley, capers, and pickle, and pulse to chop finely. Add the egg, sour cream, and ½ teaspoon salt and 1 tablespoon lemon juice and process until blended. Refrigerate until ready to serve (up to 2 days), and add salt or lemon as needed.

Heat a grill to medium, or preheat a broiler with the broiler pan in place 4 to 6 inches from the heat source. Brush the fish on both sides with oil and season with salt. If the salmon has its skin, start the fish skin side up on the grill and grill until the underside is opaque and has grill marks, 2 to 3 minutes. Turn skin side down and grill for 5 to 6 minutes longer for a slightly translucent center, or 7 to 8 minutes longer for well done. Slide a spatula under the fish, leaving the skin behind. Or, place the salmon skin side down on the preheated broiler pan and broil until the fish is done to your liking, 7 to 11 minutes. Squeeze lemon juice over the fish, and serve hot or cold with the sauce.

HOW TO CHOOSE WATERCRESS: Watercress is highly perishable. Look for a bunch with bright green leaves, and once you get it home, remove the band binding it, discard any bruised leaves, and refrigerate in an open plastic bag for up to 2 days. Use kitchen scissors to snip off tough stems.

Grilled Albacore Skewers with Bay Laurel and Bacon

Seasoning these skewers with the classic Portuguese flavoring trio of onion, garlic, and bay laurel was inspired by a barbecued whole albacore I enjoyed at the home of Steve Correia, a Santa Monica artist and the son of a Portuguese tuna fisherman. Once local albacore season starts in July, I am on the lookout for this lean white-fleshed tuna at Anjin II's stand. The kebabs are great stuffed into pita with aioli (page 46), or in smaller portions as appetizers. Mediterranean bay laurel has an invigorating clean taste and a camellia-shaped leaf; don't confuse it with nonedible California laurel, whose leaves are more eucalyptus-like. Available year-round, laurel is at its peak in summer and fall. You need fresh leaves for this dish, which will not break when you thread them onto the skewer.

MAKES 6 SERVINGS

Spring, Summer

½ cup extra-virgin olive oil
3 large cloves garlic, minced
Grated zest of 1 lemon, with lemon
    reserved for finishing
About 36 fresh bay leaves, large
    leaves broken in half

2 pounds albacore or ahi tuna, 1 inch
    thick, cut into 36 1-inch cubes
1 onion, cut into 1-inch chunks
½ pound sliced bacon, cut crosswise into
    1-inch pieces
Kosher or sea salt and freshly ground
    black pepper

Soak 12 bamboo skewers in water to cover for 30 minutes. Meanwhile, in a small pot, warm the oil over medium heat until hot, about 2 minutes. Stir in the garlic and lemon zest, then crush 2 bay leaves and add them as well. Set aside to infuse. Cook the onion in salted boiling water for 1 minute, and drain. Don't worry if the pieces separate into layers. Drain the skewers. Without crowding, thread the bay leaves, bacon, onion, and tuna onto each skewer in the following order, using 3 pieces of fish per skewer: bay leaf, a couple of onion layers, bacon, fish, and ending with an extra set of bay and onion. Lay the skewers in a shallow baking dish and pour the cooled oil-garlic mixture over them. Let stand for 15 minutes or refrigerate for 1 hour. Just before grilling, season with salt and pepper.

Heat a grill to medium-high. Grill the skewers, turning once, until the edges of the tuna are browned but the fish still has give and the bacon is cooked, about 4 minutes total. Place the skewers on a platter, squeeze lemon juice over, and finish with salt.

SHRIMP VARIATION: Use 1 pound (36) peeled and deveined medium-sized shrimp in place of the tuna. Thread onto skewers as for the albacore, using 3 shrimp per skewer. Push the skewer through both the head and tail end to keep the shrimp in place. Marinate as directed, then grill over medium heat, turning once, until the shrimp are pink and the bacon is cooked, 4 to 5 minutes total.

This robust chopped salsa goes well with hearty fish such as ahi (bluefin) tuna, bonito, or *hamachi* (yellowtail), is a great "ketchup" for grilled chicken or for sandwiches, and keeps well in the refrigerator. Chopped fine, it makes a zesty topping for bruschetta (page 37). Tuna can dry out on the grill in the blink of an eye. See the Cook's Tip below for suggestions on how to manage this temperamental fish.

MAKES 6 SERVINGS

Summer

1½ pounds Roma or other meaty tomatoes such as Costoluto Genovese

2 tablespoons extra-virgin olive oil

2 to 3 tablespoons red wine vinegar

¼ to ½ teaspoon red pepper flakes

2 large cloves garlic, unpeeled

Grated zest of 1 lemon, with the lemon reserved for finishing

¾ cup Kalamata olives, pitted and coarsely chopped

2 tablespoons capers

¼ cup fresh Italian parsley leaves

Kosher or sea salt and freshly ground black pepper

2½ pounds tuna steaks, 1 inch thick

3 tablespoons olive oil

Slow roast the tomatoes as directed on page 103, tossing them with the extra-virgin olive oil, 1 tablespoon of the vinegar, and ¼ teaspoon of the red pepper flakes before they go in the oven. Chop the roasted tomatoes, capturing their juices, and set aside. Toast the unpeeled garlic cloves in a small skillet or on a griddle over medium heat until browned in spots, 5 to 10 minutes. Peel when cool enough to handle. Finely chop together the garlic, lemon zest, olives, capers, and parsley. Stir into the tomatoes along with 1 tablespoon of the vinegar and ½ teaspoon salt. Let the mixture stand for 1 hour, taste, and add vinegar, salt, or red pepper flakes as needed. The salsa should be zesty and tangy. You should have about 1½ cups.

Heat a grill to medium-high. Brush the fish liberally with the oil and season well with salt and pepper. Grill the tuna, turning once, until medium-rare (see Cook's Tip), about 4 minutes total. Squeeze the juice from the lemon over the fish and serve with the salsa.

COOK'S TIP: Watch the sides of the tuna steaks as they cook, as they are a guide to doneness. When the fish is opaque and light colored to a depth of ¼ inch, turn the fish. Grill until the second side is done to a similar depth, with the center still a deeper rose. If you like your tuna more cooked, grill until the opaque part extends deeper, but be sure to leave a little rose in the center or the fish will be dry.

White Seabass with Fennel

It's a red-letter day when Dennis Tsunoda brings white seabass, an excellent moist, mildly firm fish that is highly regulated by the Department of Fish and Game in an effort to rebuild its numbers after overfishing for the last fifty years. A member of the croaker family (unlike other sea bass, which are groupers) that grows to ninety pounds, it has delicate flesh that readily absorbs flavorings. Wrapping the fillets in fennel fronds before roasting perfumes the fish without overwhelming it (look for spring wild fennel for this, which has a more pronounced flavor than common bulbing Florence fennel). The fish is pan-crisped and finished in the oven, a convenient technique I learned from Anne Willan, founder of La Varenne Cooking School, but it is also delicious grilled. When white seabass is unavailable, use other mildly firm fish such as California halibut. The fish is nice with Meyer Lemon Relish (page 49) and roasted fennel (page 104).

MAKES 6 SERVINGS

Winter, Spring

Fennel fronds from 1 or 2 bunches fennel bulbs, or 1 bunch wild fennel

2 pounds skin-on white seabass fillet, about 1 inch thick

Olive oil

Kosher or sea salt and freshly ground black pepper

1 large clove garlic, peeled

1 Eureka or Meyer lemon, thinly sliced and seeded

Preheat oven to 425 degrees. Choose the longest fennel fronds and discard the thickest part of the stems. Cut the fillet into 6 equal pieces, pat dry, rub with oil, and season with salt and pepper. Wrap the fronds around the fish pieces, starting and ending on the skin side. Place skin side down on a plate.

In a large, heavy ovenproof skillet, preferably well-seasoned cast iron, heat 2 teaspoons oil and the garlic clove over medium-high heat until the garlic is golden and the oil is very hot. Discard the garlic. Working in batches if necessary to avoid crowding, add the fish, skin side down. Cook the fish without moving the pieces until the skin is crisped and brown, about 4 minutes. The fennel will adhere to the fish. If your skillet is large enough, return all the fish to the pan skin side up, or transfer to an oiled baking sheet. Transfer to the oven and roast until the fish is opaque at the center when tested with a knife tip, 4 to 6 minutes. Use scissors to cut through fronds to make it easier for guests to peel away the fennel. Serve with lemon slices.

COOK'S TIP: This technique works well with small whole fish. Season the cavities of 3 whole fish (1½ pounds each) with salt and pepper and fill with the lemon slices and some of the fennel and wrap with the remaining fronds. Brown the fish in the skillet as above, about 4 minutes per side, and finish in the oven, about 10 minutes more. A general timing rule for cooking fish is 10 minutes per inch of thickness.

You wouldn't expect to find a selection of meats listed on a farmer's growing certificate, but that's exactly the kind of "crop" farmers like Greg and Lisa Nauta and Bill and Barbara Spencer are raising, and the results are a gift to home cooks.

"Ever since I graduated college in 1989, I dreamed of having a farm where we'd use everything and throw away nothing," says Greg Nauta of Rocky Canyon Produce in Atascadero. "Cattle would graze the fields first, then the chickens. The animals would eat market and field leftovers and help nourish the soil." Today, the Nautas' cattle, chickens, and pigs dine on leftover fruits and vegetables and green and sere grasses and grains, and graze, peck, and wallow in mud holes at will.

The result is free-range Duroc and Hampshire pork and Angus-bred beef with rounded flavors influenced by season and varied diet. Sales are brisk for the Nautas' meat, minimally aged for tenderness and sold in vacuum-sealed packages that keep refrigerated for up to a week and frozen for up to a year. Success is due to the repeat business of home cooks not chefs. Restaurants require a lot of one cut, and because there are only two tri-tip roasts or two to three pounds of skirt steak from each animal, for example, it would take a lot more than Greg and Lisa's twenty to forty cattle to meet those needs. Home cooks who want a specific cut or a side from a small producer must reserve ahead.

In neighboring Paso Robles, Bill and Barbara Spencer of Windrose Farm decided sheep make perfect "weeders." Under the shade of cottonwood trees, the animals "mow" the fragrant rosemary, basil, purslane, pigweed, and the soil-replenishing crop known as green manure, a mix of legumes and vetch. "It's part of our particular integrated farm system," Bill explains to interested customers.

And part of what makes their Fresian-Suffolk lamb so tasty. The Spencers "harvest" thirty to thirty-five six- to eight-month-old lambs ("more respectful and more flavorful than just-weaned spring lamb," says Bill) each summer and ten to twelve one-year-olds, or hoggets, and three "fat and tasty" older sheep, or mutton, each fall.

The Santa Monica Farmers' Market also offers lean, protein-rich bison from Lindner Ranch in Lassen and free-range naturally fed chickens and ducks by special order from Lily's Eggs in Santa Barbara. All the meat sold at the market has been inspected by the USDA.

Because free-range animals get exercise and eat a varied diet, the meat is a little firmer and has a more complex flavor than meat from conventionally raised animals. Long-cooking cuts, such as short ribs or shoulder, take more time to get tender, but the payoff in flavor is worth the wait. Grill quicker-cooking steaks over a medium, not a hot, fire to prevent drying out.

Chicken Legs with Kumquats, Prunes, and Green Olives

Curious kumquats—sweet skin and puckery pulp—must be eaten in one bite to experience their range of flavors. Oval-shaped Nagami is the most common variety, but Armando Garcia also brings the sweeter, round Meiwa from winter through spring. Schaner Farms and Betty B's have Nagamis beginning late winter into September. This dish was inspired by Moroccan braises with preserved lemons and an old favorite Silver Palate recipe. Serve it with couscous or its Sardinian cousin, *fregola*, or with plain white rice, and spike it with *harissa*, Moroccan hot sauce. Dark meat does better than white in long cooking, so save breasts for another use.

MAKES 6 TO 8 SERVINGS

Winter, Spring

½ pound prunes, or 6 ounces pitted prunes
1 cup boiling water
½ pound kumquats
1 tablespoon olive oil
3½ pounds whole chicken legs (drumstick and thigh)
Kosher or sea salt and freshly ground black pepper

1 large onion, chopped
1 large clove garlic, finely chopped
¾ cup dry white wine
1 cup mild green olives such as Adams Olive Ranch Manzanillo
About ½ cup chicken stock
Harissa (optional)

Pour the boiling water over the prunes to soften, about 15 minutes. Drain and use scissors to pit and quarter the prunes. Quarter the kumquats lengthwise, remove the seeds and center pith, and if you feel energetic, cut the quarters in half again lengthwise. Set the prunes and kumquats aside.

In a wide pot, heat the oil over medium heat. Working in batches if necessary to avoid crowding, add the chicken pieces, season with salt and pepper, and brown, turning as needed, until golden on all sides, 10 to 12 minutes. Remove the chicken to a plate. Pour off all but 1 to 2 tablespoons of the fat from the pot, reduce the heat to medium-low, and add the onion. Stir well, scraping the pan bottom to loosen the brown bits, and cook, stirring occasionally, until the onion is translucent and soft, 5 to 7 minutes. Add the garlic, stir, and cook for 1 minute more. Add the wine, raise the heat to medium, and cook, stirring to deglaze the pot, until the liquid is reduced by slightly more than half, about 3 minutes. Return the chicken to the pot and add the prunes, kumquats, olives, and a little salt and pepper. Stir, cover, reduce the heat to low, and simmer for 20 minutes. Add ¼ cup of the stock, stir (the sauce develops as the chicken cooks), and simmer covered until the chicken is very tender, about 1 hour, basting occasionally with the sauce and adding stock if needed to keep the chicken half submerged in the sauce. The dish may be made a day ahead and reheated. Serve with the *harissa*.

Blackberries, balsamic vinegar, and lemon verbena team up in a tangy-sweet marinade that lacquers game hens to a nice mahogany. Fragrant lemon verbena, with its rough, pointed leaves, tastes and smells like lemon but isn't sour on the tongue, so it extends the tartness of the berries here without adding acidity. Use only the most tender leaves for flavoring and garnishing this dish. These game birds are nice with Real Creamed Corn (page 65).

MAKES 4 TO 6 SERVINGS

Summer

- 2 half-pint baskets blackberries
- ½ cup torn fresh lemon verbena leaves
- 1 cup balsamic vinegar
- 1½ tablespoons crushed toasted black peppercorns (page 34)
- 2 large shallots (about 2 ounces total), grated
- ½ cup olive oil
- Kosher or sea salt
- 4 game hens, butterflied

Set a food mill fitted with the fine disk over a medium bowl. Put 1 basket of the blackberries and ¼ cup of the lemon verbena through the mill, scraping the underside of the disk to capture all the puree. In a small pot, cook ½ cup of the balsamic vinegar over medium heat until syrupy and reduced by half, about 10 minutes. Add the reduced vinegar to the blackberry-verbena puree, and stir in 1 tablespoon of the pepper, the shallots, oil, and 1 tablespoon salt and set aside to cool. Place a large resealable plastic bag in a large bowl. Place the hens in the bag, pour the marinade over, and seal the bag, squeezing out the air. Turn the hens to coat with the marinade and refrigerate for at least 4 hours or up to overnight. Remove from the refrigerator 1 hour before grilling.

Heat a grill to medium for indirect cooking (see Cook's Tips for Grilling, page 159). Remove the hens from the marinade, pat dry, and season with salt. Place skin side up on the grill, cover the grill, and cook until the meat is firm to the touch and the skin is a nice mahogany, 35 to 40 minutes. If desired, turn the hens skin side down during the last few minutes to crisp the skin further.

While the hens are grilling, reduce the remaining ½ cup balsamic vinegar over medium heat to about 3 tablespoons very thick syrup, watching closely so it doesn't burn. Stir in the remaining basket of berries to warm and remove from the heat. Place the hens on a platter, season with salt and pepper, and spoon the blackberry-balsamic syrup over. Top with the remaining lemon verbena.

COOK'S TIP: To butterfly a game hen, use kitchen scissors to cut the bird open along one side of the backbone, then cut away backbone and discard. Open out the hen skin side up on a work surface. With the heel of your hand, press sharply on the breastbone to crack it and flatten the bird. If desired, make a slit in the skin at base of each thigh and tuck the end of each drumstick in the slit to anchor it.

Prosciutto and Persimmon Sandwiches

Jam-ripe Hachiya persimmons are a ready-made sweet-spicy spread for these sandwiches, ideal for an autumn brunch, lunch, or picnic. Unlike flat Fuyu persimmons that are eaten firm, oblong Hachiyas must be very soft or they'll be mouth-puckeringly astringent. Persimmons take a while to ripen, but Mary Hillebrecht of Farmstand West, Laura Ramirez of J.J.'s Lone Daughter Ranch, and Vilma Causey of Briar Patch, among others, carefully bring soft Hachiyas to market in boxes and trays. Hachiyas are the most common astringent variety, but look for acorn-shaped, mango-flavored Tamopan persimmons from Penryn Orchard. In summer, make this sandwich with figs, substituting 6 ripe Black Mission figs, sliced, for the persimmons. No mascarpone on hand? Use softened butter instead.

MAKES 6 SERVINGS

Autumn

1 to 2 ripe Hachiya persimmons

¼ pound mascarpone cheese, or 4 tablespoons unsalted butter, softened

6 thin panini rolls, split horizontally, or 12 thin slices country bread, lightly toasted if desired

6 ounces prosciutto, thinly sliced

Freshly ground black pepper or crushed toasted black peppercorns (page 00)

3 ounces arugula or other spicy green such as pepper cress, mizuna, or radish sprouts

Stand the persimmon on its blossom end on a cutting board and, using a serrated knife, cut thin vertical slices. Don't worry if the slices break down into pulp. Spread a thin layer of mascarpone on each roll bottom (or half of the bread slices). Top with prosciutto and persimmon slices. (If the persimmon was too soft to slice, spoon the fruit onto the meat.) Season generously with pepper and top with arugula. Close the sandwiches and cut in half to serve.

FARMER'S TIP: Mary Hillebrecht speed-ripens Hachiyas by freezing them. When thawed, the pulp will be soft and the tannins will have disappeared. Leave them in the freezer for use later in the year.

COOK'S TIP: For an easy autumn or winter appetizer, serve a platter of prosciutto with carefully cut wedges of ripe Hachiyas seasoned with crushed toasted black peppercorns.

One wintry day, I had a hankering for a comforting but interesting bowl of pasta. I found some McGrath La Estrella pumpkin and Rocky Canyon hot Italian sausage in my freezer and was soon on my way to a tasty dinner. A sort of inside-out take on northern Italy's pumpkin-filled ravioli, the slightly sweet squash and spicy sausage became a sauce for *garganelli*, rolled, ridged tubular egg pasta. (If you can't find *garganelli*, use other egg noodles such as fettuccine or *pappardelle*.) Green Swiss chard, if you have some, adds earthy color and flavor.

MAKES 4 SERVINGS

Autumn, Winter

½ pound hot Italian sausage meat

1 small or ½ medium onion, chopped

Kosher or sea salt and freshly ground black pepper

1 tablespoon extra-virgin olive oil

1 bunch Swiss chard, leaves only, cut into thin ribbons

¼ cup dry white wine

1 cup roasted pumpkin or other winter squash (page 25)

1 cup Chicken Stock (page 53), or ½ cup canned diluted with ½ cup water

½ pound *garganelli*

½ cup grated Parmigiano-Reggiano cheese

In a deep skillet or wide pot large enough to accommodate the pasta, brown the sausage meat over medium heat, breaking it up with a fork, about 5 minutes. Remove the meat from the pot and add the onion, a little salt, and the oil (if you want a more refined sauce, start the onion in a clean pot). Reduce the heat to medium-low and cook the onion, stirring occasionally, until translucent and soft, 5 to 7 minutes. Stir in the chard and cook until it wilts, about 2 minutes. Add the wine, raise the heat to medium, and cook, stirring to scrape up any brown bits, until the wine evaporates, 2 to 3 minutes. Stir in the pumpkin, stock, and salt and pepper to taste. Reduce the heat to low and simmer until the flavors are blended, about 5 minutes. Return the sausage to the pot and heat through.

Meanwhile, cook the pasta in a generous amount of boiling salted water until just al dente. Drain, reserving about 1 cup of the cooking water. Add the pasta to the sauce and stir to coat, adding a little pasta water if needed to smooth out the sauce. Cook over medium-low heat for 2 to 3 minutes, then remove from the heat and stir in the cheese. Season with salt and pepper and serve.

COOK'S TIP: Rocky Canyon sells sausages seasoned in a variety of ways. For an easy winter market meal, serve them with roasted potatoes and Moessner Orchard's homemade mild sauerkraut.

Roast Pork Loin with Red Currants and Provençal Herbs

The Pudwills are among the few California farmers who grow the red and rare white currants that remind me of late summer in France, when the tart berries are enjoyed in savory as well as sweet dishes. Currants look like miniature grape clusters but are actually in the gooseberry family. This meal-in-a-pot, perfumed with classic Provençal herbs that are also California favorites, includes La Ratte potatoes, a French variety nearly identical to Russian Banana Fingerlings. If fresh currants aren't available, use ¼ cup finely chopped tart dried plums from Harvest Pride.

MAKES 6 TO 8 SERVINGS

Summer, Autumn

Kosher or sea salt

1 boneless pork loin roast, 3½ to 4
    pounds, rolled and tied

8 fresh bay leaves

8 long sprigs thyme

8 long sprigs rosemary

8 shallots, unpeeled

4 carrots, peeled and cut in half

2 pounds La Ratte, Russian Banana,
    or other yellow-fleshed potatoes,
    unpeeled, cut into chunks

2 tablespoons extra-virgin olive oil

1 bunch fresh red currants, stemmed
    (about ½ cup)

½ cup water

1 tablespoon fruit vinegar such as
    black currant

Preheat oven to 475 degrees. Rub salt over the surface of the roast. Thread the herbs under the string lengthwise along the roast, alternating the bay, thyme, and 4 of the rosemary sprigs. Select a roasting pan just large enough to accommodate the roast and the vegetables in a single layer, and lay the remaining 4 rosemary sprigs in the center. Place the roast on the sprigs. Toss the shallots, carrots, and potatoes with salt and the oil and arrange around the meat.

Roast until the pork looks crisp and the vegetables begin to brown, 20 to 30 minutes. Baste with the juices, and stir in enough water to create a thin layer of liquid in the bottom of the pan. Reduce the heat to 350 degrees and continue roasting, basting often and adding water as needed, until the meat is nearly firm to the touch and still slightly pink at the center, or a thermometer inserted into the thickest part of the roast registers 140 degrees, 30 to 50 minutes longer.

Remove the meat and vegetables to a platter and tent with foil. Discard the rosemary in the pan. Place the pan over medium-low heat, add the currants, water, and vinegar to the pan juices, and stir, scraping up any brown bits. Raise the heat to medium and cook until the sauce takes on flavor from the currants, 3 to 5 minutes. Season to taste with salt and pour over the roast and vegetables. Remove strings and herbs from the roast and slice to serve.

Roast Pork Loin Sandwiches
with Seasonal Fruit-Onion Relish

Leftovers from the preceding roast pork recipe are ideal here. For an autumn sweet-tart relish, use late-season Autumn Royale grapes—large, almost black, and oblong, with a firm, meaty texture and deep grape taste—from Chandler Farms and Nicholas Orchard. These are not juicy summer fruits, but spicy and dense, making them a good choice for roasting (I found that Red Flame and Thompson don't work well). In early summer, substitute 2 pounds apricots, halved and pitted; in late summer, use ¾ pound figs, halved lengthwise.

**MAKES 2 CUPS,
ENOUGH FOR ABOUT 12
SANDWICHES**

Summer, Autumn

FOR THE RELISH

3 large onions (about 1½ pounds
    total), halved
3 tablespoons extra-virgin olive oil
3 tablespoons balsamic vinegar
Leaves from 5 large sprigs thyme
Kosher or sea salt and freshly ground
    black pepper
1¾ cups Autumn Royale grapes (about ½
    pound on the stem)

FOR THE SANDWICHES

Country bread slices, large baguette,
    or *batarde*
Extra-virgin olive oil
1 clove garlic, cut in half
Roast pork loin slices, 3 to 4 ounces
    per sandwich
Arugula, preferably wild, or stemmed
    watercress, handful per sandwich

To make the relish, preheat oven to 400 degrees. Cut each onion half into 6 to 8 wedges. Finely chop 2 of the wedges, rinse in cold water, and set aside. On a baking sheet, toss together the remaining onion wedges, oil, 1½ tablespoons of the vinegar, thyme, and a generous sprinkling of salt and pepper. Roast for 30 minutes. Add the grapes and the remaining 1½ tablespoons vinegar, toss, and return to the oven until the onions are soft with crisped edges and the grapes are browned and melting, about 30 minutes more. Let cool briefly, then hand chop or pulse in a food processor to a coarse texture. Spoon into a bowl and stir in the chopped raw onion. Allow to stand for 1 hour, then taste and add salt, pepper, and/or more vinegar to yield a bright sweet-tart flavor. You should have about 2 cups. The relish will keep refrigerated for up to 2 weeks.

Heat a grill to medium, or preheat a broiler. If using a baguette or *batarde*, cut into sandwich-sized portions and split horizontally. Brush one side (or cut side) of each bread piece generously with oil. Toast both sides on the grill or under the broiler. Rub the oiled surface with the cut side of the garlic and lay 3 or 4 pork slices on the oiled side of half of the bread pieces. Top each with a handful of arugula, spread the relish on the remaining bread, close the sandwiches, and cut in half.

Beans, Greens, and Pork Stew

Soon after they started Windrose Farm in 1990, Barbara and Bill Spencer realized their microclimate was similar to New Mexico's climate, so they decided to grow heirloom Southwest beans, chiles, and tomatoes. That's what farmers call "appropriate production," growing what is logical for the land. This richly textured dish is a good example of market bounty: other than salt, every ingredient from meat to seasonings is farm produced. A rarity at market stands until chefs asked farmers to grow it, deep blue-green *cavolo nero* (Tuscan kale) is now an abundant winter and spring market staple. Also called *lacinato*, it is more savory and tender than common kale. Since the meat, beans, and kale have different cooking times, cook them separately and combine them shortly before serving to keep the flavors and colors bright. Serve with grilled thick slices of country bread.

MAKES 6 SERVINGS

Winter

2 tablespoons extra-virgin olive oil

1 pound boneless pork stew meat such as shoulder, cut into 1-inch cubes

Kosher or sea salt

1 large red onion, chopped

3 large cloves garlic, peeled

3 smoked dried tomatoes, cut into small pieces

1 cup water, plus more as needed

2 chipotle chiles

1 cup (½ pound) dried beans such as Windrose Farm's Anasazi, Dos Mesas, or Indian Woman Yellow

2 large bunches *cavolo nero* or Swiss chard (about 1½ pounds total), stemmed and coarsely chopped

½ pound hot Italian sausages, cooked and cut into 1-inch slices

In a large, wide pot, heat the oil over medium-high heat. Working in batches if necessary to avoid crowding, add the pork, season with salt, and brown on all sides, about 5 minutes. Remove the pork to a plate. Add the onion and garlic, reduce the heat to medium, and cook, stirring occasionally, until the onion is tender and the garlic is lightly browned, about 5 minutes. Return the meat and its juices to the pot and add the tomatoes, water, and 1 chile. Reduce the heat to low, cover, and simmer until the meat is very tender, 1½ to 2 ½ hours (if you use free-range meat, it takes longer to cook), adding water as needed so there is always a little sauce.

Meanwhile, cook the beans with the remaining chile as directed on page 25, then drain, reserving the liquid. Cook the greens in a large pot of boiling salted water until tender, about 5 minutes for chard, and 10 minutes for *cavolo nero*. Drain and set aside. When the pork is tender, add the sausages, greens, and beans, along with enough of the bean liquid to enrich and thicken the stew. Cook over medium-low heat to blend the flavors, about 15 minutes, adding more bean liquid as needed to keep the stew saucy. Season to taste with salt and serve.

Roast Leg of Lamb
with Oil-Cured Black Olives and Herbs

When you carve this crusted leg, zesty ribbons of olive-garlic-herb stuffing are revealed running through each slice. And any leftovers make terrific sandwiches. The oil-cured black olives with Celtic salt from Adams Olive Ranch are a good choice here. To grill the lamb instead of roasting it, use a boneless, butterflied leg and make shallow incisions for the filling (see page 159 for grilling tips).

MAKES 8 TO 10 SERVINGS

Spring, Summer

1 bone-in leg of lamb, 5 pounds
5 large cloves garlic, peeled
1 teaspoon kosher salt
¾ cup pitted oil-cured black olives
½ cup fresh Italian parsley leaves, coarsely chopped

¼ cup fresh summer savory leaves, coarsely chopped
¼ cup fresh rosemary leaves, finely chopped, plus sprigs for pan
½ cup olive oil
Freshly ground black pepper
1 cup dry white wine or stock

Cut at least 12 slashes, each 1 to 2 inches deep and 2 inches long, in the leg of lamb, spacing them evenly. With a mortar and pestle, mash the garlic with the salt. Add the olives and herbs in batches, adding a little olive oil with each addition (using up to ¼ cup total), and mash to make a textured paste. Or, with a food processor running, drop the garlic through the feed tube to mince. Add the salt, olives, herbs, and ¼ cup of the oil and pulse to make a textured paste. Stuff the olive-garlic paste into the slashes, and don't worry about being too neat. Rub the remaining ¼ cup olive oil over the lamb and season with pepper. Lay the rosemary sprigs in a roasting pan just large enough to hold the roast, and place the lamb on the rosemary. Cover and let stand in a cool place for 1 hour or in the refrigerator for up to 6 hours. Bring to room temperature before roasting.

Preheat oven to 425 degrees. Roast the lamb, turning once, for 12 minutes per pound for rare, and 15 minutes per pound for medium. A thermometer inserted into the thickest part of the leg away from bone should register 120 degrees for rare and 140 degrees for medium. (The temperature will continue to rise a few degrees outside the oven.) Remove the meat to a warmed platter, tent with foil, and let rest for 15 to 20 minutes before carving.

Discard the rosemary from the pan, place the pan over medium-low heat, pour in the wine, and stir to scrape up any brown bits. Skim the fat from the surface, season with salt and pepper to taste, and pour through a fine-mesh sieve into a warmed serving bowl. Add any juices that have collected on the meat platter. To carve the roast, hold at an angle by the shank bone and rest the meaty end on the platter. Carve long, thin slices with the grain, parallel to the bone. Serve with the sauce.

Grilled Filet Mignon Sandwiches with Roasted Peppers and Eggs

I have learned a lot about grilling meat from Rodolfo, my Argentine son-in-law, including the technique of browning larger cuts of meat at the *end* of the cooking time, which gives the cook better control. Here's his favorite sandwich, dressed with *chimichurri*, the piquant sauce considered the Argentine ketchup. It's available at specialty markets, or make your own using market herbs.

MAKES 8 SERVINGS

Summer, Autumn

1 piece beef tenderloin, 2 pounds
2 to 3 teaspoons kosher or sea salt
Freshly ground black pepper
Marinated Grill-Roasted Lipstick Peppers
  (page 40)
1 white onion, thinly sliced

3 hard-boiled eggs, sliced
Mayonnaise or aioli (page 46)
Chimichurri, purchased or homemade
  (recipe follows)
8 large French rolls, split

Heat a grill to medium with an area of indirect heat and direct heat (see opposite). Rub the meat with the salt and some pepper. Place the beef over indirect heat and grill until juices appear on top, 10 to 15 minutes. Turn the meat and continue grilling over indirect heat until almost done, about 10 minutes. Move the meat over direct heat for 3 to 5 minutes to crisp the crust and finish cooking (the meat will be medium-rare). Remove the meat to a platter and let stand for 10 minutes.

Thinly slice the meat across the grain. Place the condiments—peppers, onion, eggs, mayonnaise, and *chimichurri*—and rolls on the table and let guests assemble their own sandwiches.

Chimichurri

MAKES 1⅔ CUPS

Evergreen

10 cloves garlic, finely chopped
2 tablespoons *ají molido* (page 28) or
  1 teaspoon each chile powder and
  paprika
¼ cup chopped fresh Italian parsley
1 tablespoon crushed fresh Greek

  oregano leaves
2 teaspoons kosher or sea salt
1 teaspoon freshly ground black pepper
2 fresh bay leaves, torn
½ cup corn, canola, or olive oil
1 cup red wine vinegar

Place all the ingredients in a bowl and mix well. Transfer to a jar with a tight-fitting lid and allow to age in the refrigerator for 1 to 3 days before using. It will keep for several weeks.

COOK'S TIPS FOR GRILLING

- For maximum cooking control when grilling outdoors, create direct (hotter) and indirect (cooler) areas of heat in your gas or charcoal grill.
- Gas grills usually have multiple controls, allowing two or more areas of the grill to be heated to different temperatures. Turn one section (preferably the middle area) to low or off, and put the food over the cooler area for indirect-heat grilling.
- For a kettle-type charcoal grill, mound most of the charcoal to one side, or make two equal piles, one on either side, and put the food over the cooler area for indirect-heat grilling. Do not start to cook until the coals are glowing and covered with white ash, 30 to 40 minutes after lighting (hardwood charcoal takes longer than briquettes).
- For Santa Maria–type grills, raise and lower the pulley-operated grates to control the distance of the food from the heat of the glowing coals.
- Grill quick-cooking foods such as steaks and burgers over direct heat. Start on medium, then brown at the end on high.
- Grill long-cooking foods such as whole chickens or roasts over indirect heat to allow food to cook all the way through without burning. If additional browning or crisping is needed, move food to the hotter part of grill at the end of the cooking time.
- Grill delicate foods such as fish over indirect or medium to low direct heat.
- Season meat with salt before cooking to deepen the flavors you get from browning and to help develop a crust. You'll be surprised at the tasty difference such a simple technique produces, especially with grass-fed beef. A good salt rub works wonders with all grilled and broiled meats and poultry.
- You can test meat for doneness with your fingertip. Press on the steak. If it is blood-rare, it will feel squashy; if is medium-rare, it will be springier and have some give; and if it is medium-well, it will be heading toward firm. Pull the meat off the heat before it reaches the feel you want. It will continue to cook from its own residual heat, as the heat from the hot exterior moves toward the cooler center.

Steak with Bloomsdale Spinach Chiffonade

Alex Weiser's sweet, dense Bloomsdale spinach makes an interesting change from the traditional arugula with steak found in the classic Italian *tagliata*. Bloomsdale and other Savoy (bumpy-leaved) spinaches have no tannin pucker and hold up better in salads and cooking than flat-leaved varieties. Even the stems are sweet. Season meat with salt before cooking to deepen the flavors you get from browning and to help develop a crust. This dish travels well for picnics.

MAKES 8 SERVINGS

Summer

2 top sirloin, skirt, or rib-eye steaks,
about 1 pound each
Kosher or sea salt

1 pound Bloomsdale or other Savoy
spinach
1 tablespoon extra-virgin olive oil
Freshly ground black pepper

Heat a grill to medium. Rub about 1 teaspoon salt into the meat and fat of each steak. Grill, turning once, to desired doneness, about 4 minutes on each side per inch of thickness for medium-rare.

Cut the spinach crosswise into ½-inch-wide ribbons (chiffonade) and place in a bowl. Add the oil, a little salt, and generous grinds of pepper and toss. Mound the spinach on a platter. Cut the steaks, across the grain and on the diagonal, into thin slices. Lay the steak slices over the spinach and serve.

Short Ribs Braised in Red Wine

This may not sound like a farmers' market recipe, but except for the wine, that's where I bought all the ingredients. Lean, flavorful grass-fed beef short ribs become meltingly tender after long, slow cooking in robust red wine. Cook the ribs a day ahead to allow time for the flavors to blend and so you can easily defat the sauce. Serve with a mix of roasted carrots, leeks, and parsnips (page 104).

MAKES 6 SERVINGS

Winter

3½ pounds meaty beef short ribs
Kosher or sea salt
2 tablespoons olive oil
1 onion, finely chopped
2 carrots, peeled and finely chopped
2 ribs celery, finely chopped
1 tablespoon chopped fresh Italian
   parsley

1 tablespoon chopped fresh marjoram
2 bay leaves, preferably fresh
1 large clove garlic, minced
About 2½ cups hearty, spicy red wine
   such as Zinfandel
1 tablespoon minced sun-dried tomato
About 2 cups Beef Stock (page 54), or 1
   cup canned diluted with 1 cup water

Heat a large, wide pot over medium heat. Season the ribs with salt and add them to the pot, working in batches if necessary to avoid crowding. Brown well on all sides, about 10 minutes. Remove the ribs to a plate and drain off the fat from the pan. Reduce the heat to medium-low and add the oil, onion, carrots, celery, parsley, marjoram, and bay leaves. Season the vegetables with salt, stir to scrape up any brown bits, and then cook, stirring occasionally, until the vegetables are tender, about 10 minutes. Add the garlic and cook for 1 minute more. Pour in 2 cups of the wine, add the tomato, raise the heat to high, and bring to a boil. Cook until the wine has reduced by half, 8 to 10 minutes. Return the meat to the pan, rib bones upright, and reduce the heat to low. At this point, the liquid in the pan should reach no more than halfway up the sides of the ribs. Cover and braise the meat until very tender, 2 to 2½ hours, turning the ribs once after the first hour. Check the meat every 30 minutes during cooking to be sure there is sufficient liquid, adding stock as necessary to keep the ribs covered about halfway, and that it is simmering rather than boiling vigorously.

Remove the meat to a plate. Remove and discard the bay leaves and pour the sauce and vegetables into a liquid measure or bowl. You should have about 2 cups. Skim the fat from the sauce. Return the ribs and sauce to the pot and heat, adding a little stock if you feel there isn't enough sauce. Or, refrigerate the sauce and ribs until closer to serving time; the fat will harden and be easy to lift off. To reheat, return the ribs and defatted sauce to the pot and add ½ cup wine and ½ cup stock. Bring to a boil, reduce the heat to a medium-low, and simmer until the ribs are heated through, 15 to 20 minutes, or reheat in a 350-degree oven.

162 Sweets

When it comes to capturing the intricate flavors of ripe farmers' market fruit, less is more. Dessert recipes often call for so much sugar, butter, and flour that the elusive complexities of such wonders as white Snow Queen nectarines or blushing Blenheim apricots are masked. Or, once the fruits are cooked, their natural sweetness recedes and their tart notes advance. The obvious solution is to consume these gems only in their natural state. Indeed, few desserts are more elegant than a perfect—in taste, if not always in looks—piece of fruit served the temperature of a foggy summer morning. Such simplicity also shows off a fruit's *terroir*—that particular year's sun and soil conditions—and honors the farmer who raised it to excellence.

But sometimes we want to put the fruit through its paces. In this chapter, you will find such simple techniques as searing and roasting that maintain and heighten flavors; crisps, crumbles, and tarts that use just enough sugar to draw out a fruit's juices and just enough topping to offer textural contrast; and introductions to such exotics as sapotes, cherimoyas, and dragon fruits that you may have passed up before.

Choose recipes appropriate to the fruit. Delicate Meyer lemons, white or low-acid peaches, and melting Persian mulberries deserve gentle treatment. Assertive Eureka lemons, yellow and red stone fruits, blackberries, and winter squash can tolerate more forward approaches. When seasoning "to taste," start with the barest minimum of a complementary flavor—a tablespoon of sugar, a squeeze of lemon, a pinch of black pepper—and then taste. You can always add more, but you may be surprised by how little you will need. Let your accompaniments defer to the star ingredient. A too-sweet ice cream can make fruit seem sour by comparison. Yogurt, heavy cream, crème fraîche, or an earthy cheese will provide a mellower contrast.

Strawberry Shortcakes

These cream-biscuit shortcakes from Annie Miler, owner of Clementine café, and Nancy Silverton, founder of La Brea Bakery, are so easy, even strawberry grower Phil McGrath, who insists he can't cook, can make them. Molly Gean, of Harry's Berries, suggests Seascape strawberries here; their higher acidity stands up to the biscuits and whipped cream. Organic Pastures Dairy unpasteurized cream from grass-fed cows reminds me of the cream in France or Italy: rich in color and tasting of the field.

MAKES 12 SERVINGS

Spring, Summer

3 to 4 pint baskets strawberries, hulled
    and quartered lengthwise
2 to 4 tablespoons sugar
1 to 2 tablespoons lemon juice
1 cup heavy cream

FOR THE BISCUITS

2 cups plus 2 tablespoons flour
¼ cup sugar, plus more for sprinkling
1 tablespoon baking powder
1 teaspoon salt
1½ cups heavy cream

Preheat oven to 425 degrees. Line a large baking sheet with parchment paper. Place the berries in a bowl and sprinkle with the sugar and lemon juice to taste. Stir gently, then let stand until some syrup forms, at least 30 minutes. Whip the cream to soft peaks, and refrigerate until serving.

To make the biscuits, in a bowl, stir together the flour, sugar, baking powder, and salt. Use a fork to make a well in the dry ingredients and pour in the cream. Working from the center toward the edge of the bowl, use the fork to stir the dry ingredients into the cream until just blended. The dough will be sticky and lumpy. Using a large spoon, scoop dough portions the size of small lemons onto the prepared pan. You should have 12 biscuits. Sprinkle the tops with sugar. Bake until lightly golden, 15 to 17 minutes. Let cool for at least 15 minutes on the pan on a rack, then slice in half horizontally. The biscuits are best served within a couple of hours of baking, but may be refreshed in a hot oven. Or, freeze some unbaked for another time (bake frozen biscuits for 30 minutes).

Place the biscuit bottoms, cut side up, in individual bowls, top with some strawberries and syrup and whipped cream, and then the biscuit tops. Surround with more berries.

HOW TO CHOOSE STRAWBERRIES: Midspring is peak strawberry season. Look for completely red berries (with the exception of early-season Galantes, which are almost pink and can have white shoulders) with no dulling or soft spots. Small or medium berries are often the most flavorful. Store them unwashed in a paper towel–lined airtight container in the refrigerator, but serve at room temperature. Rinse just before serving, using very little water. Pull out the stem and core with the tip of a vegetable peeler, a small knife, or an inexpensive strawberry huller.

You won't find heirloom strawberries at the farmers' market. That's because the world's most popular berry is strictly a cultivated hybrid, born of a lucky mid-eighteenth-century European cross between species from North America and South America. Ever since, fruit breeders and growers have struggled to develop and deliver tasty varieties that hold up more than a day.

Too often, the solution has been sturdy, lifeless berries bred for size, shipping, and storage capabilities. But local farmers can grow varieties developed primarily for flavor and fragrance. "The decision to sell locally allows us to focus strictly on taste, our number one criterion," explains Molly Gean, whose late father, Harry Iwamoto, founded Harry's Berries in Oxnard in 1967. It's a choice that requires nerves of steel and constant oversight. Strawberries, which don't improve a bit after harvest, must be picked fully ripe to reach their aromatic peak and then rushed to market within a day. Although best consumed soon after purchase, carefully grown strawberries will keep well for several days, since their postharvest life is spent in our homes, not in cold storage.

Strawberries, which don't like too much heat or direct contact with water, grow exceptionally well in cool coastal areas such as Oxnard, explains Phil McGrath, who farms not far from Molly and Rick Gean, on land that has been in his family since the arrival of his great-grandfather from Ireland in 1867. "They love that morning fog and sandy soil," says the ag-land preservationist. "The area is an ancient diluvial plain, and I've read it's got the deepest topsoil in the world."

Today, the most popular (read juicy, not crisp) strawberries at the Santa Monica Farmers' Market are the round, low-acid Gaviota, with a distinctive ruby color, and the pointed, higher-acid Seascape, with more complex flavors. According to Molly, these have pretty much replaced the beloved 1983 Chandler hybrid, "because hybrids just don't last more than twenty or thirty years and need to be retired after several generations."

Such commercial hybrids as Camarosa, Ventana, and Diamante are tasty if picked ripe, but they still can't compare to varieties developed with flavor at the top of the list. The fragrant, supple Galante that Jerry Rutiz grows farther north in coastal Arroyo Grande illustrates the struggle between flavor and durability. Developed by a fruit breeder friend in the mid-1990s, the Galante was intended to be a tasty commercial berry that could be grown without the use of the pesticide gas methyl bromide (a once-common industry practice being phased out), but the delicious result proved too soft for commercial use. It is cultivated in Europe, but Jerry is one of the few growers who plants the Galante in this country.

Fraises des bois, the small, highly aromatic alpine summer strawberries much beloved in Europe, are a different species. About the size of the tip of your little finger, they are ruddy outside, rich and creamy (color and texture) inside, and have a mellow, floral sweetness best enjoyed served plain. They are a rare treat at California farmers' markets. In midsummer, Jaime Farms in The City of Industry and Pudwill's in Nipomo bring them to the Santa Monica market. *Fraises des bois* are highly perishable; refrigerate them immediately and serve within a day of purchase.

Bumbleberry Crisp

Bumbleberry is an old term meaning mixed berries. Blackberries, raspberries, and strawberries are used here, but blueberries or boysenberries can be added or substituted. Or, make a single-berry or other fruit crisp, such as sour cherry (with 2 pounds fruit and ½ cup sugar). Start with flavorful fruit and keep sugar to a minimum. A little instant tapioca lightly thickens juices more effortlessly and delicately than cornstarch. This recipe can easily be doubled. Accompany each serving with a drizzle of heavy cream or a scoop of vanilla ice cream.

MAKES 8 SERVINGS

Summer

1 cup flour

¼ cup packed light brown sugar

¼ cup granulated sugar, plus more
    for berries

¼ teaspoon salt

Grated zest and juice of 1 lemon

6 tablespoons unsalted butter, softened

2 cups each strawberries, blackberries,
    and raspberries

1½ tablespoons instant tapioca

Preheat oven to 375 degrees. To make the topping, in a bowl, stir together the flour, brown and granulated sugars, salt, and lemon zest. Add the butter and work it into the dry ingredients with your fingertips or a fork until the mixture is the texture of coarse sand. Set aside.

Using the tip of a vegetable peeler or a small knife, hull the strawberries and quarter them lengthwise. Place all the berries in a 2-quart baking dish. Sprinkle with the tapioca and with sugar and lemon juice to taste and stir gently. Sprinkle the topping over the berries. and bake until the berries are bubbly, about 40 minutes. Increase the heat to 400 degrees and bake until the topping is a rich golden brown, about 5 minutes longer. Serve the crisp warm or at room temperature.

COOK'S TIP: Freeze unbaked crisps to enjoy later in the year. Do not thaw before baking, and bake at 375 degrees for about 1 hour.

West Coast blackberries, raspberries, and the like grow on long canes much like rambling roses, to which they are related. Raspberries slip from their cores when plucked, yielding the familiar hollow fruit. Some raspberries are also ever-bearing, producing late into the year. In coastal Nipomo, prolific berry producer Randy Pudwill plants numerous varieties to get the longest possible season, and protects them in hoop houses during cold weather. Lower acid orange, yellow, and white raspberries are variants of red ones and have a more delicate flavor and texture. Black raspberries are a different species, with much tighter, firmer drupelets (the little, round vesicles) and a wilder flavor. Red raspberries come in shades light to bright; avoid fruit that has turned dark and dull, signs of overripeness and fermented flavors. Store blackberries and raspberries unwashed in shallow, airtight containers in the refrigerator and use within a couple of days.

Boysen, olallie, and young (among others) are the progeny of crosses between blackberries and raspberries. These hybrids possess plumper, juicier drupelets than raspberries and mellower, richer flavors than tart blackberries. Standouts are Robert Poole's brief early-summer display of youngberries and boysenberries from Redlands (Bob is also known for his giant sweet summer onions). With blackberries and their offspring, look for fruit with large, full drupelets, no sign of red, and a white, pithy core stained with juice.

Blueberries, one of the few native North American fruits, are related to the cranberry, another native. Until recently, the best large highbush berries (as opposed to the very different Maine small, wild lowbush berries) required many cold-weather hours to set sweet fruit and were primarily grown in the Pacific Northwest. But California growers like Rachel Whitney of Whitney Ranch in Carpinteria have worked hard to produce excellent local sweet fruit from recently developed warmer-weather varieties. Blueberries are the sturdiest berry: toss them unwashed into an uncovered bowl, and they will keep fine on the counter for a couple of days or for a week in the refrigerator. Choose smooth, plump berries with a powdered (bloom) look and no green or reddish spots.

Persian mulberries are the *ne plus ultra* of berries. Dripping from tall trees, almost black, and with twice the sugar of raspberries when fully ripe, mulberries are meltingly tender and overflowing with intoxicating winelike juices. Underripe, they are puckeringly tart; overripe, they are dry and cloyingly sweet. No wonder these demanding berries that grow on trees are a connoisseur's expensive delight. They are available midsummer at Weiser Family Farms, Tenerelli Orchards, Circle C Ranch, and Flora Bella Farm. It is impossible to improve on their exquisite flavor, so serve them plain, with a bit of unsweetened cream if you must. If you are feeling flush, buy extra and follow Spago pastry chef Sherry Yard's suggestion: freeze them on baking sheets, store in freezer bags or plastic containers, and use them later in the year to create mulberry sauces, ice creams, and sorbets.

Cherry and Goat Cheese Gratin

Here, goat cheese, red wine, and amaretti dress up the first stone fruits of summer. The distinctive flavor of the Italian cookies (available in most supermarkets) comes from bitter almonds, which are also used to make amaretto liqueur and certain almond flavorings. Rusty Hall of Paso Almonds considers bitter almonds the most interesting of the four varieties he grows and sells them in small quantities by special order. For more about cherries, see page 80.

MAKES 6 TO 8 SERVINGS

Summer

½ pound mild goat cheese such as Redwood Hill plain chèvre or Montrachet, at room temperature

½ cup crème fraîche

3 tablespoons sugar

1¼ pounds (about 3 cups) cherries such as Bing or Garnet, pitted and halved

Finely shredded zest of 1 lemon

⅓ cup light red wine such as Beaujolais

⅓ cup crushed amaretti

⅓ cup almonds, toasted (page 25) and chopped

Fleur de sel or other finishing salt

Preheat the broiler, positioning the rack close to the heat source. In a bowl, lightly whisk together the goat cheese and crème fraîche. Place a large, nonreactive ovenproof skillet over medium-high heat and sprinkle the sugar evenly over the bottom. When the sugar just starts to melt, after 1 to 2 minutes, add the cherries and lemon zest and cook, without stirring, until the sugar is melted and bubbly, about 2 minutes. Pour the wine evenly over the cherries and cook until the juices are thickened, about 2 minutes more. Remove from the heat. (The gratin may be prepared to this point up to 2 hours ahead and held at room temperature.)

Scatter the amaretti crumbs over the cherries, and then spoon dollops of the goat cheese mixture evenly over the surface. Place under the broiler until the cheese is lightly browned, about 2 minutes. Strew the almonds over the gratin and finish with a generous sprinkling of *fleur de sel*. Serve warm or at room temperature.

Goat Cheese Coeur à la Crème
with Blackberry–Blood Orange Sauce

Edged in dark chocolate, this goat cheese version of the easy, no-cook French classic is cool, creamy, and tangy. The sauce, made with early-season blackberries and late blood oranges, pairs well with a fruity bittersweet chocolate, such as Scharffen Berger 70%. Traditional heart-shaped perforated porcelain molds are available at cookware stores; a wide 1-quart sieve or perforated pie pan can be substituted.

MAKES 12 SERVINGS

Spring

¾ pound mild goat cheese such as Redwood Hill plain chèvre or Montrachet, at room temperature

3 ounces cream cheese, at room temperature

3 tablespoons powdered sugar

1 cup heavy cream

2 ounces bittersweet chocolate

2 cups mixed berries

FOR THE SAUCE

⅓ cup granulated sugar

¼ cup water

2 half-pint baskets blackberries

Juice of 1 blood orange

1 tablespoon Crème de Cassis

Line a 1-quart perforated mold with a 16-inch square of cheesecloth, allowing the ends to overhang the sides. Using an electric mixer, whip together the cheeses and powdered sugar until fluffy, about 3 minutes. In a separate bowl, whip the cream to firm peaks. Fold one-fourth of the whipped cream into the cheese mixture to lighten it, and then gently fold in the remaining cream. Pile mixture into the prepared mold and smooth the top with a spatula. Fold the ends of the cheesecloth over the top, cover with plastic wrap, and place on a pie plate to catch the whey. Refrigerate for at least 6 hours.

Melt the chocolate in a microwave or double boiler. Peel back the cheesecloth from the mold. Working quickly, and using an offset spatula, spread the chocolate evenly over the cheese. Do not let the chocolate overlap onto the edge of the mold. Refrigerate until serving.

To make the sauce, in a small pot, heat the granulated sugar and water over medium heat, stirring frequently, until the sugar dissolves, about 1 minute. Remove from the heat and let cool slightly. Put the sugar syrup, berries, orange juice, and cassis in a blender and process until smooth. Strain the sauce through a fine-mesh sieve. You should have about 1½ cups.

To serve, run a knife along the inside edge of the mold to a depth of ½ inch to loosen the cheese. Invert the mold onto a serving plate, keeping the edges of the cheesecloth free. Lift off the mold and peel away the cheesecloth. Drizzle a little sauce decoratively around the *coeur*, then scatter the berries on and around it. Cut into wedges to serve. Pass the remaining sauce at the table.

Grandmother Rachel's Fresh Apricot Preserves

Sweet-tart, juicy Blenheims are not to be missed in their month-long season, beginning around the end of June. Once, they were *the* apricot, but their fragility and less-than-perfect looks made them commercially unviable, and sturdy but mealy varieties have become the norm. Fortunately, dedicated farmers like Mike Cirone of Cirone Farms and Eric Todd of Forcefield are willing to grow and handpick Blenheims. Several other cultivars are also worth seeking at the market, including Fitzgerald's Elgin Marbles and Tenerelli's Golden Sweets. When I was a child, my family had a Blenheim tree. If it was apricot season when my Grandmother Rachel came to visit, she would make jars of these chunky preserves, the best way to prolong the Blenheim's all-too-short season. This recipe may be multiplied, always keeping the same proportions.

MAKES 2 TO 3 CUPS

Summer

2 pounds very ripe apricots, halved and pitted

2¼ cups sugar

1 lemon, if needed

Put the apricots in a large, wide nonreactive pot. Pour the sugar over them and let stand until the apricots release their juices, for several hours at room temperature or overnight in the refrigerator (remove from the refrigerator 1 hour before cooking).

Place over medium heat and bring to a boil. Reduce the heat to a gentle boil and cook uncovered, making sure the liquid is always bubbling and stirring often with a wooden spoon to prevent scorching, for 45 minutes. Put a small amount of the mixture on a plate, let cool briefly, and test for thickening with your finger. The preserves should mound, not drip off your fingertip, and the fruit should still be chunky. Continue to cook as needed until the desired consistency is achieved, up to 1 hour longer. Add a little water if the preserves become too thick. Taste and add a squeeze of lemon if needed to regain sweet-tart balance.

Ladle into sterilized jars, seal with canning lids, and store in a cool, dry place for up to 1 year. Or, ladle into airtight containers and refrigerate for up to 1 month or freeze for up to 6 months.

South of San Luis Obispo, See Canyon is a deep coastal box canyon where the rainfall, climate, and water table allow Mike Cirone to dry-farm Blenheim apricots, heirloom apples, and pears with minimal irrigation. "The mouth of the canyon might get twenty-five inches of rain in a year, but three miles in there may be seventy-five inches," Mike explains. "Because of this high water table, the trees reach their roots down to find water without irrigation. The less water used in growing, the more concentrated the sugars." In the same way vintners believe vines must suffer to produce great wine, the Cirones "challenge the fruit to get flavor."

Even on a July morning, it is surprisingly cool at Cirone Farms, the perfect environment for growing Blenheims, the gold standard for apricots. The first orchard we visit is small, embraced by steep oak-covered hills that protect the gnarled, squat seventy-year-old apricot trees whose branches are laden almost to the ground. The heart-shaped leaves form a rich green canopy, the abundant fruit peeking through, reddened and luminous in the foggy morning's white light. The air smells of the damp grass and earth, but the trees offer no fragrance. It's quiet as three helpers gently take the apricots from the trees by hand. They pack them in flat boxes and store them on the back of the open truck, where they will remain overnight at the ambient temperature until they are driven before dawn to market. They will not spend any time in a cooler.

Protected by a deer fence, the next small orchard is full of smooth, slender young trees. The perk of early-morning picking is all-you-can-eat, and the taste of a cool apricot straight from the tree, vital with juices, is a pleasure startlingly different from the sun-warmed apricots at the market.

A higher canyon orchard, farther from the road and into the wild, is laid out like an amphitheater. It is Mike's first and favorite grove, and if you are quiet, the only sound you will hear are the blue jays overhead. Occasionally, mountain lions and bobcats stroll the orchard, tracking the birds and squirrels that typically plague urban fruit-tree owners.

This remarkable year (2001), which happens once every five or seven years, Cirone's orchards will yield twenty-five hundred boxes full of sun-kissed apricots in a month or so of furious picking. Mike tries to lengthen the season as much as possible by winter-pruning the trees to create a shade canopy so some fruits will ripen a little later. "But," he laments, "I don't have the final say—the trees do."

Even if the next year's growing conditions are equally superb, Mike won't hope for more than a thousand boxes, because the trees will be too worn out from this year's labors to match the harvest. (At the time of writing, 2006 promised to be a boom year, but the caprice of weather dropped the harvest back to one thousand boxes.) "Blenheims are a challenging crop; they'll take you right over the edge," Mike says. "Even after more than twenty years, that's the crop that still keeps me up at night. You gotta be willing to play the stress game. You can't pick them green; you just have to wait it out. But they can go from green to fully ripe in one day, and then you've got to get them off the tree and to market."

Seared White Nectarines with Burnt Honey

A great white nectarine is unforgettable—sweet, floral, with hints of burnt sugar, qualities that can be easily overpowered. A quick sear in a little butter heightens caramel notes, keeps raw flavors intact, and protects the fruit from discoloring, which means you can prepare this simple dessert ahead. Look for Snow Queens from Honey Crisp and Harvest Pride (labeled Stanwick there), and Lovely Lolitas from Fitzgerald. These white nectarines aren't the prettiest girls at the dance, but they are the most fascinating. Fitzgerald's or Pritchett's white donut peaches and Tenerelli's late-season Indian Blood peaches are also delicious prepared this way. Too often, white stone fruits are sweet but uninteresting, so taste before you buy. Use a full-flavored honey, such as earthy buckwheat or molasses-like eucalyptus from Bee Canyon Ranch in Saugus.

MAKES 8 SERVINGS

Summer

2 tablespoons full-flavored honey, warmed

2 tablespoons water or dessert wine such as muscat

2 teaspoons unsalted butter

4 fresh bay leaves (optional)

4 ripe nectarines or peaches, halved and pitted

Boysenberries, blackberries, or raspberries

In a small bowl, stir together the honey and water. Heat a large, heavy skillet over medium-high heat. Film the pan with 1 teaspoon of the butter and add the bay leaves. When the butter sizzles and the bay leaves start to blister, add half of the fruit, cut side down. Cook until the cut surface is browned, about 2 minutes. Transfer the fruit, cut side up, and the bay leaves to a platter. Repeat with the remaining fruit and 1 teaspoon butter.

Reduce the heat to medium-low and pour the honey mixture into the pan. Stir, scraping up any brown bits, and then simmer until deep brown, about 2 minutes. To serve, divide the fruit among dessert plates, lightly drizzle the fruit with the honey, and then scatter the berries around the fruit.

HOW TO CHOOSE WHITE NECTARINES: Look for burgundy-russet rather than pink tones to the blush and dusky gold skin tones. Some sugar cracking is fine.

FARMER'S TIP: In autumn, sear buttery D'Anjou pears from Cirone Farms or Penryn Orchard. The trick to choosing a good pear lies in the orchard. "Pears should be picked firm and mature," Mike Cirone explains. "If left on the tree until ripe, they get grainy and pithy." Slightly underripe D'Anjous can be refrigerated several weeks, then ripened on the kitchen counter. When ready, the skin will have turned from green to light yellow, and the fruit will have a slight give. Consume ripe pears within a few days.

Seared Peach Open-Faced Rustic Tart

I've created countless farmers' market treats with inspiration from the galettes in Deborah Madison's *Vegetarian Cooking for Everyone*. Here, seared fruit adds another dimension to this rustic fruit tart. This recipe works well with other fruits, seared or raw, and with full-flavored honey or the burnt honey, opposite. For helpful hints on how to acheive crisp, flaky pastry, see page 193.

MAKES 12 SERVINGS

Summer

FOR THE PASTRY

2 cups flour

1 tablespoon sugar

½ teaspoon salt

¾ cup (12 tablespoons) cold unsalted butter, cut into ½-inch pieces

⅓ to ½ cup ice water

FOR THE FILLING

3 pounds white peaches or nectarines (about 12 small)

2 tablespoons burnt honey (opposite)

3 tablespoons crushed amaretti or ground almonds

4 tablespoons unsalted butter, melted

1 tablespoon sugar

To make the pastry, in a large bowl, stir together the flour, sugar, and salt with a fork. Add the butter and cut in using your fingertips or a pastry blender until the mixture resembles coarse sand with some flattened pieces of butter still visible. Stir in ice water a little at a time until the dough just sticks together when pressed between your fingertips. Gather the dough into a ball, wrap in plastic wrap, and flatten into a thick rectangle. Refrigerate for 15 minutes. The dough may be made up to 1 day ahead and refrigerated; let it sit at room temperature for a bit before rolling.

Preheat oven to 425 degrees. To make the filling, lightly scrub the peaches to remove the fuzz, then halve and pit. Sear the fruit as directed opposite, omitting the bay leaves, and prepare the burnt honey. Cut each peach half into 3 to 6 wedges. On a lightly floured surface, roll out the dough into a 12-by-18-inch rectangle about ⅛ inch thick. Transfer to an ungreased large, rimless baking sheet (if you don't have a rimless pan, turn a rimmed pan upside down). Sprinkle the amaretti crumbs evenly over the dough, leaving a 2-inch border all around. Arrange the fruit slices, seared side up, in overlapping rows on the dough, staying within the border. Fold the border over to cover the edge of the fruit. Brush the dough edge with some of the butter and sprinkle with the sugar. Stir the honey into the remaining butter and drizzle over the fruit.

Bake for 15 minutes. Reduce the heat to 375 degrees, and bake until the crust is golden and the fruit is bubbly and its edges are browned, about 25 minutes more. Let cool on the pan on a rack for 5 minutes. Use a large offset spatula to loosen the tart from the pan, but leave it on the pan for 30 minutes. Slide the tart onto a platter and serve warm or at room temperature.

Nifty Nectarines and Peaches

You can tell a farmer's passions by the peaches and nectarines he grows. At Fitzgerald's Premium Ripe Tree Fruit in Reedley, Fitz Kelly dabbles in fruit so unusual that sometimes he's the only one in the country to grow it for sale. His neighbor in nearby Dinuba, octogenarian Art Lange of Honey Crisp, pushes the envelope of tree ripening to the max, leaving intricately flavored heirloom varieties hanging to the last possible moment to raise sugar to insane levels, yet maintain the fruit's integrity, a pomological high-wire act. Mike Cirone grows old, mellow varieties like fuzzy, subtle Elbertas and delicate, white Babcocks, while John Hurley of Summer Harvest picks powerful commercial varieties at peak perfection. John believes "it's not so much the variety, but how you grow it, pick it, and store it, if you do store it, that matters." That's why he doesn't list varieties at his stand: "I want customers to focus on the flavor, not the name."

Fresno County, where Kelly, Lange, Hurley, and Troy Regier of Regier Farms grow dozens of varieties, is prime stone-fruit country, but the high-desert conditions in Los Angeles County's Antelope Valley also yield superb fruit, especially in late season. "Late August, September is the best for Littlerock peaches and nectarines," says John Tenerelli of Tenerelli Orchards in Littlerock. Cool nights and warm days through October and into November allow the Tenerelli family to grow tasty Autumn Lady, September Sun, and Indian Blood peaches long after the last San Joaquin harvest.

In addition to differences in color, flavor, and texture and whether it is a peach or a nectarine (a single gene—the fuzz gene—separates them), time of harvest is key to understanding the countless peach and nectarine varieties at the market. Each variety matures in a seven- to fourteen-day blitz, so farmers plan their orchards to stagger harvests through the summer. If you find a variety you love, carpe diem.

Tasting is the best way to choose. Flavors range from mild low acid to complex, floral subacid, and from subtle sweet-acid balanced fruits to high acid–high sugar "flavor bombs." Select fruit with a little give when gently palmed and look for warm depth of all-over skin color, not just the rosy blush. Also, ask the farmer the optimal time to consume the fruit. Here are some notable varieties.

YELLOW PEACHES

EARLY SEASON: June Lady, Springcrest, Rich Lady (Lady in Red).

MIDSEASON: Elegant Lady (bright, sweet flavor), Flamecrest, Elberta and Fay Elberta (fuzzy old varieties, mild sweet-acid balance, luminous yellow-orange when ripe; hold shape in cooking), Honey Zee (intensely sweet, low acid yet complex), O'Henry (excellent sturdy, all-around peach), Rio Oso Gem (buttery, subtle sweet-acid; at Pritchett).

LATE SEASON: Sangre de Toro (Tenerelli name; deep berry flavor and color in firm, juicy orange flesh), Fairtime (excellent Elberta type), September Sun (juicy, berry notes), Last Chance (pale yellow, creamy texture, best if fairly firm), Autumn Lady (for die-hard peach fans; very firm texture).

WHITE PEACHES
EARLY SEASON: Saturn (floral donut peach with melting flesh; at Fitzgerald and Pritchett).
MIDSEASON: Glacier (very sweet), Babcock (delicate, melting flesh; floral with honey notes).
LATE SEASON: Indian Blood (greenish skin with burgundy blush; firm, juicy; intense floral, round flavors; at Tenerelli).

YELLOW NECTARINES
EARLY SEASON: Diamond Bright (the most tree-ripened of Tenerelli's harvests), Ruby Diamond.
MIDSEASON: Fantasia (old-fashioned, delicate), Zee Glow (intense, sweet), Flavortop (red-flecked flesh, excellent sweet-acid balance), Honey Kist (a.k.a. Carmen Miranda; mango flavor, low acid).
LATE SEASON: September Red (rich cherry flavors in a good year).

WHITE NECTARINES
EARLY SEASON: Snow Queen (complex flavors, tendency to cracking), Lovely Lolita (Fitz Kelly's name for several low-acid varieties).
MIDSEASON: Arctic Rose (extremely high sugar, similar to Snow Queen but less rich), Arctic Queen (burnt-sugar notes similar to Snow Queen).
LATE SEASON: Arctic Snow (sweet, juicy),

Plums and Pluots

Plums divide into three main groups: Japanese, European, and American. Most of the juicy, sweet-tart plums we enjoy fresh are Japanese varieties, including Santa Rosa, Mariposa, Burgundy, Elephant Heart, Sweetheart, Frontier, Friar, Nubiana, Eldorado, and Satsuma. Red-skinned cultivars range from bright with a yellow glow to purple-black with anywhere from meaty yellow to melting wine-red meat.

European plums, which include the damson and greengage types not commonly seen in California, tend to be smaller and often meatier, such as the tiny apricot-flavored golden mirabelles at Harvest Pride, a French favorite for preserves. Oval-shaped prunes, also in the European category, have a high percentage of sugars and solids. They dry well as we know, but fresh late-season blue-black Italian Prunes and dusty purple Sugar Plums, both with sweet, tawny meat, are excellent in baked desserts.

Small, tart indigenous American plums such as beach or Sierra, which is native to northern California and Oregon, generally grow wild on shrubs and are best used in preserves or liqueurs. James Birch brings to market the wild Sierra-type plums growing on his land.

The latest plum craze is the apricot-plum cross known variously as Pluot, Aprium, and plumcot. They range from dappled to purple skinned and from yellow to pink to crimson fleshed, with names like Flavorella, Flavor Queen, and Dapple Dandy. Harvest Pride, Balderama, Burkart, Nicholas, Pritchett, Cirone, and Flora Bella and more bring a plethora of plums to the market.

Peach Pavlova

Slices of ripe, sunny peaches are piled into a Pavlova, a crisp meringue shell with a marshmallow-like center named for the famed ballerina's 1926 visit to Australia (but originally created in New Zealand). This peach version is crowned with raspberry sauce, evoking another famous dessert created for Australian opera star Nellie Melba. You will want a sweet-acid yellow peach that will stand up to the sweet meringue, such as Maycrest, Fiesta Gem, June Lady, Elegant Lady, or O'Henry from Fitzgerald, Honey Crisp, Regier, Summer Harvest, or Tenerelli. This easy two-egg Pavlova recipe comes from my friend Claudia Stafinski, who lived in New South Wales for several years.

MAKES 10 SERVINGS

Spring, Summer, Autumn, Winter

FOR THE PAVLOVA

2 egg whites, at room temperature

1½ cups superfine sugar

½ teaspoon vanilla extract

1 teaspoon vinegar or strained
  lemon juice

1 teaspoon cornstarch

4 tablespoons boiling water

FOR THE SAUCE

⅓ cup granulated sugar

¼ cup water

2 half-pint baskets raspberries

Juice of 1 orange

2 teaspoons kirsch (optional)

4 or 5 large, ripe peaches

2 tablespoons granulated sugar

½ cup heavy cream, whipped (optional)

Preheat oven to 350 degrees. Line a large baking sheet with aluminum foil, shiny side down. Place all the meringue ingredients in an impeccably clean bowl of an electric mixer, and beat on high speed until very stiff and glossy, 7 to 15 minutes, depending on the power of your mixer. Working quickly, and using a spatula, spread the mixture onto the prepared baking sheet into a circle or oval about 10 inches in diameter, swirling the edges of the meringue into free-form peaks and creating a "valley" in the center. Or, for individual shells, spoon 10 dollops of meringue mixture several inches apart on the pan, and shape as directed.

Bake for 10 minutes and reduce the heat to 250 degrees. Bake a large Pavlova for 45 minutes longer in an electric oven, or for 1 hour longer in a gas oven. Bake individual shells 30 or 45 minutes, respectively. Allow to cool completely in the oven with the oven door ajar, about 3 hours or up to overnight, then peel the foil away. The shell(s) may be stored in an airtight container at room temperature for up to 2 weeks.

To make the sauce, in a small pot, heat the granulated sugar and water over medium heat, stirring frequently, until the sugar dissolves, about 1 minute. Remove from the heat and let cool slightly. Put the sugar syrup, berries, orange juice, and kirsch in a blender and process until smooth. Strain the sauce through a fine-mesh sieve. You should have about 1½ cups.

To assemble the dessert, peel the peaches (page 24) and cut into ½-inch-thick slices. Place in a bowl, stir in the granulated sugar, and let stand, or macerate, until the juices run, 30 to 60 minutes. Place the large shell on a platter, or the smaller shells on individual plates. Spread the center with the whipped cream and pile the peaches on top, allowing some to tumble onto the edge of the plate. Cut the large Pavlova into wedges to serve. Pour raspberry sauce over, or around, each serving.

SPRING PAVLOVA VARIATION: Substitute 6 to 8 cups sliced stawberries for the peaches.

AUTUMN AND WINTER PAVLOVA VARIATIONS: Substitute 4 cups peeled, sliced kiwifruits for the peaches. In winter, substitute 1 cup sliced Meiwa kumquats for 1 cup of the kiwifruits.

Plum Crisp with Cornmeal Topping

Plums are the last stone fruits to leave the market as summer turns to fall, my favorite time to enjoy them. They've had plenty of time to sweeten on the tree, and their slightly spicy flavor lends itself to transitional menus as our thoughts move to cooler weather. Try a mix of plum varieties—sweet, tart, firm, soft—for a richly textured dssert.

MAKES 8 TO 10 SERVINGS

Summer, Autumn

3½ pounds plums, one kind or a mixture, halved, pitted, and large plums quartered
1 to 2 tablespoons honey, warmed
2 tablespoons dessert wine, such as muscat
1 cup flour
⅔ cup cornmeal
¼ teaspoon salt

¼ cup granulated sugar
¼ cup packed light brown sugar
2 tablespoons chopped crystallized ginger
Grated zest of 1 lemon
¾ cup (12 tablespoons) unsalted butter, cut into small pieces
Heavy cream, crème fraîche, or vanilla ice cream for serving

Preheat oven to 400 degrees. Arrange the plum pieces, cut side up, in a shallow 3-quart baking dish. They should be somewhat vertical and overlapping slightly. Drizzle the honey over the fruit, and sprinkle the wine over all. Bake the fruit for 20 minutes.

Meanwhile, make the topping. In a bowl, stir together the flour, cornmeal, salt, granulated and brown sugars, ginger, and lemon zest. Add the butter and work it in with your fingertips, a pastry blender, or a fork until the mixture resembles coarse sand with some larger lumps and bumps. Remove the plums from the oven and sprinkle the topping evenly over the fruit. Continue to bake until the fruit is syrupy and the topping and the edges of the fruit are browned, about 40 minutes. Serve warm or at room temperature, accompanied with cream.

Roasted Seasonal Fruit

In summer, set a pan of peaches, plums, Pluots, nectarines, apricots, figs, and berries—or an abundance of one—on the barbeque to roast to smoky, syrupy goodness while you eat dinner. Autumn fruits—tender Golden Delicious apples (or other quick-cooking variety) and D'Anjou or Bartlett pears from Cirone Farms or Penryn Orchard, concord Grapes from Flora Bella or Nicholas Orchard, Fuyu persimmons from Schaner or J.J.'s Lone Daughter Ranch—also roast beautifully on the grill. Serve with a mild goat cheese or yogurt cheese. The Provençal addition of fresh lavender (use only culinary varieties), draws inspiration from a recipe by Patricia Wells.

MAKES 8 SERVINGS

Summer, Autumn

3 pounds assorted fruits or a single type
1 cup berries or Concord red grapes
¼ cup honey, warmed
1 or more sprigs lavender (optional)
⅓ cup muscat or other dessert wine

Yogurt Cheese (recipe follows) or other
    mild cheese such as *fromage blanc*,
    ricotta, or goat cheese

Heat a grill to low. Halve and pit or core the fruits. If using apples and pears, quarter them; if using persimmons, peel and slice them. Place the fruits, cut side up, in a shallow baking pan suitable for the grill. Scatter the berries on top, and drizzle with the honey. Crush the buds of a lavender sprig over the fruits, and pour the wine over all.

Place the pan on the grill rack and roast, basting occasionally with the pan juices, until the fruits are tender and browned, about 45 minutes. (Or bake in a 375 degree oven for 30 to 40 minutes, then, if desired, place under a hot broiler to brown the fruit.) Transfer the fruit to a platter and top with additional crushed lavender buds. Accompany each serving with a dollop of cheese.

YOGURT CHEESE: Use 2 cups whole-milk or low-fat plain yogurt. Line a fine mesh sieve with a double thickness of cheesecloth, allowing the ends to overhang the rim, and set the sieve over a deep bowl. Spoon the yogurt into the sieve, cover with the ends of a cheesecloth, and refrigerate for at least 6 hours or up to overnight to drain the whey.

CHEF'S TIP: Chef-owner Josiah Citrin of Mélisse freezes Concord grape juice in small containers to use in game sauces and granitas. Cook the grapes briefly with a little sugar, strain through a fine-mesh sieve, pressing against the pulp with the back of a spoon, and freeze.

An Apple Tasting

One autumn, my friend Angela Hunter, a former pastry chef, and I did a tasting of some of the intriguing old apple varieties available from Mike Cirone and Barbara and Bill Spencer at the Santa Monica Farmers' Market. We first noticed that apple skins run the gamut from translucent to opaque and from matte to naturally shiny. We tasted the apples raw and baked unadorned—resulting in Baked Applesauce (page 182)—and were amazed by the transformations that occurred in the oven. With some varieties, the skins clung to the meat; others lifted off in one piece or exploded off the apple. Some turned bitter, others developed deeper apple flavor. Baked textures ranged from fluffy to dissolving and from shapely to hard and dry.

This list is divided subjectively into dessert (the term once used to describe fruit served *au naturel* at meal's end) and culinary apples that show better with cooking, although some are delicious both ways. Their approximate dates of introduction are included for context. We by no means covered the dozens of varieties at the market, a fraction of the more than thousands of existing apple cultivars. Other market treasures include nectarlike Fuji dessert apples (a mid-twentieth-century cross between eighteenth-century Ralls Janet and Red Delicious) from Ha's Orchard in Tehachapi; fresh Granny Smiths (dating from 1868), raw or cooked, that are worlds away from their supermarket counterparts; crisp, sweet-tart Pink Ladies (1970s) from Pudwill's; Lady Williams (1960s) from Sherrill Orchards; and sweet Mutsu apples (1930s) from Briar Patch and Penryn Orchard.

Some apple varieties improve after harvest, but others have a fairly short shelf life and quickly turn mealy or develop off flavors, so ask the farmers. Surprisingly, apples don't hold well at room temperature. To delay deterioration (senescence), store apples uncovered in the refrigerator.

DESSERT APPLES

Braeburn (1952)
Muted red and green
Raw: crisp, tart–sweet, juicy
Cooked: firm texture, loses some complexity

Criterion (1973)
Yellow to orange
Raw: crisp, very juicy, complex
Cooked: lemon yellow flesh, loses complexity, mildly tart

Empire (1966)
Deep red with green to lighter red
Raw: sweet-tart, juicy, crisp
Cooked: skin exploded off, creamy white, soft, dissolving flesh; would mix nicely with other apples

Golden (1914)
Pale greenish yellow to yellow, freckled
Raw: sweet, floral, moderately crisp, (fresh farmers' market Goldens are not mealy!)
Cooked: skin detached, sweet, simple applesauce-like flavor and texture; would add sweetness and texture to other apples

**Golden Russet
(commercial by early 1800s)**
Small to medium, deep golden
russeting with orange blush
Raw: dense, yellow flesh,
exceptional sweet-tart nectar
Cooked: skin detached, flesh
fluffy, bright, tart cider qualities
with sweet notes; good for pie

Jonagold (1968)
Red and green stripe
Raw: juicy, simple sweet-tart;
good lunchbox apple
Cooked: insipid

Northern Spy (1800)
Freckled orange-red with green
undertones
Raw: tart, juicy, crisp, pleasing
dessert apple
Cooked: skin popped off in
one piece, golden yellow flesh
holds shape; good baking and
eating apple

CULINARY APPLES

Arkansas Black (1870)
Black-red
Raw: aromatic, tart, deep apple
flavor, slightly astringent
Cooked: golden, semifirm flesh,
slightly astringent skin

Belle de Boskoop (1856)
Russeted golden orange
Raw: very tart, wine tones,
pronounced apple flavors, juicy
yet feels dry in the mouth
Cooked: skin adhered, but
unpleasant taste; flesh rich gold
with firm, almost crisp texture

Calville Blanc d'Hiver (1627)
Pippinlike green with starburst
russet at stem
Raw: unusual texture, neither
crisp nor mealy
Cooked: greenish flesh with
improved texture, skin intense,
hints of geosmin and tannin

Cox's Orange (early 1800s)
Green but can have lots of red
by late season
Raw: surprisingly complex,
undercurrent of sweetness
Cooked: honey scent, green-
yellow flesh, softer than Golden
Russet but holds shape, good
baking and eating apple

Pink Pearl (California, 1944)
Yellow with pink undertones
Raw: bright pink flesh, crisp,
slightly astringent, sweet-tart
Cooked: pink, semifirm flesh,
tart with berry notes; lovely
for open-faced pastries or pink
applesauce

**Spitzenberg (late 1700s,
Thomas Jefferson's favorite)**
Muted light red and green striated
Raw: flavorful, complex, crisp,
sweet-tart
Cooked: warm caramel flesh, best
sugar-acid balance, moist, soft
texture, deep apple flavor

Winesap (1817)
Wine red, green tinged
Raw: tough skin, rugged texture
and taste
Cooked: slightly pink-tinged
flesh, good sweet-tart balance,
applesauce qualities similar
to Golden but with more
complexity, bitter skin

Baked Applesauce

Baking apples in their skins concentrates flavors and yields an intense pure-apple applesauce, delicious as is or enhanced with an herb, spice, and/or wine or spirit. And there's no peeling, slicing, standing over the pot, or food processor or food mill to wash. You can also roast red or green Bartlett, D'Anjou, and Bosc pears from Cirone Farms or Penryn Orchard this way.

MAKES ABOUT 3 CUPS

Autumn

3 pounds (8 or 9) tart apples such as Spitzenberg or Winesap

A few sprigs thyme (optional)

2 to 3 tablespoons water, fresh lemon juice, Calvados, hard cider, or dessert wine

Ground cinnamon or nutmeg (optional)

Preheat oven to 375 degrees. Cut the apples in half vertically and core them. Place the halves, cut side down, in 1 or more large shallow baking pans, spacing them 1 to 2 inches apart. Scatter the thyme among the apples. Cover the pan tightly with aluminum foil.

Bake the apples until tender, about 30 minutes. When cool enough to handle, slip the fruits from their skins back into the pan, scraping any pulp from the peels. Discard the skins and thyme. Mash the apples with a fork, stirring in a bit of water to help scrape up any brown bits in the pan and to lighten the texture of the applesauce. Season to taste with cinnamon or nutmeg, if desired. Serve the applesauce warm, room temperature, or cold.

Slow-Baked Quince with Honey and Cognac

Long, slow baking caramelizes this hard, fuzzy-skinned, astringent pome fruit to russet tenderness in this unusual autumn dessert I learned from my Aunt Dahlia. As with the popular Spanish tapa of quince paste and sheep's milk cheese, wedges of salty cheese mellow the fruit's assertive tartness. The dish is beautiful made with small, young, golden-skinned Pineapple quince from Cirone Farms, Nicholas Orchard, and Circle C. Without the cheese, the quinces may be used as a savory accompaniment to ham or roasted game birds. An oyster knife is the ideal tool for scooping out the core from the quince's hard surface, though a sharp paring knife or grapefruit spoon will also work.

MAKES 8 TO 10 SERVINGS

Autumn

- ⅓ cup raisins
- ⅓ cup cognac
- 2 pounds quinces, preferably 4 or 5 small
- 8 to 10 whole cloves
- 8 to 10 teaspoons honey
- ⅓ cup finely chopped walnuts
- 2 tablespoons water
- ½ pound aged sheep's milk cheese such as Rinconada Dairy pozo tomme or Manchego, cut into wedges

Plump the raisins in the cognac for at least 2 hours or up to overnight. Drain them, reserving the liquid, then chop. Preheat oven to 325 degrees. Scrub the quinces to remove the fuzz, but do not peel. If using small quinces, cut in half crosswise, and carefully cut out the core from each half (the cut surfaces will brown a bit; don't worry). For large quinces, cut each fruit into several wedges and scoop out the core from each wedge. Trim rounded ends of quince halves so they stand level, and place cut side up in a shallow 3-quart baking dish. Fill the cavity in each half or wedge with 1 clove, 1 teaspoon honey, 1 generous teaspoon chopped raisins, and a few walnut pieces. Pour 1 to 2 teaspoons of the reserved cognac into each quince, and pour the remaining cognac into the baking dish. Add the water to the dish and seal tightly with aluminum foil.

Bake the quinces until tender, 30 to 35 minutes. They will still be pale yellow at this point. Baste with the pan juices and add a little water if the pan seems dry. Reseal and continue baking, basting occasionally and adding water as necessary, until the quinces have turned a deep rosy gold and are very tender and the syrup is thick, about 1½ hours more. Serve warm with a drizzle of the pan syrup and a wedge of cheese. This dish may be made up to 6 hours ahead, held at room temperature, and then reheated, covered, in a 300-degree oven for about 10 minutes.

Meyer Lemon Sundae with Cara Caras and Tangelos

Inspired by Marcella Hazan's simple recipe for lemon ice cream, I made a version with Meyer lemons, which perfectly showcases the fruit's floral perfume and haunting flavor. Topped with pink Cara Cara navel oranges, deep orange tangelos, cool, green Persian mint, and a little *frissante* dessert wine and served with Pistachio Shortbread Cookies (page 190), these beautiful sundaes make a refreshing finish to a rich winter meal.

MAKES 6 TO 8 SERVINGS

Winter, Spring

3 Meyer lemons

1½ cups water

1 cup sugar

⅔ cup heavy cream, cold from the refrigerator

3 Cara Cara oranges

4 tangelos

Handful of fresh Persian mint leaves, torn

Raspberries for serving

1½ to 2 cups Moscato d'Asti

Use a Microplane grater to finely grate the zest from the lemons; you should have 3 to 4 tablespoons. Juice the lemons; you should have ⅔ cup juice. In a small pot, stir together the water, sugar, and lemon zest and juice. Bring to a boil over medium heat, stirring until the sugar dissolves, and boil for 2 minutes. Chill the syrup thoroughly.

Stir the cream into the lemon mixture and freeze in an ice cream maker according to the manufacturer's instructions. To assemble the sundaes, use a zester to remove the zest from the tangelos in long, thin strands and reserve. Peel and segment the oranges and tangelos into a bowl (page 24), then squeeze the juice from their membranes over the segments. Scoop the ice cream into bowls, spoon the citrus segments and their juice over and around the ice cream, and top with the tangelo zest, mint, and a few raspberries. Pour ¼ cup Moscato d'Asti into each bowl.

Ultimate-Pucker Lemon Bars

Most lemon bars just aren't lemony enough, but this one is. I got the recipe many years ago from my college roommate, whose mother got it from her Avon lady, and now my daughter Rebecca is our family's official lemon bar baker. The crust is incredibly easy: just mix and press into the pan. In winter and spring, try the tantalizing tangelo and Meyer lemon variations. Tom Brezinski, who works with San Diego citrus grower Bob Polito and loves to cook, helped me solve the problem of capturing subtle orange and tangelo flavors in baked goods: add a little Meyer lemon juice. The orange-lemon hybrid gently ups the acid and heightens the mandarin notes. For more on citrus, see page 98.

**MAKES TWENTY-FOUR
2-BY-2½-INCH BARS**

**Evergreen, Winter,
Spring**

FOR THE CRUST

½ cup powdered sugar

2 cups flour

¼ teaspoon salt

1 cup (½ pound) cold unsalted butter, cut
　　into ½-inch pieces

FOR THE FILLING

4 eggs

2 cups granulated sugar

½ cup Eureka lemon juice

¼ cup flour

Preheat oven to 350 degrees. To make the crust, in a bowl, stir together the flour, powdered sugar, and salt. Add the butter and cut it in with your fingertips or a pastry blender until the mixture resembles coarse cornmeal. Gently pat the mixture into the bottom and up the sides of a 9-by-13-inch baking pan. Bake until just lightly golden, 20 to 25 minutes.

Meanwhile, make the filling. In a bowl, whisk together the eggs, granulated sugar, lemon juice, and flour until thoroughly blended, about 1 minute.

Pour the filling over the partially baked crust. Continue to bake until the filling is set and crust is golden, 15 to 20 minutes. Let cool completely on a rack before cutting into bars.

TANGELO BARS VARIATION: Use ½ cup tangelo juice (about 2 tangelos) in place of the lemon juice, and add the grated zest of 2 tangelos, ¼ cup Meyer lemon juice, and 1 tablespoon Grand Marnier. Reduce the granulated sugar to 1½ cups.

MEYER LEMON BARS VARIATION: Use ½ cup Meyer lemon juice (about 2 lemons) in place of the Eureka lemon juice, and add the grated zest of 2 Meyer lemons. Reduce the granulated sugar to 1½ cups.

Sapote Brûlée

In the past, I didn't have a clue what to do with the round, green Vernon and Lemon–Gold sapotes and the heart-shaped Bays cherimoyas at Bill and Delia Coleman's stand. But those days are over. These custardlike South American natives, with hints of pineapple, citrus, and banana, are creamy rich as they are, or are easily adorned with sugar, lime, and California macadamia nuts and seared on top like a crème brûlée. Peaches and almonds or pears and walnuts are also lovely prepared this way.

MAKES 6 SERVINGS

Winter, Spring

6 lime-sized or 3 large sapotes

1 to 2 tablespoons raw or dark brown sugar

¼ cup chopped macadamia nuts

3 Mexican limes, cut in half, or 1 Persian lime, cut into 6 wedges

Cut the sapotes in half through the stem end and remove the seeds. Sprinkle the cut surfaces with the sugar and nuts. Use a kitchen torch, or slip under a preheated broiler close to the heat source, until the sugar is bubbly, 30 to 60 seconds. Serve at once with the limes. Or, the fruits may be prepared up to 2 hours ahead and served at room temperature.

CHERIMOYA VARIATION: Cut 1 large or 2 small cherimoyas (about 1½ pounds total) in half vertically. Scoop out the seeds and cut each half into 3 wedges. Prepare as directed for sapotes.

HOW TO CHOOSE CHERIMOYAS: Skin with large thumbprint faceting (protuberances) indicates maturity, says Bill Coleman. A ripe cherimoya will have the soft give of a ripe avocado or peach. Keep underripe fruits on the counter until ripe, then refrigerate for up to 3 days.

HOW TO CHOOSE SAPOTES: Harvesting sapotes is a tricky art, according to farmer Bill Coleman. They are fragile when ripe, but if picked too "green" (immature), they will never soften, just shrivel. Look for matte-finish, smooth, firm but not hard fruits. Store on the counter for 2 to 5 days until they give slightly and turn lightly golden (Lemon-Golds turn more yellow than Vernons). Refrigerate ripe fruits for up to 3 days.

Macadamias, the Cadillac of Nuts

Jim Russell's raw macadamia nuts are uncommonly sweet. That's because he and wife Barbara (BJ) grow *Macadamia tetraphylla,* which have more natural sugars and less oil than the more commonly cultivated *M. integrifolia*. The high sugar content of *M. tetraphylla* makes them less desirable for commercial roasting and frying, but deliciously sweet in their natural state.

Jim and BJ started two hundred trees from seeds in Fallbrook in 1978, painstakingly grafting them and nurturing the orchard to an annual production of sixteen thousand pounds of nuts. Jim boasts that their raw macadamia nuts keep nine months on the counter and five years in the freezer. He is a font of macadamia minutiae: Did you know the Australian native trees were first planted in California in 1879, eleven years before they were taken to Hawaii? The Russells sell macadamias shelled (macs are incredibly difficult to crack) whole and chopped and nut meal at the market and by mail order.

More Exotics at the Market

The dragon fruit, aptly named for its vivid magenta, scalelike skin and pink flesh dotted through with tiny black seeds, is another of the Coleman family's exotic fruit offerings (ask Bill about Surinam cherries, and some of the other 180 crops on his growing certificate). Popular in Asia and known in Central America as the pithaya, this relative of the prickly pear is often made into a refreshing agua fresca. It has a mild, sweet flavor and when contrasted with oranges or mandarins, makes a pretty winter fruit salad to serve after lunch or a simple family supper. Choose dragon fruits with bright, unblemished skin and with the give of a ripe avocado. To peel them, cut into wedges, cut the flesh away from the peel as you would a melon wedge, and then cut into bite-sized pieces.

The Colemans also grow sweet-tart passion fruits. In spring and summer, Nicholas Peter, chef-owner of the Little Door restaurant and Little Next Door café and market, orders sixty pounds at a time to make a simple sauce to serve with coconut cheesecake. Look for wrinkled, but still plump, fruits. To make the sauce, cut the fruits in half, scoop out the pulp and seeds, and cook over low heat for 30 to 45 minutes, skimming the foam as it rises, then strain the sauce. The sauce can be frozen or canned.

Dried Plum and Toasted Almond Cream Tart

Mixed dried plums (not prunes) create a stained-glass effect of reds, pinks, and burgundies in this elegant autumn or winter tart. Betty and Truman Kennedy of Harvest Pride in Dinuba grow and sun-dry interesting heirloom fruits, including Rosemary, Sweet Reedley Wrinkled, Sweetheart, and Angelina plums and Pluots, a plum-apricot cross. They pick fully ripe fruits for the best flavor and use a tiny amount of sulfur to keep them moist and plump (but also dry some without sulfur). Dried in the valley's hot, dry breezes on century-old wooden grape trays, the fruits are sold within the year, so you're never buying old goods. This tart has a press-in cookie-type crust. Infusing the cream with toasted almonds perfumes the custard filling.

MAKES 12 SERVINGS

Autumn, Winter

½ pound mixed dried plums and Pluots, quartered

⅓ cup cognac

½ cup boiling water

½ cup whole raw almonds, toasted (page 25) and finely chopped or coarsely ground

1½ cups plus 2 tablespoons heavy cream

5 tablespoons sugar

1¼ cups flour

¼ teaspoon salt

½ cup plus 1 tablespoon (9 tablespoons) unsalted butter, cut into ½-inch cubes

3 egg yolks

Place the fruits in a bowl and pour in the cognac and boiling water. Cover and allow to plump for at least 4 hours or up to overnight.

Measure out 3 tablespoons of the nuts and reserve. Put the remaining almonds, 1½ cups of the cream, and 3 tablespoons of the sugar in a pot over medium-low heat. Heat, stirring occasionally, until the cream just comes to a boil. Remove from the heat, cover partially, and let steep for 15 minutes. Strain through a fine-mesh sieve, pressing on the almonds to extract all the cream and then discard the almonds. Allow the almond cream to cool to lukewarm. In a large bowl, whisk the egg yolks until blended. Gradually whisk the almond cream into the yolks.

Preheat oven to 375 degrees. In a bowl, stir together the flour, the remaining 2 tablespoons sugar, and salt with a fork. Add the butter and cut it in with your fingers or a pastry blender until the mixture is crumbly. Stir in the remaining 2 tablespoons cream. The dough will be very crumbly. Gather it together and place in a deep 9-inch tart pan with a removable bottom. Pat the dough evenly along the bottom and sides of the pan, being careful that it is not too thick where the sides and the bottom meet. The dough may not reach to the rim of the pan. If the dough feels dry, the warmth of your hands will bring it together; if it feels sticky, dust your hands with flour as you pat. Chill for 15 minutes.

Line the tart shell with parchment paper or paper coffee filters. Fill with pie weights, dried beans, or raw rice. Bake until the edges of the shell start to color, about 15 minutes. Remove the weights and parchment, and use a large spoon or the bottom of a measuring cup to gently smooth the bottom and sides of the shell, sealing any cracks. Return the pan to the oven and bake until the bottom is a deep gold, about 20 minutes. Let cool briefly on a rack. Reduce the oven temperature to 325 degrees.

Sprinkle the reserved almonds evenly over the tart shell and place on a baking sheet. Drain the plums, gently squeezing out any excess liquid, and reserve the liquid. Scatter the plums evenly over the crust, and pour the almond cream evenly over the plums. Bake until the filling is set, 28 to 30 minutes. Let cool on the rack.

In a small pan, cook the plum soaking liquid over medium-low heat until reduced to 2 to 3 tablespoons thick syrup, about 10 minutes. Brush the syrup lightly over the cooled tart to glaze it.

Harvesting Almonds

"Come fall, we don't just go pick almonds and dry them," explains Betty Kennedy, whose husband's family has been farming since the mid-nineteenth century. "We watch the limbs. First they start to get heavy and droop. When they start to rise again, that's our sign that the nuts inside their shells are starting to dry a little and are ready. We wait until the limbs are about halfway back up before we knock the trees [with mauls, rubber-coated mallets] to harvest the nuts."

"The most beautiful time of year in the orchard is during the bloom in late January and February," says confectioner and former architect Rusty Hall, who dry-farms (using little irrigation) a ninety-year-old orchard in Paso Robles. "But the most satisfying moment is the harvest. My crew and I roll tarps out under the trees, 'knock' the trees, and the nuts tumble down onto the tarps. It's the most satisfying sound, the sound of almonds hitting the tarps and our shoulders—like pennies from heaven. Or, in the case of almonds, nickels from heaven."

Pistachio Shortbread Cookies

Pastry chef Kimberley Boyce helped develop this elegant slice-and-bake cookie. Farmers are always looking for ways to use every last bit of a crop, and Santa Barbara Pistachio Company packages the pistachio meal that is a by-product of its oil production. Owner Gail Zannon advises using up to ¼ cup meal per 1 cup flour in recipes for flavor, richness, and texture. If you don't have pistachio meal, grind ½ cup raw pistachios with 1 tablespoon sugar and measure out the correct quantity.

MAKES 20 TO 24 COOKIES

Evergreen

½ cup plus 2 tablespoons raw pistachios
1 cup flour
½ teaspoon salt
½ cup (8 tablespoons) unsalted butter, softened

½ cup powdered sugar, sifted
¼ cup pistachio meal
1 egg, lightly beaten

Set aside 24 whole pistachios. Finely chop the remaining pistachios. Sift together the flour and salt and set aside. Using an electric mixer, cream together the butter and sugar on high speed until blended, about 3 minutes. Add the pistachio meal and beat until well blended and creamy, 1 to 2 minutes more. On low speed, beat in the flour mixture until a stiff, slightly sticky dough forms.

Scrape the dough onto a lightly floured piece of parchment or waxed paper, and shape into a log 8½ inches long and 1¾ inches in diameter, using the paper to help you (think sushi rolls). Press firmly so there are no cracks in the dough. Even through the paper, the heat of your hands will help bring the dough together. Brush all sides of the log, but not the ends, with the egg. Lay out 2 sheets of plastic wrap, and sprinkle the chopped pistachios across the middle of 1 sheet. Place the dough log on the pistachios, and roll to coat evenly on all sides. Transfer the log to the clean sheet, wrap, and chill for at least 1 hour or up to 3 days. The log can be frozen for up to 2 weeks; thaw to slice.

Preheat oven to 350 degrees. Remove the dough from the refrigerator 5 to 10 minutes before slicing so it softens slightly. Cut into ⅜-inch-thick slices, place on an ungreased baking sheet 1 inch apart, and press 1 reserved whole pistachio in the center of each cookie. Bake until lightly golden and slightly puffed, about 16 minutes, rotating the pan 180 degrees halfway through the baking time to ensure evenness. Let cool on the pan for 5 minutes, then transfer to a rack to cool.

CHEF'S TIP: After the fall harvest, the Zannons bring soft-shelled, fresh pistachios, known rather redundantly as green, that is, young, pistachios. Chef-owner Joe Miller of Joe's Restaurant likes their "slightly gelatinous" texture and uses a truffle slicer to grate day-old nuts, shell and all, over salads and almond *panna cotta*. Chef-owner Mark Peel of Campanile restaurant uses "green" pistachios in an autumn pesto.

Holiday Persimmon Pudding

This California-style holiday pudding is rich with naturally spicy, ripe Hachiya persimmons, plump golden raisins, and meaty walnuts from local farmers such as Scott Peacock and Elmer Lehman. I got the original recipe for this dessert years ago from my neighbor Laurie Malley. Serve the pudding warm with the heavy cream that Organic Pastures Dairy brings to market from the San Joaquin Valley.

MAKES 6 TO 8 SERVINGS

Autumn

2 tablespoons unsalted butter, melted

1⅓ cups flour

¾ cup sugar

1 teaspoon baking soda

½ teaspoon baking powder

½ teaspoon salt

¾ teaspoon ground cinnamon

¼ teaspoon ground ginger

¼ teaspoon ground nutmeg

1 egg

¾ cup whole milk

2 to 3 Hachiya persimmons, cored but not peeled and mashed or pureed to a pulp (2 cups pulp)

½ cup golden raisins, coarsely chopped

½ cup chopped walnuts (optional)

Heavy cream for serving

Preheat oven to 350 degrees. Brush a shallow 2-quart baking dish with 1 tablespoon of the butter. In a medium bowl, sift together the flour, sugar, baking soda, baking powder, salt, and spices. In a large bowl, whisk together the egg, the remaining 1 tablespoon butter, and the milk. Stir the dry ingredients into the wet ingredients until well blended. Stir in the persimmon pulp, raisins, and nuts. Pour into the prepared baking dish, and place the dish on a baking sheet.

Bake the pudding until it is set and lightly puffed, the edges are crisped, and a toothpick inserted in the center comes out clean, 35 to 40 minutes. If a uniformly delicate texture is desired, bake the pudding in a water bath (put the filled baking dish in a large roasting pan, and add hot water to reach halfway up the sides of the dish). Let the pudding cool slightly (it will fall in the center) before serving. It may be made a day ahead and reheated in a 350-degree oven until hot, about 15 minutes. Spoon into dishes, and pour a little cream over each serving.

COOK'S TIP: For a simple autumn or winter treat, quarter firm-ripe Hachiya or Tamopan persimmons and freeze. Pull them out 30 minutes before serving time to thaw partially, then serve with a squeeze of lemon and a sprinkle of crushed toasted black peppercorns (page 34). They will have a cold, custardy texture, like a spicy persimmon ice cream or *semifreddo*.

Classic Pumpkin Pie

This is the real thing. Pumpkins have been baked with spices and cream at least since the seventeenth century, and in a crust since the end of the eighteenth. Use any variety of roasted meaty, slightly sweet winter squash—which pumpkins are—for a pie with a deep, full flavor. For more on pumpkins, see page 69. The pie can be made a day ahead, a big help at holiday time.

MAKES 8 SERVINGS

Autumn

FOR THE CRUST

1½ cups flour

Generous ¼ teaspoon salt

2½ teaspoons granulated sugar

6 tablespoons cold unsalted butter, cut into ½-inch pieces

3 tablespoons shortening, chilled

⅓ to ½ cup ice water

FOR THE FILLING

2 eggs

2 cups roasted pumpkin or other winter squash puree (page 25)

¾ cup whole milk

¾ cup heavy cream

1 cup packed dark brown sugar

1 teaspoon ground cinnamon

¾ teaspoon ground ginger

¼ teaspoon ground nutmeg

1 cup heavy cream, whipped to soft peaks

To make the crust, in a large bowl, stir together the flour, salt, and granulated sugar with a fork. Toss the butter pieces with the flour mixture and chill for 10 minutes in the freezer. Using your fingertips or a pastry blender, cut in the butter until the dough is the texture of coarse meal with some chunks of butter flattened but still whole. When dough is almost to this point, work in the shortening with fingertips or a pastry blender. Using the fork, stir in the ice water 1 to 2 tablespoons at a time just until a piece of dough holds together when pressed between your fingertips. Gather the dough into a ball, wrap in plastic, press into a disk, and chill for 15 to 30 minutes.

On a lightly floured surface, roll out the dough into a round ⅛ to ¼ inch thick. Transfer the dough to a 9-inch glass pie dish or perforated metal pie pan, guiding the dough downward to hug the sides of the pan. Use scissors to trim the dough, leaving a ¾-inch overhang. Fold the overhang under to create a rim, then use the side of your index finger and thumb and the index finger of your other hand to flute the edge of the dough. Chill the crust until ready to fill. It may be made a day ahead and refrigerated; remove it from the refrigerator when you begin to make the filling.

Preheat oven to 425 degrees. To make the filling, in a large bowl, whisk together the eggs until blended. Add the pumpkin, milk, cream, brown sugar, and spices and whisk until thoroughly mixed. Pour the filling into the prepared crust. (If there is too much filling, and it threatens to run over the sides, reserve some until the pie has baked for 5 to 10 minutes, then add it.) Bake on the lowest oven rack for 15 minutes. Reduce the heat to 350 degrees and continue to bake until the filling is still slightly jiggly in the center, 35 to 45 minutes longer. Let cool completely on a rack before serving. The pie can be made a day ahead and refrigerated. Remove from the refrigerator 1 hour before serving. Serve with whipped cream.

COOK'S TIPS FOR CRISP, FLAKY CRUSTS

- For an extra-flaky crust, use all shortening or lard.
- For a more meltingly tender, or "short," crust, use all butter.
- Chill pastry ingredients and the bowl before making the dough.
- Use cool fingertips, not warm hands, or a pastry blender to work in the butter.
- Add only enough ice water for the dough barely to adhere. It will look dry, but will come together when pressed into a disk with warm palms and then chilled.
- Use a light touch when rolling dough, loosen frequently from the work surface with a large offset spatula, and give the dough a quarter-turn and flip it over now and again as you work.
- A glass pie dish or perforated metal pie pan will help the bottom of the crust brown.

Although you will find some of these crops year-round at the Santa Monica Farmers' Market, they are listed here according to their peak season(s) in California. Those that show up for a very brief but inexact season (for example cardoons might be late winter or early spring) are listed in more than one season. As usual, check with the farmer for availability.

WINTER
Gwen avocados
Brussels sprouts
Cabbage
Cardoons
Cauliflower (baby)
Cavolo nero (Tuscan kale)
Celery root
Cherimoyas
Citrus
   Grapefruits
   Meiwa and Nagami kumquats
   Meyer lemons
   Mandarins
   Blood oranges
   Washington navels
   Pummelos
   Tangelos
Dates
Dragon fruits
Escarole
Fennel
Kohlrabies
Leeks (baby)
Mushrooms
   Black trumpet
   Chanterelle
   Yellow-footed chanterelle
Nettles
Parsnips
Treviso radicchio
Radishes

Rutabagas
Sapotes
Sorrel
Sweet potatoes
Swiss chard
Turnips
Winter squash

SPRING
Green almonds
Artichokes
Arugula flowers
Asparagus
Fuerte, Gwen, and
   Pinkerton avocados
Beets
Sprouting broccoli
Cabbage
Cardoons
Carrots
Cherimoyas
Citrus
   Grapefruits
   Meiwa and Nagami kumquats
   Meyer lemons
   Pink Eureka lemons
   Bearss limes
   Mandarins
   Blood oranges
   Cara Cara navel oranges
   Pummelos
   Tangelos

Eggs
Fava beans
Fennel
Fiddlehead ferns
Green garlic
Grape leaves
Herbs (dill, leek-chives, Italian
   parsley, tarragon, mint)
Lettuce
Mushrooms
   Yellow-footed chanterelle
   Hedgehog
   Morel
   Porcini
Nettles
Spring onions
Parsnips
Passion fruits
English peas
Pea shoots
New potatoes
Treviso radicchio
Radishes
Ramps
Rapini
Romanesco
Sapotes
Snap peas
Sorrel
Strawberries
Watercress

SUMMER

Amaranth
Apricots
Arugula
Asian pears
Hass, Lamb Hass, and Reed
  avocados
Bay leaves
Shell beans
Berries
Cherries
Green chickpeas
Citrus
  Nagami kumquats
  Eureka lemons
  Bearss limes
  Key (Mexican) limes
  Valencia oranges
Corn
Cucumbers
Red currants
Edamame
Eggplants
Figs
Fraises des bois
Grapes
Grape leaves
Herbs (basil, wild fennel, lemon
  verbena, summer savory)
Lamb's quarters
Leeks
Mangoes
Melons
Nectarines
Okra
Maui- and Walla Walla–type onions
Passion fruits
Peaches
Peanuts
Peppers
Plums
New potatoes
Purslane
Radicchio

Shallots
Snap beans
Snap peas
Bloomsdale spinach
Squash blossoms
Summer squash
Swiss chard
Tomatoes

FALL

Apples
Wild arugula
Asian pears
Hass and Reed avocados
Bay leaves
Shell and dried beans
Snap beans
Beets
Sprouting broccoli
Brussels sprouts
Celery root
Citrus
  Buddha's hand
  Key (Mexican) limes
Corn
Crosnes
Red currants
New-harvest dates
New-harvest dried fruits
Eggplants
Autumn Royale and Concord grapes
Kiwifruits
Mangoes
Mushrooms
  Chanterelle
  Crimini
  Porcini
Mustard greens
New-harvest nuts
Okra
Olives
Indian Blood peaches
Pears
Snap peas

Peppers
Fuyu and Hachiya persimmons
Pomegranates
Quinces
Treviso radicchio
Rapini
Rutabagas
Bloomsdale spinach
Sweet potatoes
Tomatillos
Late-harvest tromboncino squash
Winter squash

Locations, Days, and Hours

WEDNESDAY
8:30 am to 1:30 pm
Second Street at Arizona
Manager: Laura Avery

SATURDAY
8:30 am to 1:00 pm
Third Street at Arizona
Manager: Mort Bernstein

SATURDAY—PICO
8:00 am to 1:00 pm
Virginia Avenue Park
Pico/Cloverfield
Manager: Ted Galvan

SUNDAY—MAIN STREET
9:30 am to 1:00 pm
2640 Main Street at Ocean Park Boulevard
Manager: Jodi Low

OFFICE
200 Santa Monica Pier
Santa Monica, California 90401
Telephone 310.458.8712
Fax 310.393.1279

www.farmersmarket.santa-monica.org

This is a list of all the growers at all the Santa Monica markets, from beekeepers to flower farmers, as of fall 2006. Each entry, when possible, includes the farm name, location, number of acres, number of years farming, primary crop(s), and Web site or contact information for mail order. Growers who are certified organic are indicated with an asterisk.

Adams Olive Ranch
Lindsay, CA
55 acres
53 years farming
Olives
www.adamsoliveranch.com

Anjin II
Port Hueneme, CA
20 years fishing
Seafood

Aroma Orchids
Rowland Heights, CA
4 acres
10 years farming
Orchids

David Avila
Hanford, CA
65 acres
38 years farming
Dried fruits, nuts

Jack Balderama
Orosi, CA
16 acres
27 years farming
Fruits, grapes

Ballard Ranch
Santa Ynez, CA
2.25 acres
10 years farming
Lavender

Barbagelata
Linden, CA
40 acres
89 years farming
Cherries

Basiltops*
Cardiff-by-the-Sea, CA
1 acre
28 years farming
Pesto
www.basiltops.com

Bautista Family Organic
Date Ranch*
Mecca, CA
5 acres
6 years farming
Dates

Bautista Ranch
Stockton, CA
39 acres
50 years farming
Cherries

Bee Canyon Ranch
Whittier, CA
40 years farming
Honey

Bernard Ranches
Riverside, CA
40 acres
26 years farming
Citrus

Betty B's
Ramona, CA
12 acres
35 years farming
Citrus

Beylik Farms
Fillmore, CA
20 acres
33 years farming
Hydroponic tomatoes
www.beylikfarms.com

Arria Brasseur
Santa Barbara, CA
10 acres
10 years farming
Lavender

Briar Patch
Kingsburg, CA
43 acres
20 years farming
Asian pears, vegetables

Burkart Farms*
Dinuba, CA
105 acres
40 years farming
Stone fruits, grapes

Longino Cabral
Ontario, CA
6 acres
30 years farming
Vegetables, strawberries

California Organic Fruit*
De Luz, CA
15 acres
5 years farming
Citrus

Cal-Pecan
Clovis, CA
80 acres
30 years farming
Pecans

Miguel Cervantes
Riverside, CA
10 acres
10 years farming
Vegetables

Chandler Farms
Sanger, CA
25 acres
15 years farming
Grapes, walnuts

Circle C Ranch*
Lake Hughes, CA
25 acres
20 years farming
Cherries, mulberries

Cirone Farms
San Luis Obispo, CA
55 acres
23 years farming
Apricots, apples, pears

Clearwater Farms
Delano, CA
11 years farming
Mushrooms

Coastal Farms
Santa Paula, CA
15 acres
25 years farming
Vegetables

Coleman Family Farm
Carpinteria, CA
10 acres
23 years farming
Vegetables, herbs,
tropical fruits

Cosgrove Cymbidium
Leucadia, CA
1 acre
34 years farming
Orchids
www.coscymcoorchids.com

Davall Date Gardens
Indio, CA
20 acres
30 years farming
Dates

Maria Durazo
South Gate, CA
1 acre
1 year farming
Sprouts

David Eakin
Riverside, CA
18 acres
50 years farming
Citrus

Energy Bee Farm
Los Angeles, CA
32 years farming
Honey

Etheridge Farms
Dinuba, CA
35 acres
31 years farming
Tree fruits

Fair Hills Farm★
Paso Robles, CA
45 acres
15 years farming
Apples

Fairview Gardens★
Goleta, CA
12 acres
25 years farming
Vegetables
www.fairviewgardens.org

Farmstand West
Escondido, CA
55 acres
100 years farming
Fruits, vegetables

Fitzgerald's Premium Ripe
Tree Fruit
Reedley, CA
35 acres
33 years farming
Stone fruits

Flora Bella Farm★
Three Rivers, CA
25 acres
53 years farming
Vegetables
www.florabellafarm.net

Flying Disc
Thermal, CA
10 acres
34 years farming
Dates

Forcefield
Santa Paula, CA
3 acres
25 years farming
Apricots, water hyacinths

Four Apostles Ranch★
Bermuda Dunes, CA
10 acres
26 years farming
Dates
www.fourapostles.com//
virtualstore/storefront.asp

Fresno Evergreen
Fresno, CA
13 acres
11 years farming
Asian vegetables

Friend's Ranch
Ojai, CA
30 acres
115 years farming
Citrus
www.friendsranches.com

Garcia Organic Farm★
Fallbrook, CA
25 acres
17 years farming
Citrus, avocados

Garden Organics★
Los Angeles, CA
0.5 acre
2 years farming
Garden starts

Gless Ranch
Riverside, CA
1,000 acres
100 years farming
Citrus
www.glessranch.com

Green Farms
Lompoc, CA
Artichokes, asparagus

David Ha★
Tehachapi, CA
120 acres
20 years farming
Apples

Harry's Berries
Oxnard, CA
39 acres
30 years farming
Strawberries, vegetables

Harvest Pride★
Dinuba, CA
20 acres
34 years farming
Dried fruits and nuts

Heritage Garden
Los Angeles, CA
40 acres
26 years faming
Bedding plants

Holy Guaca-Moly
Fallbrook, CA
6 acres
20 years farming
Avocados

Honey Crisp
Reedley, CA
17 acres
35 years farming
Stone fruits
www.honeycrispfarm.com

Honey Pacifica
Long Beach, CA
30 years farming
Honey
www.treepilot.com:2006/
TreePilotClient

Tsugio Imamoto
Moorpark, CA
8 acres
50 years farming
Vegetables

Ipatzi Nursery
Oxnard, CA
7 acres
30 years farming
Bedding plants

It Began in the Garden
Mountain Center, CA
0.5 acre
8 years farming
Potted herbs

Jaime Farms
City of Industry, CA
45 acres
19 years farming
Vegetables

JJ Farming
Santa Maria, CA
15 acres
20 years farming
Vegetables

J.J.'s Lone Daughter Ranch
Bryn Mawr, CA
70 acres
57 years farming
Citrus, avocados,
persimmons

Johna's Orchard★
Tehachapi, CA
60 acres
27 years farming
Apples

Lynn Johnson
El Segundo, CA
20 years farming
Tillandsia (air plants)

K & K Farms
Fresno, CA
40 acres
30 years farming
Stone fruits

Kenter Canyon Farms★
Sun Valley, CA
10 acres
15 years farming
Salad greens, herbs

Jack Kohara
Oxnard, CA
5 acres
30 years farming
Flowers

Kowalke Family Sprouts
Culver City, CA
0.5 acre
20 years farming
Sprouts
kowalke.itgo.com

Ken Lee
Reedley, CA
30 acres
20 years farming
Stone fruits

Elmer Lehman
Fresno, CA
10 acres
65 years farming
Grapes, peaches

William Lewis
Lake View Terrance, CA
35 years farming
Honey

Lily's Eggs★
Santa Barbara, CA
4 acres
20 years farming
Eggs

Lindner Bison
10 years farming
Bison
www.lindnerbison.com

Maggie's Farm★
Agoura, CA
10 acres
25 years farming
Salad greens, herbs

Martinez Farms
Fillmore, CA
40 acres
15 years farming
Vegetables
www.martinezfarms.net

McGrath Family Farms★
Camarillo, CA
30 acres
134 years farming
Vegetables, strawberries

Mike & Sons Egg Ranches
Ontario, CA
2 acres
44 years farming
Eggs

Mill Road Orchard
Paso Robles, CA
70 acres
26 years farming
Apples

Moessner Orchard
Tehachapi, CA
13 acres
26 years farming
Preserves, pickles

Munak Ranch★
Paso Robles, CA
60 acres
30 years farming
Tomatoes, melons

Nakamura Farms★
Oxnard, CA
40 acres
12 years farming
Vegetables, strawberries

Nicholas Orchard
Orange Cove, CA
20 acres
60 years farming
Cherries, grapes, kiwifruits

Ocean Breeze
Carpinteria, CA
30 acres
33 years farming
Flowers

Olson Family Farms★
Kingsburg, CA
800 acres
118 years farming
Stone fruits
www.olsonfamilyfarms.com

Organic Pastures Dairy Co.★
Fresno, CA
400 acres
18 years farming
Raw dairy
www.organicpastures.com

Paso Almonds
Paso Robles, CA
40 acres
20 years farming
Almonds

Peacock Farms
Dinuba, CA
21 acres
60 years farming
Stone fruits, grapes,
vegetables
www.peacockfamilyfarms.
com

Penryn Orchard
Penryn, CA
15 acres
6 years farming
Asian pears, persimmons
www.
penrynorchardspecialties.
com

Polito Family Farms
Valley Center, CA
80 acres
38 years farming
Citrus
www.politofarms.com

Robert Poole
Redlands, CA
3 acres
29 years farming
Blackberries

Daniel Pritchett
Visalia, CA
40 acres
30 years farming
Stone fruits

Pudwill Farm
Nipomo, CA
86 acres
20 years farming
Berries

Ramos Nursery
Whittier, CA
5 acres
15 years farming
Bedding plants

Rancho La Viña
Lompoc, CA
150 acres
48 years farming
Walnuts
www.rancholavina.com

Rancho Mi Familia
Santa Maria, CA
20 acres
40 years farming
Vegetables

Redwood Hill Farm★
Sebastopol, CA
10 acres
17 years farming
Goat's milk cheese
www.redwoodhill.com

Regier Farms
Dinuba, CA
50 acres
33 years farming
Stone fruits, mandarins

Rinconada Dairy★
Santa Margarita, CA
52 acres
8 years farming
Sheep's milk cheese
www.rinconadadairy.com

Rivas Farms
San Marcos, CA
18 acres
18 years farming
Vegetables

Rocky Canyon★
Atascadero, CA
60 acres
16 years farming
Free-range meat, melons,
squash, sweet potatoes

Rodriguez Ranch★
Escondido, CA
40 acres
45 years farming
Flowers, vegetables

Roots Brother Grows★
Van Nuys, CA
2 acres
10 years farming
Lavender

Russell Family Farms
Fallbrook, CA
6 acres
28 years farming
Macadamia nuts
888.549.9126

Rutiz Farms
Arroyo Grande, CA
30 acres
26 years farming
Vegetables, herbs
www.rutizfarms.com

Santa Barbara Pistachio
Ventucopa, CA
380 acres
15 years farming
Pistachios
www.santabarbarapistachios.
com

Scattaglia
Little Rock, CA
800 acres
52 years farming
Stone fruits

Schaner Farms
Valley Center, CA
42 acres
24 years farming
Citrus, alliums

Scott Farms
Dinuba, CA
21 acres
20 years farming
Stone fruits, grapes

Spring Hill Cheese★
Petaluma, CA
320 acres
19 years farming
Cheese
www.springhillcheese.com

Sherrill Orchards
Arvin, CA
58 acres
25 years farming
Pomegranates, apple juice

Skyline Flower Growers
Oxnard, CA
250 acres
55 years farming
Flowers
www.skylineflowers.com

McKay Smith★
Irvine, CA
25 acres
25 years farming
Vegetables and strawberries

Sproutime
Sun Valley, CA
10 acres
25 years farming
Sprouts

Stackhouse Bros.
Hickman, CA
Almonds

Sugar Bush Proteas
Valley Center, CA
18.2 acres
20 years farming
Proteas

Summer Harvest Farms★
Dinuba, CA
30 acres
20 years farming
Stone fruits, grapes

Suncoast Farms
Lompoc, CA
35 years farming
Artichokes, asparagus

Sunny Spot Flowers
Santa Paula, CA
21 acres
15 years farming
Flowers

Sunrise Ranch
Redondo Beach, CA
80 acres
50 years farming
Flowers

Sweet Peach Farm
Lancaster, CA
10 acres
20 years farming
Peaches

Sycamore Hill★
Fillmore, CA
75 acres
45 years farming
Citrus, green garlic

Tamai Farms
Oxnard, CA
40 acres
75 years farming
Vegetables, corn,
strawberries

Tenerelli Orchards
Little Rock, CA
50 acres
26 years farming
Stone fruits

Vang Thao
Fresno, CA
13 acres
6 years farming
Asian vegetables

Tomato Man
Ridgecrest, CA
0.5 acre
11 years farming
Tomatoes

Mario Trevino
Lompoc, CA
18 acres
30 years farming
Vegetables, strawberries

Tutti Frutti Farms★
Lompoc, CA
210 acres
20 years farming
Vegetables, tomatoes
www.tuttifruttifarms.com

Two Peas in a Pod
Arroyo Grande, CA
22 acres
22 years farming
Peas, beans

Vaca Evergreen Nursery
Compton, CA
12 acres
45 years farming
Bedding plants

Valdivia Farms
Carlsbad, CA
120 acres
24 years farming
Baby vegetables

Valley Center Orchards
Valley Center, CA
12 acres
20 years farming
Citrus, avocados

Phong Vang
Fresno, CA
5 acres
12 years farming
Asian vegetables

Venegas Creek
Vista, CA
20 acres
15 years of farming
Flowers

Lanie Villalobos★
Pauma Valley, CA
21 acres
26 years of farming
Citrus, rhubarb

Weiser Family Farms★
Lucerne Valley, CA
220 acres
25 years farming
Potatoes, melons

Whitney Ranch
Carpinteria, CA
6 acres
6 years farming
Blueberries

Winchester Cheese
Winchester, CA
80 acres
55 years farming
Gouda cheese
www.winchestercheese.com

Windrose Farm★
Paso Robles, CA
20 acres
11 years farming
Dried beans, tomato plants
www.windrosefarm.org

Wong Farms
North Shore, CA
4 acres
22 years farming
Tomatoes (hydroponic),
mangoes

Worm Wrangler
Menifee, CA
5.5 acres
25 years farming
Worms

Yamaoka Flowers
Carpinteria, CA
10 acres
20 years farming
Flowers

Kanji Yasutomi
Pico Rivera, CA
5 acres
12 years farming
Hydroponic vegetables
and herbs

Zuckerman
Stockton, CA
400 acres
30 years
Asparagus, potatoes

Acton, Eliza. *Modern Cookery for Private Families.* London: Longnan, Brown & Co. 1845.
Reprint, London: Elek, 1966.

Aidells, Bruce, and Denis Kelly. *The Complete Meat Cookbook.* New York: Houghton Mifflin, 2001.

Bayless, Rick. *Rick Bayless's Mexican Kitchen: Capturing the Vibrant Flavors of a World-Class Cuisine.*
New York: Scribner, 1996.

Facciola, Stephen. *Cornucopia II: A Source Book of Edible Plants.* Vista, California: Kampong Publications, 1998.

Fisher, Mary Frances Kennedy. *With Bold Knife and Fork.* New York: Putnam, 1968.

Goldman, Amy. *The Complete Squash: A Passionate Grower's Guide to Pumpkins, Squashes, and Gourds.*
New York: Artisan, 2004.

Goldman, Amy. *Melons for the Passionate Grower.* New York: Artisan, 2002.

Harder, Jules Arthur. *Physiology of Taste: Harder's Book of Practical American Cookery, Volume I (Treating of American Vegetables, and All Alimentary Plants, Roots and Seeds).* San Francisco: Harder, 1885.

Hazan, Marcella. *Marcella Cucina.* New York: Morrow Cookbooks, 1997.

———. *Marcella's Italian Kitchen.* New York: Knopf, 1987.

Herbst, Sharon Tyler. *Food Lover's Companion.* Hauppauge, NY: Barron's Educational Series, 2001.

Hieatt, Constance D., and Sharon Butler, eds. *Curye On Inglysch.* London: Early English Text Society, 1985.

Kasper, Lynne Rosetto. *The Splendid Table.* New York: Morrow Cookbooks, 1992.

Kennedy, Diana. *From My Mexican Kitchen: Techniques and Ingredients.* New York: Clarkson Potter, 2003.

Kiple, Kenneth F., and Kriemhild Conee Ornelas, eds. *The Cambridge World History of Food.* Cambridge:
Cambridge University Press, 2000.

The Landmarks Club. *The Landmarks Club Cook Book.* Los Angeles: The Out West Company, 1903.

McGee, Harold. *On Food and Cooking.* London: Hodder & Stoughton Ltd, 2004.

Madison, Deborah. *Vegetarian Cooking for Everyone.* New York: Broadway Books, 1997.

Miller, Daniel J., and Robert N. Lea. "Guide to the Coastal Marine Fishes of California." *California Fish Bulletin, no. 157.* University of California and State of California Department of Fish and Game (August 1976).

Rosso, Julee, and Sheila Lukins. *Silver Palate Cookbook.* New York: Workman Publishing Company, 1982.

Schneider, Elizabeth. *Vegetables from Amaranth to Zucchini.* New York: Morrow Cookbooks, 2001.

Waldheim, Lance. *Citrus.* Ironwood Press, Tucson, 1996.

Weaver, William Woys. *Heirloom Vegetable Gardening: A Master Gardener's Guide to Planting, Seed Saving, and Cultural History.* New York: Henry Holt & Company, 1997.

Wells, Patricia. *Patricia Wells at Home in Provence: Recipes Inspired by Her Farmhouse in France.* New York: Scribner, 1996.

Yepsen, Roger. *Apples.* New York: W. W. Norton & Company, 1994.

Yu, Su-mei. *Cracking the Coconut: Classic Thai Home Cooking.* New York: Morrow Cookbooks, 2000.

Zaslavsky, Nancy. *A Cook's Tour of Mexico.* New York: St. Martin's Press, 1995.

This book owes much to the generous farmers of the Santa Monica Farmers' Market. Many farmers have opened their homes to me, cooked for me, and even endured the makeup artist's brush as my guests on *Fresh from the Farmers' Market*. They have offered me countless samples of their latest discoveries, and have patiently answered my never-ending questions, sometimes by cell phone as they sowed seeds or tilled the soil. Special thanks to Maryann Carpenter, Mike Cirone, the Coleman family, Molly Gean, Fitz Kelly, Phil McGrath, Greg Nauta, Bob Polito, Laura Ramirez, Peter Schaner, Bill and Barbara Spencer, Alex Weiser, and the late Dede Thogmartin.

I am also indebted to the many chefs for their cooking advice and for painting a vivid picture of their days at the market. Special thanks to Josiah Citrin, Alain Giraud, Suzanne Goin, Chris Kidder, Evan Kleiman, Michael McCarty, Mary Sue Milliken, Mark Peel, Nicholas Peter, and Brian Wolff.

Laura Avery's boundless passion, energy, and ideas for the Santa Monica Farmers' Market never cease to amaze me, and I thank her for the many opportunities she has provided me, including hosting and producing *Fresh from the Farmers' Market*, a joint project spearheaded by Robin Gee, manager of Santa Monica CityTV, with funds from the Buy California Campaign. Thank you to Jennifer Ferro, assistant general manager of KCRW, who has given me a radio presence with her numerous invitations to "do a recipe" (many of the book's recipes evolved from these on-the-spot creations) on *Good Food*'s "Market Report." I am also grateful to market staffers Mort Bernstein, Ted Galvan, Jodi Low, and particularly to Darra Adler for her help with cooking demonstrations and with assembling the book's detailed farmers' list.

Sharon Silva's sensitive editing and guidance have given the book its polish and accuracy. It was a joy to work with her, and I am indebted to author William Rubel for suggesting I contact her (and for much mentoring as well). Ken dellaPenta provided the thorough index, and Traci Swartz carefully proofread the book. I am grateful to Michael Hodgson of Ph.D, for creating such a beautiful, user-friendly book, and for his tutelage of this first-time author and publisher. Hilary Laffer, also of Ph.D, often smoothed the way. Dear friends Betty Mallorca and Lawrence Manning of Hill Street Studios generously gave their photographs to the farmers, the market, and me to enrich our projects. I am also fortunate to have the photographs of the gifted Anne Fishbein in these pages.

The multitalented Angela Hunter was instrumental in the early days of the book's creation. Pilar Perez brought her publishing expertise to the project, and Lezlie Lee-French, Debbie White, Sarah Strayer, and Laurie Hughes helped in numerous ways.

Thank you to pastry chef Kimberly Boyce for her work on the Pistachio Shortbread Cookies and Dried Plum and Toasted Almond Cream Tart recipes; to Ret. Lt. Mark Caywood of the

208 California Department of Fish and Game, Seafood Extension Program Manager Pamela D. Tom of the University of California at Davis, David Karp, and Southland Farmers' Market Association Executive Director Howell Tumlin for vetting many facts; to Ellen Rose, Carl Chu, Judy Bart Kancigor, Don Michel, Suzanne Wickham-Beiard, Lisa Ekus, Claudia Luther, and Nancy Zaslavsky for their advice; and to Jill and John Walsh, keen tasters and recipe testers. Special thanks to Jill and to Tomi-Jean Yaghmai for their willing help with my farmers' market cooking demonstrations.

I am grateful to those who have inspired and encouraged me as a cook and chronicler: Marion Cunningham, Barbara Haber, Marcella and Victor Hazan, Joan Nathan, Lisa See, and Anne Willan and Mark Cherniavsky. From the moment Deborah Madison and I first worked together in 1996, during her book tour for *The Vegetarian Table*, and then again in 1997, when she toured with *Vegetarian Cooking for Everyone*, she has been a generous teacher, kindred spirit, and friend.

If a writer is lucky, she finds herself blessed with friends who are willing to nurture, sustain, read and reread, and brainstorm beyond all reasonable asking. I have been fortunate indeed to have the wisdom and friendship of Laura Avery, Jennifer Ferro, Alice Medrich, Constance Pollock, and Angela Rinaldi to guide me on this journey.

To my family: my parents, Serilla and Benjamin Ben-Aziz, for their loving support; my husband, Ralph, whose impeccable ear for language has improved the cadence of mine; my daughter Jessica, who is willing to "talk food" day or night; my daughter Rebecca, for her incisive editorial queries throughout; my son, Adam, writing compatriot, who supplied me with the gritty details of what it's really like to farm; my son-in-law, Rodolfo Buonocore, designer of Web sites (with his partners at Caffini/Communication & Design) and logos; and darling Delfina, the newest addition to our family, who has reawakened the wonder of taste for all of us. It is a joy to cook for and with all of you.

Lastly, thank you to the City of Santa Monica for its unwavering commitment to the Santa Monica Farmers' Market.